新编实用英语写作教程

NEW PRACTICAL ENGLISH WRITING COURSE

主编 张 松 刘志强

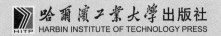
哈尔滨工业大学出版社
HARBIN INSTITUTE OF TECHNOLOGY PRESS

内 容 简 介

本书主要包括两大部分：英语基础写作知识和实用文体写作，是一本适合广大英语学习者提高英语写作能力的实用性写作教材。基础写作知识部分包括：英语句子、标点、英语作文的写作过程以及不同类型的英语作文的写作。实用文体写作包括：求职应用文写作与日常工作文写作，其具体内容涵盖求职信、简历、电子邮件、通知、备忘录、便条、会议纪要等常用文体。

本书可作为大学英语专业写作课教材，也可作为毕业生求职和日常工作所需的英文写作参考书。

图书在版编目(CIP)数据

新编实用英语写作教程/张松,刘志强主编. —哈尔滨：哈尔滨工业大学出版社,2013.11
ISBN 978-7-5603-4227-6

Ⅰ.①新… Ⅱ.①张… ②刘… Ⅲ.①英语－写作－高等学校－教材 Ⅳ.①H315

中国版本图书馆 CIP 数据核字(2013)第 201973 号

策划编辑	杨 桦 陈 洁
责任编辑	杨 桦 何波玲
出版发行	哈尔滨工业大学出版社
社　　址	哈尔滨市南岗区复华四道街 10 号 邮编 150006
传　　真	0451－86414749
网　　址	http://hitpress.hit.edu.cn
印　　刷	哈尔滨市工大节能印刷厂
开　　本	787mm×960mm 1/16 印张 24.5 字数 437 千字
版　　次	2013 年 11 月第 1 版 2013 年 11 月第 1 次印刷
书　　号	ISBN 978－7－5603－4227－6
定　　价	48.00 元

(如因印装质量问题影响阅读,我社负责调换)

前　　言

  本书主要是为高等学校英语专业学生编写的英语写作课教材,同时也适合旨在提高英语写作能力的广大英语学习者们使用。

  本教材的目的是:提高学生基本写作能力和职场实用文体训练能力以满足学生英语书面交际及毕业之后步入职场的需求。

  本教材编写的主要思路是英语写作的教与学的两个阶段。一是基础英语写作阶段:学习者从简单的英语句子与标点学起,然后进入写作过程的学习,最后了解并掌握不同类型的英语写作。二是实用文体写作阶段:学习者在积累了一定的写作知识和技巧后,可以从容应对从求职到就职过程中所要求的办公文体写作。通过这两个阶段的教与学,教师帮助学习者完成从学习积累到实践应用的过程。

  本书的主要特点是:符合英语写作学习的自然规律,即从句子写作到语篇写作,有针对性地解决在英语写作过程中出现的常见问题。本书范文选材新颖、地道、有时代性。实用文体写作部分突出实用性,内容选取包括求职与办公文体写作,满足学生求职与就业所需的英语写作需求。

  本书包括两大部分,共6章。其中第一部分的第1章、第3章、第4章由牡丹江大学张松编写,第一部分的第2章,第二部分的第1章、第2章由牡丹江大学刘志强编写。在本书编写的过程中,得到了牡丹江大学艾厚新教授和付亚力副教授的大力支持,他们为本教材的创作提出了积极的、有建设性的意见,在此一并表示诚挚谢意,同时也感谢本书在编写过程中参考其研究成果的专家学者们。

  本书基于多年的英语写作教学实例和教案,参考与借鉴了国内外相关著作,并结合编者的教学实践编写而成。对于书中存在的疏漏之处,敬请读者给予批评指正。

编者
2013 年 6 月

Contents

Part I Basic Writing Skills

Chapter 1 **Sentences** 3
  1.1 Finding the Subject and the Verb 3
  1.2 Subject-Verb Agreement 9
  1.3 Common Errors in Pronoun Reference and Agreement 15
  1.4 Sentence Fragments, Run-on Sentences, and Comma-Splices 20
  1.5 Dangling and Misplaced Modifiers 30
  1.6 Faulty Parallelism 33
  1.7 Illogical Comparisons 37
  1.8 Mixed Constructions 38
  1.9 Building Effective Sentences 39

Chapter 2 **Punctuation and Mechanics** 59
  2.1 End Punctuation 59
  2.2 The Comma 61
  2.3 Semicolon 70
  2.4 Colon 72
  2.5 The Apostrophe 74
  2.6 Quotation Marks 75
  2.7 Other Punctuation Marks 79
  2.8 Capitalization 88

Chapter 3 **The Process of Writing an Essay** 95
  3.1 Prewriting 97
  3.2 Organizing 101
  3.3 Drafting 108
  3.4 Revising 140
  3.5 Editing 143

Chapter 4 **Modes of Essays** 147
  4.1 A Narrative Essay 147

4.2 Descriptive Essays ······ 164
4.3 A Process Essay ······ 176
4.4 An Illustration Essay ······ 187
4.5 A Comparison and Contrast Essay ······ 199
4.6 A Cause and Effect Essay ······ 211
4.7 A Classification Essay ······ 225
4.8 An Argumentative Essay ······ 242

Part II Practical Writing Skills

Chapter 5 Writing for Job Application ······ 265
    5.1 Application Letter ······ 267
    5.2 Resume (Curriculum Vitae) ······ 275
Chapter 6 Writing for Routine Job ······ 294
    6.1 Notices ······ 294
    6.2 Notes ······ 302
    6.3 Memo ······ 308
    6.4 E-mails ······ 319
    6.5 Reports ······ 338
    6.6 Minutes ······ 344
Answers ······ 357
References ······ 385

Part I Basic Writing Skills

Chapter 1 Sentences

1.1 Finding the Subject and the Verb

To improve our writing, we should master the sentence and its two main parts, the subject and the verb. This section offers some useful tips for locating the subject and verb in every sentence. Once we have mastered this skill, we will be on our way to writing clear and effective sentences.

1.1.1 The Subject and the Verb in a Sentence

The **subject** of a sentence names a person, place, thing, or idea; it tells us *who* or *what* the sentence is about. The **verb** describes action or the subject's state of being; it tells us what the subject *does*, what the subject *is*, or what the subject *receives*. A sentence is a group of words that expresses a complete thought. Every sentence contains at least a subject (a noun or a noun plus its modifiers) and a predicate (a verb, or a verb plus its modifiers). For example:

Little **streams** *feed* big rivers.
He and I *are* old friend.
Mo Yan *received* the Nobel Prize for Literature in 2012.
The gray-haired **dog** *limped* slowly to its dog bed.

Each of the previous sentences contains a subject and a verb, and each makes a complete statement. In other words, they convey a sense of completeness. In conversations, sentences often lack stated subjects and verbs, but their contexts—the words and sentences that surround them—make clear the missing subject or verb. For example:

"Studying your Science of Law?"
"Yes. Big test tomorrow."
"Ready for it?"
"Hope so. Flunked the last one."

If this conversation were written in formal sentences, the missing subjects and verbs would be supplied, and the exchange might look something like this.

"Are you studying your Science of Law?"

"Yes. I have a big test tomorrow."

"Are you ready for it?"

"I hope so. I flunked the last one."

1.1.2 The Subject

The **subject** is one or more words that indicate *who* or *what* is doing the action of the verb. The subject can be a noun or noun phrase, a pronoun, a gerund phrase, or the implied *you* of a command. In the following sentences, the subjects are in bold font, and the verbs are in *italics*.

A tree *has fallen* across the road. (noun as subject)

He *told* a joke but **it** *fell* flat. (pronoun as subject)

The old theater building *created* an old-fashioned feel to the neighborhood. (noun phrase as subject)

Grab the keys. (implied you as subject)

Smoking *is* bad for you. (gerund phrase as subject)

(1) The subject can be a noun, a noun phrase, or an infinitive.

1) Noun as subject:

A **noun** can be a person, place, thing, idea, or state of existence.

The team *are wearing* their new jerseys.

2) Noun phrase as subject:

A **noun phrase** is a noun plus its modifiers, the words that describe it.

Most people *sleep* at night. (The noun is *people*. The word that describes it is *Most*.)

3) Infinitive as subject:

Phrases beginning with *to* can be subjects.

To find your way *can be* a problem.

4) Nouns and noun phrases can be joined to form a *compound subject*:

A **compound subject** is made of two or more nouns or noun phrases joined with the word *and* or *or*.

Jane and Tom *are* absent.

Either Professor Wang or Professor Li *will teach* us English writing next semester.

(2) The subject can be a pronoun.

A **pronoun** is a word that replaces a noun that was mentioned previously: *I*, *you*, *he*, *she*, *it*, *we*, *they*, *this*, *that*, *these*, and *those* are pronouns. Pronouns can also be indefinite, or a pronoun that refers to one or more unspecified beings, objects, or places: for example, *everyone*, *someone*, *anybody*, *both*, *few*, and *many*.

You *are no*t far wrong.

Both of us *passed* the examination.

(3) The subject can be a gerund phrase.

Watching a film *is* pleasure; **making one** *is* hard work.

(4) All sentences must have a subject, but in commands, the subject you is implied.

The subject *you* is implied in a command or request directly stated to someone.

Please *return* all overdue library books by next Friday. (the subject you is implied.)

1.1.3 The Subject in Inverted Sentences

Most sentences follow the subject-verb pattern. In **inverted sentences**, however, the pattern is reversed: the subject generally comes *after* the verb. Read the following inverted sentences carefully.

Across the street *stood* the abandoned **schoolhouse**. (The abandoned schoolhouse stood across the street; schoolhouse is the subject, although street is in the subject position before the verb.)

On her desk *is* a new **computer**.

In sentences that begin with *here is*, *here are*, *there is*, or *there are*, the real subject follows the verb.

Here is a **map** of the subway route to the Bronx. (What is here? The subject, map, is here.)

There are **several reasons** to explain his refusal. (What are there? Several reasons, the subject.)

Task 1.1

Underline all of the subjects in the sentences of the following passage. Some sentences have more than one subject.

  The daring life and unexplained death of an American pilot, Amelia Earhart, have intrigued people for decades. Her love affair with airplanes bloomed when Amelia attended an air show in California with her father. Amelia received a parade and a medal from President Herbert Hoover in 1932 after she became the first woman to fly alone across the Atlantic Ocean. Her most treasured goal, however, was to be the first pilot ever to circle the earth at the equator. Amelia, along with her copilot, Fred Noon, took off from Miami in June 1937. Articles and photographs for American newspapers, together with letters to her husband, were sent by Amelia throughout her journey. The public followed Amelia and Fred's progress eagerly. Everyone was stunned when their airplane suddenly vanished one month after their quest began. The two flyers had completed 22,000 miles of the mission. A final message from <u>Amelia</u> to a Coast Guard ship indicated that her plane was near New Guinea, in the South Pacific. Neither the plane nor its pilots were ever found, though squads of Army planes and Navy ships searched thoroughly. Numerous adventurers, scholars, and Earhart fans have launched their own unsuccessful searches. Rumors about the pilots' disappearance continue to circulate today. Some say that Earhart dove into the ocean deliberately, while others claim she was on a spy mission and was captured by the Japanese. Nevertheless, many modern female pilots cite Earhart's courage and achievements among their reasons for learning to fly.

1.1.4 The Predicate Verb

  All sentences must have at least one verb or verb phrase. A verb is the action of a sentence it can be a physical action, a mental action, or a state of being.

  (1) Action Verbs.

Action verbs tell what the subject does.

Neil Armstrong *landed* on the moon in 1969. (What action takes place in this sentence? What did Neil Armstrong do? He landed. Therefore, the verb in this sentence is *landed*.)

The newlyweds *boarded* the plane for Hainan. (What did the newlyweds do? They boarded. The verb in this sentence is *boarded*.)

Oceans *cover* three-quarters of the earth's surface. (What action takes place in this sentence? What do the oceans do? They cover. Therefore, the verb in this sentence is *cover*.)

Visitors to Disneyland *buy* souvenirs for their friends at home. (What do visitors do? They buy souvenirs. The verb is *buy*.)

(2) Linking Verbs.

Some verbs do not show action. Instead, they express a condition or state of being. They are called linking verbs, and they link the subject to another word that renames or describes the subject. Most linking verbs are formed from the verb *to be* and include *am*, *are*, *is*, *was*, and *were*. Several other verbs often used as linking verbs are *appear*, *become*, *feel*, *grow*, *look*, *remain*, *seem*, *smell*, *sound*, and *taste*. The verbs in the following sentences are linking verbs. They link their subjects to words that rename or describe them.

French *is* the language of the province of Quebec in Canada. (The linking verb *is* connects the subject French with the word that renames it: language.)

Helen's face *remained* expressionless. (The verb *remained* connects the subject Helen's face with the word that describes it: expressionless.)

His explanation *sounds* all right. (The linking verb *sounds* connects the subject explanation with the word that describes them: all right.)

When looking for the verb in a sentence, we should remember that it sometimes consists of more than one word. In such cases, it is called a verb phrase, and verb phrases consist of a main verb and a helping/auxiliary verb. Any helping/auxiliary verbs in front of the main verb are part of the verb, as in the following examples.

The child *is* crying because he's been stung by a bee.

The idea *was* given up years ago.

I wish he *had*n't gone.

When *did* he go home?

Task 1.2

Circle the verbs in the sentences of the following passage, including any helping/auxiliary verbs. Some sentences have more than one verb.

Cheese rolling has been known as one of Britain's most unusual customs for centuries. Each year, Gloucestershire, England, is invaded by thousands of fans who can't wait for the contest. They are thrilled to watch perfectly sane men and women chase seven-pound wheels of Gloucestershire cheese that are rolled down Cooper's Hill. Once the spectators see the athletes line up along the crest of the hill, they begin chanting "Roll that cheese!" When the master of ceremonies has blown the whistle, the athletes give their cheeses a push and scramble after them. The hill is steep and lumpy, so contestants know that they might get injured; broken bones and sprains are reported each year. Some competitors win only by accidentally tumbling down the hill, past their more careful peers. At times, the cheese rolls into the crowd and strikes someone, but no one is hurt and the cheese is kicked back onto the course. The winner gets a fine prize: the cheese that he or she has chased. Cheese rolling may have evolved from early harvest or fertility rituals, and it may date back to the ancient Britons or Romans who lived in the area.

Task 1.3

Underline the subject and circle the verb in the sentences of the following passage. Some sentences have more than one subject or verb.

Many animals are friendly, helpful, or amusing, but others possess venom that can cause their victims pain or even death. Rattlesnake bites, for example, can cause severe pain, swelling, and temporary paralysis. Several old horror movies feature Gila monsters, a type of venomous lizard that frequents the southwestern United States and Mexico. Bites from Gila monsters can bring horrible pain and dangerously low blood pressure. Many people are allergic to bites from bees, wasps, hornets, and even ants. Allergic reactions can include swelling and rashes. Some victims are so allergic that they may die of shock within minutes of being bitten. Though most spiders' bites cause only itching and swelling, others are much more harmful. Black widow spider bites cause severe pain, weakness, and convulsions, though survival from their bites is likely. The brown recluse spider is often called a "fiddleback" because of its oblong body.

1.2 Subject-Verb Agreement

We all know the simple rule that the subject and the verb in a sentence must agree in number and in person. Agreement in number means that a singular subject takes a singular verb and a plural subject takes a plural verb. Agreement in person means that a subject and its verb must both be in the same person (*first*, *second*, or *third*).

Here are three steps to ensure subject-verb agreement. First, find the subject of the sentence. Second, determine whether the subject is singular or plural. Third, select the appropriate singular or plural form of the verb to agree with the subject. The following suggestions will help you with these steps.

(1) Remember that a verb must agree with its subject, not with any words that follow the subject but are not part of it. These include terms such as *as well as*, *including*, *such as*, *along with*, *accompanied by*, and *rather than*. If the subject is singular, use a singular verb; if the subject is plural, use a plural verb.

A tape-recorded confession by the suspects, as well as statements by eyewitnesses, *has* (not have) been read to the jury.

The ambassadors from the West African countries, accompanied by a translator, *intend* (not intends) to meet with the president this afternoon.

Professor Wang, together with his students, *was* (not were) present at the meeting.

(2) Do not confuse the subject with words that rename it in the sentence.

The referee's only reward *was* (not were) taunts and threats.

Transcripts of the senator's remarks *are* (not is) the basis of the article.

Automobile accidents *are* (not is) the chief cause of death on New Year's Eve.

(3) Do not be confused by sentences that are not in the usual subject-verb pattern.

Where *is* (not are) the box of paper clips that was on my desk?

Are (not is) cumulus clouds a sign of rain?

Under the sofa *were* (not was) the missing cuff links.

But: Under the sofa *was* (not were) the set of missing cuff links.

There *are* (not is) many reasons for her success.

There *is* (not are) one particular reason for her success.

(4) Subjects connected by *and* or by *both. . . and* usually require a plural verb.

Following the proper diet and getting enough exercise *are* important for maintaining one's health.

Both Brenda and her sister, Alice, *have been* to the Great Wall.

Exception: Use a singular verb when a compound subject refers to the same person or thing.

Fish and chips *is* a popular supper.

The best hunter and fisherman in town *is* Joe Patterson.

Exception: Use a singular verb when a compound subject is preceded by *each*, *every*, *many a*, or *many an*.

Many a fine man *has* died in that battle.

Every cable and pulley *receives* a monthly inspection.

Exception: Use a plural verb when a compound subject is followed by *each*.

The tenor and the soprano each *wear* different costumes in the final act.

(5) If the subject consists of two or more words connected by *or*, *either. . . or*, *neither. . . nor*, or *not only. . . but also*, the verb agrees with the subject that is closer to it.

Either you or your brother *is* in fault.

Neither the chief financial officer nor the marketing managers *were* able to convince the client to reconsider.

Not only the students but also their teacher *is* enjoying the film.

(6) Indefinite pronouns that are singular take singular verbs, and indefinite pronouns that are plural take plural verbs. Some pronouns may be either singular or plural in meaning, depending on the noun or pronoun to which they refer. An indefinite pronoun is one that does not refer to a specific thing or person.

When used as subjects or as adjectives modifying subjects, the following indefinite pronouns are always singular and take singular verbs.

Singular Indefinite Pronouns: *another*, *each one*, *everything*, *nothing*, *anybody*, *either*, *much*, *one*, *anyone*, *every*, *neither*, *somebody*, *anything*, *everybody*, *nobody*, *something*, *each*, *every one*, *no one*, *someone*.

Everybody *likes* to join this activity.

Much of the work on the engine *has* been done.

There *was* something vaguely familiar about him.

Each of these exercises *takes* one or two minutes to do.

When used as subjects or as adjectives modifying subjects, the following indefinite pronouns are always plural and take plural verbs.

Plural Indefinite Pronouns: *both*, *several*, *others*, *few*, *many*.

Few *survive* more than a week without water.

Many of the parts in an American car *are* manufactured in other countries; several *come* from Japan.

When used as subjects or as adjectives modifying subjects, the following indefinite pronouns may be singular or plural, depending on the nouns or pronouns to which they refer.

Pronouns that May Be Singular or Plural: *all*, *any*, *more*, *most*, *none*, *some*.

All of his bodyguards *are* big and strong.

All of the snow *has* melted.

Most of the food *tastes* too spicy for me.

Most of the houses in this village don't have indoor plumbing.

None is considered a singular pronoun in formal usage. According to informal usage, however, it may be singular or plural, depending on the noun to which it refers. Note the difference in the following sentences.

Formal usage: None of us *knows* for certain.

Informal usage: None of the others *have* lived.

(7) If the subject is *who*, *which*, or *that*, be careful: all of these pronouns can be singular or plural, depending on their antecedents. When one of them is the subject, its verb must agree with its antecedent in number.

Sergei is one of those musicians who are able to play music at first sight. (Who refers to musicians; several musicians are able to play music at first sight, and Sergei is one of them.)

Hoang *is* the only one of the musicians who has forgotten his music. (Who refers to one. Among the musicians, only one, Hoang, has forgotten his music.)

I ordered one of the word processors that *were* on sale. (That refers to word processors and therefore takes a plural verb.)

I also bought a desk that *was* reduced 40 percent. (That refers to desk and therefore takes a singular verb.)

(8) Collective nouns take singular verbs when the group is regarded as a unit, and plural verbs when the individuals of the group are regarded separately. A collective noun is a word that is singular in form but refers to a group of people or things. Some common collective nouns are *army*, *assembly*, *committee*, *audience*, *company*, *couple*, *crowd*, *faculty*, *family*, *flock*, *group*, *herd*, *jury*, *pair*, *squad*, and *team*.

When the group is thought of as acting as one unit, the verb should be singular.

To an actor, the audience *is* a big dark animal waiting to be fed.

The committee *has* published the list of finalists.

The couple *was* married last week.

If the members of the group are thought of as acting separately, the verb should be plural.

The audience *were* coughing and shuffling their feet.

The committee *are* unable to agree on the finalists.

The couple constantly *argue* over their jobs and their children.

(9) Some nouns appear plural in form but are usually singular in meaning and therefore require singular verbs. The following nouns are used this way: *athletics*, *economics*, *electronics*, *measles mathematics*, *mumps*, *news*, *physics*, *politics*, and *statistics*.

This news *bodes* ill for her.

Statistics *is* the study and analysis of numerical information about the world.

When the items they refer to are plural in meaning, these words are plural.

My measles *are* spreading.

Recent statistics *show* a marked decline in the U. S. birthrate during the past twenty years.

(10) Subjects plural in form that indicate a quantity or number take a singular verb if the subject is considered a unit, but a plural verb if the individual

parts of the subject are regarded separately. Such expressions include *one-half of* (*and other fractions*), *a part of*, *a majority of*, and *a percentage of*.

If a singular noun follows *of* or is implied, use a singular verb.

Two-thirds of her fortune *consists* of stock in computer companies.

Part of the story *is* not true.

If a plural noun follows *of* or is implied, use a plural verb.

A large percentage of our foreign students *come* from Russia.

A majority of the students *have* completed their assignment.

Words that refer to distance, amounts, and measurements require singular verbs when they represent a total amount. When they refer to a number of individual items, they require plural verbs.

More than six hundred dollars *was* spent on my dental work.

Many thousands of dollars *were* collected for Thanksgiving meals for the poor.

Two miles *is* the maximum range of his new rifle.

The last two miles *were* paved last week.

Six months *is* a long time to wait for an answer to my complaint.

Six months *have* passed since we last heard from you.

(11) When *the number* is used as the subject, it requires a singular verb. *A number* is always plural.

The number of students who work part-time *is* increasing.

A number of students *receive* financial support from government loans.

Task 1.4

Read the sentences carefully to decide which verb should be used.

1. Tom's car alarm (are, is) a source of irritation for her neighbors.
2. For years, a problem facing the city (was, were) killer bees.
3. On the curb (was, were) sitting my brothers.
4. The topic of my essay (was, were) the various kinds of tropical fish, as well as how to care for them.
5. Goalies, rather than defensive players, often (receive, receives) the most media coverage.
6. Cable news channels sometimes (announce, announces) the winner of an election before all citizens have gone to the polls to vote.

7. In his movies, Johnny Depp always (know, knows) when the outlaws are about to attack.
8. On his Web site, Carlos (offer, offers) cell phone accessories at discounted prices.
9. Why (is, are) there so much traffic on Interstate 405?
10. Many tourists are surprised to learn that there once (was, were) a lot of steelhead trout in the canyons of Malibu, California.
11. People now (begin, begins) smoking at a younger age than ever before.
12. Senator Diaz (has, have) promised not to raise taxes.
13. Did you know that cross-country skis (is, are) much cheaper than downhill skis?
14. The Ice Hotel, built each winter in Arctic Sweden, (melt, melts) in May or June.
15. To win horseracing's treasured Triple Crown, a horse (have, has) to win the Kentucky Derby, Preakness, and Belmont races.
16. At nearly one hundred years old, Lloyd Moore (is, are) Nascar's oldest former driver.
17. The founder of Craigslist.com, one of America's twenty most popular Web sites, (are, is) actually a man named Craig Newmark.
18. Laker player Kobe Bryant won the league's Most Valuable Player award in 2008, and many fans thought it (was, were) long overdue.
19. Just how many chiles (was, were) in those enchiladas we ate?
20. We all know not to disturb Caitlyn when her favorite show, *Desperate Housewives*, (is, are) on.
21. To ascend the St. Louis Arch, you must ride in a cramped capsule that (resemble, resembles) an egg.
22. After watching a season of *Boston Legal*, Linda (has, have) decided to become an attorney.
23. The television special *Lewis and Clark* (has, have) lured many people into learning about early American explorers.
24. Tim said that there (is, are) two assignments due next Monday.
25. (Has, Have) anyone met the new dormitory advisor?

1.3 Common Errors in Pronoun Reference and Agreement

1.3.1 Avoiding Unclear Reference with Pronouns

A pronoun should clearly refer to its antecedent, the noun it is replacing. A pronoun reference error occurs when a pronoun does not have a clear connection to its antecedent (the word or word group that a pronoun refers to).

(1) Ambiguity.

Ambiguous pronoun reference occurs when a pronoun could refer to two possible antecedents.

Julie told Mary that *she* needed to see a doctor.

Who needs to see a doctor, Julie or Mary? The reader cannot tell. The simplest way to eliminate the ambiguity is to change the indirect speech into direct speech.

Revised: Julie told Mary, "*You* need to see a doctor."

Julie told Mary, "*I* need to see a doctor."

Or you can change or add some words to avoid the ambiguity.

Revised: Julie advised Mary to see a doctor.

Julie told Mary that she herself needed to see a doctor.

(2) Vague Reference.

The antecedent of a pronoun should be specific rather than implied. Do not use a pronoun to refer to something merely implied by what precedes it.

Marilyn was so impressed by the lecture given by the psychologist that she decided to major in *it*.

Marilyn decided to major in what? *It* has no antecedent in this sentence although you may guess the writer is referring to psychology from the word *psychologist*.

Revised: Marilyn was so impressed by the lecture given by the psychologist that she decided to major in *psychology*.

(3) Broad Reference.

For clarity, the pronouns *this*, *that*, *which*, and *it* should ordinarily refer to specific antecedents rather than to whole ideas or sentences.

Parks in the community do not allow pets, *which* many residents did not like.

Do the tenants referred to not like pets or not like the policy prohibiting pets? The relative pronoun *which* refers to the entire situation of pets being prohibited, which creates ambiguity. In order to correct this broad pronoun reference error, an antecedent for *which* must be supplied or the sentence restructured to indicate a clear subject.

Revised: Parks in the community do not allow pets, a policy which many residents did not like.

Or: Parks in the community do not allow pets, because many residents objected to them.

Another example:

Some people insist that a woman should go out to work, while others say that she should stay at home. *This* is unfair.

Does *this* refer to the whole sentence, to the first half, or to the second? To avoid the broad pronoun reference error, the meaning of *this* should be stated explicitly.

Revised: This contradictory set of demands is unfair.

(4) Indefinite *you*.

The pronoun *you* is appropriate only when the writer is addressing the reader directly: *Before steaming bun, you should ferment the dough first.* Pay attention to the precision of your sentences if you use you for your reader alone.

You didn't have computers in ancient times.

In this sentence, *you* cannot possibly refer to any reader now living. The word *you* should be replaced.

Revised: People didn't have computers in ancient times.

(5) Faulty Point-of-view Shifts.

Be consistent in the use of pronouns; don't shift from one person to another.

One can pass the examination as long as *you* work hard.

The most common point-of-view shift error involves switching to the second-person pronoun *you*. In casual speech, people often use the generic *you* to mean people in general. However, in formal writing, this substitution is not acceptable. The pronouns used should be consistent.

Revised: *One* can pass the examination as long as *he or she* works hard.

Note: In this sentence, we should use *he or she* instead of *he* to avoid sexism.

Task 1.5

Correct pronoun reference errors in the following sentences. In some cases, you will need to decide on an antecedent that the pronoun might logically refer to.

1. Before putting the antique ceramic plate on the shelf, she dusted it.
2. I did not go to the solo concert, which was depressing.
3. I checked the weather forecast yesterday, but they didn't predict the sleet we are having today.
4. When my dog kept barking at the parrot, I put it in the other room.
5. Anyone who is interested in volunteering at village-schools should write your name on the list.
6. I had a good time collecting shells on the beach. When people looked carefully at low tide, you could see many different kinds of shells.
7. She had decorated her sitting room with posters from chamber music festivals. This led her boyfriend to believe that she was interested in classical music. Actually she preferred rock.
8. In my high school, you didn't need to get all A's to be considered a success; you just needed to work to your ability.
9. Zoe told Amy that she was worried about her mother's illness.
10. Though the little boy cried for several minutes after colliding with a chair, eventually it subsided.

1.3.2 Pronoun-Antecedent Agreement in Number

A pronoun should agree with its antecedent in number. If the antecedent is singular, the pronoun must be singular. If the antecedent is plural, the pronoun must be plural.

A pronoun agreement error occurs when the writer neglects the number of the antecedent.

When *someone* travels outside *their* country for the first time, *they* need to apply for a passport.

The plural pronouns *their* and *they* do not agree with the singular antecedent *someone*. They should be replaced.

Revised: When *someone* travels outside *their* country for the first time, *he or she* need to apply for a passport.

Revised: When *people* travels outside *their* country for the first time, *they* need to apply for a passport.

Revised: *Anyone* who travels outside *his or her* country for the first time needs to apply for a passport.

Sometimes it is not easy to determine the number of the pronouns. The following guidelines could be helpful.

(1) Two or more nouns or pronouns joined by *and* usually need plural pronoun.

Peter and I handed in *our* papers last week.

(2) But the nouns joined by *and* call for singular pronoun when they refer to one person or thing.

The philosophy professor and principal assistant left *his* coat in the dining hall.

(3) When two nouns are joined by *or* or *nor*, the pronoun normally agrees with the one closer to it.

Either the employees or Mr. Lee will make *his* presentation.

Neither Roger nor Simon admitted *he* had cheated.

(4) Collective nouns can be either singular or plural, depending on the meaning of the nouns.

The couple *was* honored for *its* contribution to the earthquake-stricken area.

The couple is regarded as a unit, so it takes singular pronoun *its*.

The couple often quarrel over the education of *their* children.

Since the two of the couple act separately, the plural pronoun *their* should be used.

(5) Some indefinite pronouns are singular, some are plural, and some can be either singular or plural.

The indefinite pronouns that are always singular include: *another, anybody, anyone, anything, each, each one, either, every, everybody, everyone, everything, many a, neither, nobody, no one, none, nothing, one, some-*

body, *someone*, and *something*. When they are used as antecedents, pronouns referring to them are always singular.

The indefinite pronouns that are always plural include: *both*, *few*, *many*, *others*, and *several*. When they are used as antecedents, pronouns referring to them are always plural.

The following indefinite pronouns are sometimes singular and sometimes plural: *all*, *any*, *most*, *some*. Antecedents referring to them will be either singular or plural, depending on their meaning and the noun they represent.

Everybody in the team finished *his or her* task in time.

In this company, no one lost *his or her* job during the recession.

Both of the girls had *their* hair cut.

Several of the students admitted *they* had never previewed.

Many of the teachers in my school treat the students as *their* friends.

Some of the spaghetti sauce left *its* mark on my dress.

Some of mothers try to act out *their* unrealized dreams through *their* daughter.

On Fridays each of the children in this kindergarten carries *his or her* own toys.

On Fridays the children in this kindergarten *each* carry *their* own toys.

As the list indicates, *each* is always singular. But when each immediately follows a plural noun, you should use plural pronoun to agree with the plural antecedent. So in the last sentence plural pronoun *their* should be used.

(6) The number of a relative pronoun depends on the number of its antecedent.

Linda is one of those able women *who* have *their* successful career.

Tim is the only one of this group *who* finished *his* assignment in time.

Task 1.6

Correct the pronoun agreement errors in the following sentences. Cross out the error, and write the correction over it. If a sentence is correct, write "C" in front of it.

1. When the belly dancer asked for a volunteer partner, everyone in the men's gym class raised their hand.
2. The faculty of the foreign languages school was praised by the president for

their dedication to the college.
3. Each of the children were responsible for arrange their own stationery.
4. For a child, stories are magical, and it improves the child's imagination.
5. A parent reading aloud to their children fosters lifelong love of reading in them.
6. When studying a foreign language, one should avoid translating each word separately into their own language.
7. Each dog and cat was classified according to its breed.
8. All of the airline passengers must pass through the security check before he or she may board the airplane.
9. That kinds of puzzles make me confused.
10. Many a students earn their tuition by working part time.

1.4 Sentence Fragments, Run-on Sentences, and Comm-Splices

1.4.1 Sentence Fragments

A sentence is a group of words containing at least one independent clause. It has a subject and a verb, and it conveys a certain sense of completeness. A sentence fragment, in contrast, is a group of words lacking an independent clause. Although it looks like a sentence because it begins with a capital letter and ends with a period or other end punctuation, it leaves the reader "hanging," waiting for more to follow.

Sentence fragments are common in conversation, particularly in responses to what someone else has said or as additions to something we have just said. Their meanings an missing parts are usually clear because of the context of the conversation and the speaker's gestures. In writing, however, it is best to avoid sentence fragments. Although professional writers occasionally use them for special effect, fragments usually suggest that the writer is careless and unable to formulate a complete thought.

We should not be fooled by the length of a so-called sentence. A long string of words without an independent clause is still a sentence fragment, despite its length. Here is an example of such a fragment.

The election of Nelson Mandela, an end to news censorship, abolition of executions, and power sharing with former white leaders, among other dramatic changes for South Africa.

At first glance this "sentence" is complete—after all, it begins with a capitalized word and concludes with a period. Despite its length, however, it is a sentence fragment because it does not contain an independent clause and therefore cannot convey a complete thought.

1. Common errors that create fragments

(1) Missing subject: leaving out the subject of the sentence.

Forgot to close the car door. (Subject missing: *Who* forgot to close the car door?)

Revised: *Mahad* forgot to close the car door.

(2) Missing, incomplete, or incorrect form of verb: leaving out the verb, using an incomplete verb, or using the wrong form of a verb.

A good variety of dining options in the cafeteria. (No verb. Add one to make the sentence complete.)

Revised: A good variety of dining options *is* available in the cafeteria.

Margaret studying for the test. (Incomplete verb: add the helping verb *is* or *was* before *studying*.)

Revised: Margaret *is studying* for the test.

Margaret *was studying* for the test.

The machine running the elevator. (Wrong form of verb: change to *runs* or *ran*.)

Revised: The machine *runs* the elevator.

The machine *ran* the elevator.

(3) Including a subordinating word or phrase before the subject and the verb: adding a word or phrase which makes a clause dependent on another clause for meaning.

Since she travels every spring. (Subordinating word: the word *Since* makes this a dependent clause. Either delete the word *Since*, or add an independent clause before or after it.)

Revised: She *travels* every spring.

2. Identifying sentence fragments

A complete sentence contains a subject and a verb and does not have a subordinating word or phrase before the subject. Here are three steps you can use to identify sentence fragments:

Find the verb.

Find the subject.

Check for a subordinating word or phrase.

(1) Find the verb. Ask yourself: *What* is happening in this sentence? If there is no verb (or if an auxiliary verb is needed), then you have a sentence fragment. For example:

The kitten in the living room. (*What* is the kitten doing in the living room? The sentence needs a verb.)

Revised: The kitten *is sleeping* in the living room.

Tom *taking* a nap. (The above sentence needs a helping verb.)

Revised: Tom *is taking* a nap.

Or, change the *-ing* form to a regular verb:

Revised: Tom *takes* (or *took*) a nap.

(2) Find the subject. Ask yourself: *Who* or *what* is the subject of the action/verb I found? If there is no noun serving as the subject, then the word group is a sentence fragment. For example:

Takes the bus almost every day. (*Who* is taking the bus? *Who* is the subject of this sentence?)

Revised: *Lori* takes the bus almost every day.

Exception: The one exception is when the subject is implied, as in the word *you* in a command. For example:

Don't drop that glass. (Although not stated, the subject of this sentence is the implied: You)

(You) Don't drop that glass.

(3) Check for a subordinating word or phrase that creates a dependent clause.

When we put a subordinating conjunction such as *whenever* in front of the subject of a sentence, the sentence becomes a dependent clause. It is incomplete because it now depends on the addition of more information to make sense. For example:

Whenever she works on weekends. (The word *whenever* makes this a dependent phrase. Either delete the subordinating word *whenever*, or add an independent clause before or after the phrase.)

Revised: She works on weekends.

Her partner complains whenever she works on weekends.

Whenever she works on weekends, *her kids don't get to see much of her.*

A subordinate clause is patterned like a sentence, with both a subject and a verb, but it begins with a word that marks it as subordinate. The following words commonly introduce subordinate clauses: *after*, *before*, *so that*, *until*, *while*, *although*, *even though*, *than*, *when*, *who*, *as*, *how*, *that*, *where*, *whom*, *as if*, *if*, *though*, *whether*, *whose*, *because*, *since*, *unless*, *which*, *why*, etc.

3. Find other forms of fragments

(1) Fragmented phrases.

After delaying it several weeks, Jeff finally began his term paper. *On the subject of religious cults in America.* (A prepositional phrase never contains a subject and a verb. So it can never stand alone as a sentence.)

Revised: After delaying it for several weeks, Jeff finally began his term paper on the subject of religious cults in America.

Scientists have repeatedly warned us. *To stop polluting our water before it is unsafe for human use.* (The infinitive phrase can not be used as verb. Besides, there is no subject in it.)

Revised: Scientists have repeatedly warned us to stop polluting our water before it is unsafe for human use.

Exercising every day, cutting down on calories, and avoiding ice cream and other desserts. I was able to lose twenty pounds last summer. (The present participle can not be confused with the main verb in a sentence.)

Revised: Exercising every day, cutting down on calories, and avoiding ice cream and other desserts, I was able to lose twenty pounds last summer.

Because I exercised every day, cut down on calories, and avoided ice cream and other desserts, I was able to lose twenty pounds last summer.

(2) Fragmented lists.

Sometimes terms like *especially*, *namely*, *like*, and *such as* introduce fragmented lists. Such fragments can usually be attached to the preceding sentence.

It has been said that there are only three indigenous American art forms. *Musical comedy, jazz, and soap opera.* (The list can not stand alone. It should be attached to the preceding sentence.)

Revised: It has been said that there are only three indigenous American art forms: musical comedy, jazz, and soap opera.

In the twentieth century, the South produced some great American writers. *Such as Flannery O'Connor, William Faulkner, Alice Walker, and Tennessee Williams.* (The list should be attached to the preceding sentence.)

Revised: In the twentieth century, the South produced some great American writers, such as Flannery O'Connor, William Faulkner, Alice Walker, and Tennessee Williams.

Expressions that introduce examples or explanations can lead to unintentional fragments. Although you may begin a sentence with some of the following words or phrases, make sure that what follows has a subject and a verb:

also, for example, mainly, for instance, in addition, that is, etc.

In his memoir, Primo Levi describes the horrors of living in a concentration camp. *For example, working without food and suffering emotional abuse.* (The phrase can not stand alone. It should be attached to the preceding sentence.)

Revised: In his memoir, Primo Levi describes the horrors of living in a concentration camp, for example, working without food and suffering emotional abuse.

4. Correcting sentence fragments

We can correct most fragments in one of two ways:

(1) Pull the fragment into a nearby sentence.

(2) Rewrite the fragment as a complete sentence.

Fragment: The kids playing on the lawn.

Revised: The kids are playing on the lawn.

The kids play on the lawn.

Fragment: Needs to find a good career.

Revised: *Clay* needs to find a good career.

Fragment: The pilots ejected from the burning plane, landing in the water not far from the ship. *And immediately popped their flares and life vests.*

Revised: The pilots ejected from the burning plane, landing in the water not far from the ship. They immediately popped their flares and life vests.

Fragment: We had just sat down to dinner. *When the cat leaped onto the table.*

Revised: We had just sat down to dinner when the cat leaped onto the table.

Fragment: The world's oldest living trees are the bristlecone pines. *Which grow in California.*

Revised: The world's oldest living trees are the bristlecone pines, which grow in California.

Fragment: I tripped and twisted my ankle. *Running for the bus.*

Revised: Running for the bus, I tripped and twisted my ankle.

Fragment: This recording of the symphony's latest concert is so clear you can hear every sound. *Including the coughs and whispers of the audience.*

Revised: This recording of the symphony's latest concert is so clear you can hear every sound, including the coughs and whispers of the audience.

Fragment: Deborah Tannen's research reveals that men and women have different ideas about communication. *For example, that a woman "expects her husband to be a new and improved version of her best friend".*

Revised: Deborah Tannen's research reveals that men and women have different ideas about communication. For example, Tannen explains that a woman "expects her husband to be a new and improved version of her best friend".

Task 1.7

Correct any sentence fragments in the following word groups, using any of the methods explained earlier. If the sentence is correct, write "C" in front of it. Answers for fragments may vary.

1. Believe it or not, there is a set of rules about how to display the American flag. Which the War Department wrote in 1923.
2. Citizens may display their flags any time they want to. Although it is traditional to fly them only from sunrise to sunset.
3. The White House, unusual because its flag flies both day and night.
4. The awesome sight of the flag above Baltimore's Fort McHenry inspired Francis Scott Key to write "The Star Spangled Banner."
5. No other flag may be flown above or to the right of the U. S. flag. Except at the United Nations headquarters in New York City.
6. A rule that most Americans are familiar with, that the flag should never tou-

ch the ground or floor.
7. A flag may cover the casket of military personnel or other public officials. If it is not permitted to touch the ground or be lowered into the grave.
8. Disposal of a worn or damaged flag in a dignified way, preferably by burning.
9. The U.S. Supreme Court's decision to allow destruction of the flag as a means of political protest was a disappointment to many Americans.
10. Politicians still debate whether American schoolchildren should be required to pledge their allegiance to the flag. Although reciting that oath is not mandatory now.

5. A fragment can be used for effect

Writers occasionally use sentence fragments for special purposes.

For emphasis: Following the dramatic Americanization of their children, even my parents grew more publicly confident. *Especially my mother.*

—Richard Rodriguez

To answer a question: Are these new drug tests 100 percent reliable? *Not in the opinion of most experts.*

Transitions: *And now the opposing arguments.*

Exclamations: *Not again!*

In advertising: *Fewer carbs. Improved taste.*

Although fragments are sometimes appropriate, writers and readers do not always agree on when they are appropriate. That's why you will find it safer to write in complete sentences.

Sentence fragments are often used in conversations ("yes" "maybe" "just a minute") and in informal or personal writing (notes, letters, e-mail, etc.). In some professional and academic writing, *intentional fragments* or abbreviated sentences may be used occasionally for emphasis or to convey a particular tone, such as playfulness, anger, or scorn. However, intentional fragments should be just that: created on purpose to achieve a specific rhetorical goal.

6. Intentional fragments

After cleaning out the attic, Eloise felt terrible. *Hot. Tired. Cranky with the world.*

She agreed to hand over the jewels. *Just exactly what he had had in mind all along.*

As a general rule, fragments should be avoided in formal writing.

1.4.2 Run-on Sentences and Comma-Splices

A **run-on sentence**, sometimes called a *fused sentence*, occurs when you combine two or more independent clauses (complete sentences) with no punctuation to separate them. It is just the opposite of a sentence fragment. For example:

Air pollution poses risks to all humans it can be deadly for asthma sufferers.

A **comma-splice** is a particular type of run-on that occurs when you combine two or more independent clauses (two complete sentences, each with a subject and a verb) with just a comma. For example:

Air pollution poses risks to all humans, it can be deadly for asthma sufferers.

1. Four methods to revise run-on sentences and comma-splices

(1) Use a comma and a coordinating conjunction (*and*, *but*, *or*, *nor*, *for*, *so*, *yet*).

Run-on: The indicted police chief submitted his resignation the mayor accepted it gratefully.

Revised: The indicted police chief submitted his resignation, and the mayor accepted it gratefully.

(2) Use a semicolon (or, if appropriate, a colon or a dash). A semicolon may be used alone or with a transitional expression.

Run-on: St. Augustine, Florida, is America's oldest city it was settled by Spain in 1565.

Revised: St. Augustine, Florida, is America's oldest city; it was settled by Spain in 1565.

Comma-splice: Crossing so many time zones on an eight-hour flight, I knew I would be tired when I arrived, however, I was too excited to sleep on the plane.

Revised: Crossing so many time zones on an eight-hour flight, I knew I would be tired when I arrived; however, I was too excited to sleep on the plane.

Conjunctive adverbs like *however*, *nonetheless*, *therefore*, *hence*, *otherwise*, *besides*, *moreover*, etc., should not be used as a coordinating conjunctions to link two coordinate clauses.

(3) Make the clauses into separate sentences.

Comma-splice: Lena said I'd like the new Leona Lewis CD, she was right.

Revised: Lena said I'd like the new Leona Lewis CD. She was right.

(4) Restructure the sentence, perhaps by subordinating one of the clauses.

Comma-splice: Bob guards his blood pressure carefully, once in a while he enjoys a salty bowl of tomato soup.

Revised: Although Bob guards his blood pressure carefully, once in a while he enjoys a salty bowl of tomato soup.

2. Comma-splices and conjunctive adverbs

Some comma-splices are the result of the writer's confusing a conjunctive adverb with a coordinating conjunction. A conjunctive adverb is a kind of connecting word that looks like a conjunction but is actually an adverb.

Some Conjunctive Adverbs: *accordingly*, *also*, *besides*, *consequently*, *furthermore*, *hence*, *however*, *moreover*, *nevertheless*, *nonetheless*, *otherwise*, *therefore*, etc.

When one of these words appears *within* an independent clause, it is usually set off by commas. For example:

It was obvious from her face, however, that she was disappointed.

I believe, nevertheless, that Maxim will continue to play.

Venezuela and Peru, moreover, also plan to sign the treaty.

When a conjunctive adverb appears *between* main clauses, it must be preceded by a semicolon or a period (and often followed by a comma). If the semicolon or period is omitted, the result is a comma-splice.

Comma-splice: Hershey is famous for its chocolate, however, the company also makes pasta.

Revised: Hershey is famous for its chocolate; however, the company also makes pasta.

Revised: Hershey is famous for its chocolate. However, the company also makes pasta.

Remember: Conjunctive adverbs are not conjunctions and can never be used by themselves to link clauses or sentences.

Task 1.8

Revise any run-on sentences or comma-splices using a technique that you find effective. If a sentence is correct, write "C" after it.

1. Wind power for the home is a supplementary source of energy, it can be combined with electricity, gas, or solar energy.
2. Aidan viewed Sofia Coppola's *Lost in Translation* three times and then wrote a paper describing the film as the work of a mysterious modern painter.
3. In the Middle Ages, the streets of London were dangerous places, it was safer to travel by boat along the Thames.
4. "He's not drunk," I said, "he's in a state of diabetic shock."
5. You are able to endure extreme angle turns, high speeds, frequent jumps, and occasional crashes, then supermoto racing may be a sport for you.

Task 1.9

Revise the following sentences. If a sentence is correct, write "C" after it.

1. Rodney's goal is to take piano lessons and play in the school orchestra then he'll try to make some spending money by playing in local jazz clubs.
2. Smiling and clapping her hands, clearly a healthy and happy baby.
3. The Lagat family of Kenya having produced several of the world's top distance runners.
4. Of the six party pictures that Matt emailed to me, I printed out three for my bulletin board.
5. We arrived too late to the movie theatre, Rico and Zack had arrived on time and gone inside without us.
6. Yankees player Robinson Cano telephones his father in the Dominican Republic after every game they dissect Robinson's batting performance swing by swing.
7. In an economic recession, even filmmakers find it difficult to raise sufficient funds from investors.
8. The humidity was high, the children did not feel like playing outside.
9. Because Cesar bought Lisa a sweater that matches her new skirt perfectly.

10. You won't believe what Jack just told me go ahead try to guess!

1.5 Dangling and Misplaced Modifiers

1.5.1 Dangling Modifiers

A dangling modifier is a modifier that has no headword in the sentence for it to modify. It is left "dangling" and as a result it ends up accidentally modifying an unintended headword, as in the following example.

Arriving home after midnight, the house was dark.

This sentence seems to say that the house arrived home. Since *arriving home after midnight* is a modifier, we expect to see its headword immediately after it, to find out *who* arrived home. Instead, what turns up in the headword slot is *the house*, and there is nothing else in the sentence that could do the arriving. The opening phrase, therefore, is a dangling modifier. It has nothing to support it.

A dangling modifier results from the miscombination of two sentences. In this case they are:

I arrived home after midnight.

The house was dark.

These two sentences have different subjects: *I* and *the house*. When we combine two sentences like these by making one of them modify the other, we must normally keep both of their subjects.

When I arrived home after midnight, the house was dark.

This combination turns the first sentence into a subordinate clause. When we combine two sentences, we can normally drop the subject of one only if it is the same as the subject of the other.

I arrived home after midnight.

I found the house dark.

Combined: Arriving home after midnight, I found the house dark.

Here both subjects are the same, so the writer can drop one of them.

Here are more sentences with dangling modifiers.

To satisfy her mother, the piano had to be practiced every day.

Deciding to join the navy, the recruiter enthusiastically pumped Joe's hand.

Upon entering the doctor's office, a skeleton caught my attention.

By supplying subjects and rewording these sentences, we can make their meanings clear.

To satisfy her mother, Linda had to practice the piano every day.

When Joe decided to join the navy, the recruiter enthusiastically pumped his hand.

As I entered the doctor's office, a skeleton caught my attention.

Upon entering the doctor's office, I noticed a skeleton.

Task 1.10

Rewrite any of the following sentences that contain dangling modifiers. If a sentence is correct, write "C" in front of it. Answers to dangling modifiers may vary.

1. When watching an exciting movie on television, commercials are especially irritating.
2. Raised in Colorado, it is natural to miss the snow-covered mountains.
3. Although only a sophomore, the field hockey team selected Kathy as its captain.
4. Although it was nearly finished, we left the concert early because we had to study for our biology exam.
5. As a child, his father bought him a violin in the hope that he would become a violinist.
6. Walking on the beach, the sand warmed my bare feet.
7. While walking across the manicured golf course yesterday, the sprinklers suddenly came on.
8. After offering a toast to the guest of honor, dinner was served.
9. Breathless and exhausted, the winner of the marathon could not talk.
10. Driving across the country last summer, the differences in regional accents could be detected.

1.5.2 Misplaced Modifiers

A misplaced modifier is one that is not close to the headword it modifies and as a result modifies the wrong headword. Sentences with misplaced modifiers are usually confusing and often result in unintended, though sometimes humorous, meanings.

Notice the unintended meanings in the following sentences. In each sentence, the modifier has been misplaced.

Jerry was chased by a dog *wearing his tuxedo*.

This sentence seems to say that the dog was wearing a tuxedo, because the modifier *wearing his tuxedo* is in the wrong spot: It is closer to *dog* than to *Jerry*. We should put the modifying phrase right after its headword *Jerry*.

Revised: Jerry, wearing his tuxedo, was chased by a dog.

Or place the modifier at the beginning of the sentence.

Revised: Wearing his tuxedo, Jerry was chased by a dog.

The racer returned to the hospital where he had undergone emergency surgery last year *in a limousine sent by Toyota*.

The sentence seems to say that the racer underwent the emergency surgery in a limousine. The modifier should be corrected.

Revised: Travelling in a limousine sent by Toyota, the racer returned to the hospital where he had undergone emergency surgery last year.

Andrew *only* jogs on the track.

If Andrew *only jogs* on the track, he may do nothing else at all. So the adverb *only* should limit *on the track*, not *jogs*.

Revised: Andrew jogs only on the track.

The modifiers like *only*, *merely*, *nearly*, *scarcely*, *simply*, *even*, *exactly*, *just*, *hardly*, etc. should be placed just before the word or phrase modified.

Her parents encouraged her regularly to diet and exercise.

Did her parents encouraged her regularly, or did she diet and exercise regularly? Here regularly is the **squinting modifier**, a modifier that usually appears in the middle of a sentence so that it can modify either the word that precedes it or the one that follows it. As a result, the squinting modifier makes the sentence ambiguous. To make the meaning of the sentence unambiguously clear, we must clearly connect the modifier with one headword or the other.

Revised: Her parents regularly encouraged her to diet and exercise.
Her parents encouraged her to diet and exercise regularly.

Task 1.11

Edit the following sentences to correct misplaced or awkwardly placed modifiers.

1. Many students graduate with debt from college totaling more than fifty thousand dollars.
2. It is a myth that humans only use 10 percent of their brains.
3. A cool-hunter is a person who can find in the unnoticed corners of modern society the next wave of fashion.
4. The bank robber was described as a short man wearing a baseball cap weighing 175 pounds.
5. Growing at the bottom of the swimming pool, Kevin found some mold.
6. On the wall above his desk is a photograph of his daughter in a gold frame.
7. The patient was referred to a cardiac specialist with symptoms of heart disease
8. Professor Jenkins is teaching a course on criminal behavior at Fairview College.

1.6 Faulty Parallelism

1.6.1 Parallelism

Parallelism (or parallel structure) involves using a consistent grammatical form or word form in sentences that have a series of verbals or phrases in order to keep them in balance.

When writing two or more items in a list, a series, a contrast, a choice, a statement of equivalence, a formal definition, a statement of evaluation, or a comparison, we should put all of the items into the same grammatical form.

(1) I have nothing to offer but *blood*, *toil*, *tears*, and *sweat*. (parallel nouns)

—Winston Churchill

(2) Let every nation know, whether it wishes us well or ill, that we shall *pay any price*, *bear any burden*, *meet any hardship*, *support any friend*, *oppose any foe* to assume the survival and the success of liberty. (parallel verb-object phrases)

—John F. Kennedy

(3) *In matters of principle, stand like a rock*; *in matters of taste, swim with the current.* (parallel clauses)

—Thomas Jefferson

(4) *We must indeed all hang together*, or most assuredly, *we shall all hang separately.* (parallel clauses)

—Benjamin Franklin

(5) *What I'm going to do* is just *what you refused to do*. (parallel noun clauses)

(6) *Robotics* is *the study* of robots designed to work like human beings. (parallel nouns)

(7) *The first violinist* is *the most important member* of a symphony orchestra. (parallel noun phrases)

(8) *Crawling down* a mountain is sometimes harder than *climbing up*. (parallel participles)

When using correlatives like both...and, not only...but also, either... or, neither...nor, whether...or, etc., be sure that the word or word group following the first member of the pair is parallel with the word or word group following the second. For example:

Mary may be either *at the office* or *on her way*. (parallel adverb phrases)

Henry not only *got the job* but also *won a promotion* after half a year. (parallel verb-object phrases)

1.6.2 Revising Faulty Parallelism

Faulty parallelism occurs when the same grammatical form or structure is not used throughout. When this happens, the form changes and the sentence becomes unbalanced.

Faulty: *To keep fit*, *to study hard*, and *spending* less time on the internet—these were Jim's New Year's resolutions. (infinitive, infinitive, and participle)

Revised: *To keep fit*, *to study hard*, and *to spend* less time on the internet—these were Jim's New Year's resolutions. (three infinitives)

Faulty: Children who study music also learn *confidence*, *discipline*, and *they are creative*. (noun, noun, and clause)

Revised: Children who study music also learn *confidence*, *discipline*, *and creativity*. (three nouns)

Faulty: Page didn't know *whether to give* Jacob her new toy or *if she should keep* it for herself. (infinitive and dependant clause)

Revised: Page didn't know *whether to give* Jacob her new toy or *keep* it for herself. (two infinitives)

Page didn't know *if she should give* Jacob her new toy or *if she should keep* it for herself. (two dependant clauses)

When using correlative conjunctions, be sure to place them as closely as possible to the words they join. For example:

Nonstandard: She neither wanted our advice nor our help.

Standard: She wanted neither our advice nor our help.

Nonstandard: Richard would neither apologize nor would he admit that he was wrong.

Standard: Richard would neither apologize nor admit that he was wrong.

Function words such as prepositions (*by*, *to*) and subordinating conjunctions (*that*, *because*) signal the grammatical nature of the word groups to follow. Although we can sometimes omit them, be sure to include them whenever they signal parallel structures that readers might otherwise miss. For example:

Faulty: Our study revealed that left-handed students were more likely to have trouble with classroom desks and rearranging desks for exam periods was useful.

Revised: Our study revealed that left-handed students were more likely to have trouble with classroom desks and *that* rearranging desks for exam periods was useful.

A second subordinating conjunction helps readers sort out the two parallel ideas: *that* left-handed students have trouble with classroom desks and *that* rearranging desks was useful.

Task 1.12

Rewrite any of the following sentences that contain faulty parallelism. If the sentence is correct, write "C" before it.

1. In computer class, Phuong learned to build Web pages, and also using the Internet.
2. Trisha complained that her counselor had neither an understanding of students' problems and he did not like people.
3. Owning a home not only requires a lot of maintenance but also it is expensive and it needs a lot of time.
4. Wally's ideas are clever, original, and they are practical.
5. The ambassador from Iran would neither apologize nor would he promise to accept the demands of the United Nations.
6. Professor Gorra is brilliant, eloquent, and helpful.
7. Winston Churchill said that victory would require blood and sweat and toil and tears.
8. The governor said that his hobbies were fly-fishing and to play video games with his grandchildren.
9. Many people join health clubs for exercise, for relaxation, and sometimes to find romance.
10. Nicolas Cage is admired as an actor because he is not only a dramatic actor but also he is good in comedy roles.
11. My Aunt Clara swears she has seen Elvis snacking at the deli, browsing at the supermarket, munching at the pizza parlor, and in the cookbook section of a local bookstore.
12. According to my husband, summer air in Louisiana is 2 percent oxygen, 8 percent water, and the rest is mosquitoes, about 90 percent.
13. Smart people learn from their own mistakes; learning from the mistakes of others is what even smarter people do.
14. Theater class helped me overcome my shyness, make new friends, and my confidence to do other activities was improved.
15. The writer Oscar Wilde, the dancer Isadora Duncan, the painter Max Ernst, and Jim Morrison, who was a rock star, are all buried in the same Paris cemetery.

1.7 Lllogical Comparisons

A comparisons should be made between items that are alike. And this comparison should be complete. Omitted words often make the comparison unclear, illogical, or awkward.

The population of China is much larger than Japan.

Population must compare with population, not with Japan.

Revised: The population of China is much larger than that of Japan.

Beijing is closer to Tianjin than Shanghai.

This sentence is not clear because the comparison is not stated fully enough. Comparisons should leave no ambiguity for readers. If more than one interpretation is possible, revise the sentence to state clearly which interpretation we intend.

Revised: Beijing is closer to Tianjin than it is to Shanghai.

Or: Beijing is closer to Tianjin than Shanghai is to Tianjin.

Mark runs faster than any players in the football team.

The word *other* should be insert to make the comparison logical:

Revised: Mark runs faster than any other players in the football team.

The examination is easier.

The comparison should be complete enough to ensure clarity. The reader should understand what is being compared:

Revised: The examination is easier than the one we took last semester.

Or there is nothing to compare:

Revised: The examination is quite easy.

Task 1.13

Revise any of the following sentences that contain illogical comparisons. If a sentence is correct, write "C" in front of it.

1. I enjoy pizza much more than Garth.
2. The Tim McGraw CD is more expensive than Faith Hill.
3. There's less rain today than there was yesterday.
4. Clothes are more fashionable at Tommy Hilfiger than other stores.

5. We'd rather listen to blues than other kinds of music.
6. The neighbors near our new house in Brownsville are friendlier than our old house in Boston.
7. Sipping coffee with my English instructor is more enjoyable than a super model.
8. Jose is younger than most professional guitarists.
9. The defense attorney's case is stronger and more interesting than the prosecutor.
10. Judy's flu has grown worse than yesterday.

1.8 Mixed Constructions

A mixed construction is a sentence in which a modifier takes the place of the subject. Consider the following examples:

Alone in the dark street frightened her.

The writer begins the sentence with a prepositional phrase *alone in the dark street*, and makes it the subject of the verb *frightened*. But a prepositional phrase can serve only as a modifier; it cannot be the subject of a sentence.

Revised: Alone in the dark street, she was frightened.

When people celebrate the Spring Festival is a momentous occasion in China.

The adverb clause *When people celebrate Spring Festival* cannot serve as the subject of the verb *is*. The revision replaces the adverb clause with a gerund phrase, a word group that can function as a subject.

Revised: Celebrating the Spring Festival is a momentous occasion in China.

The teacher, a sacred profession, requires intelligence, patience, and responsibility.

The teacher is a person, not a profession. The appositive a sacred profession and the subject the teacher are not logically equivalent. This kind of error is known as *faulty apposition*.

Revised: Teaching, a sacred profession, requires intelligence, patience, and responsibility.

The reason Bob failed the examination is because he had missed many lessons.

Grammatically, the verb *is* should not be followed by an adverb clause beginning with *because*.

Revised: Bob failed the examination because he had missed many lessons.

Task 1.14

Revise the following sentences.

1. Using radiation-proof clothes was a precaution worn by the rescuers in Japan to prevent nuclear radiation.
2. A physician, the career many young people are pursuing, requires at least ten years of challenging work.
3. The reason I did it is because they asked me to do it.
4. Raised in Inner Mongolia made Ling love the prairie.
5. In this box contains the favorite toys of my son's.
6. Early diagnosis of gastric cancer is often curable.
7. Depending on the weather condition determines our distance of travel.
8. By wearing thongs in PE class sprained Jenny's ankle.
9. On seeing the birthday gift on her desk surprised my little daughter.
10. Confident in her language gift prompted Kate to major in English-teaching.

1.9 Building Effective Sentences

1.9.1 Types of Sentences

Depending on the number and the types of clauses they contain, sentences are classified as simple sentence, compound sentence, complex sentence, and compound-complex sentence.

Clauses come in two types: independent clause and subordinate (dependent) clause. An independent clause contains a subject and a predicate, and it can stand alone as a sentence. A subordinate clause also contains a subject and a predicate, but it functions within a sentence as an adjective, an adverb, or a noun; it cannot stand alone.

1. Simple Sentence

A Simple sentence has one independent clause. The chief sentence patterns are as follows:

(1) Subject + linking verb + predicative

He is a very good teacher.

(2) Subject + intransitive verb

The river froze throughout those months.

(3) Subject + transitive verb (active voice) + direct object

The girl waters flowers every day.

(4) Subject + transitive verb (passive voice) + agent

The news was released by Foreign Ministry.

(5) Subject + transitive verb + indirect object + direct object

The teacher asked him a question.

(6) Subject + transitive verb + direct object + object complement

He found that book interesting.

2. Compound Sentence

A compound sentence is composed of two or more independent Clauses. There three ways for us to join the independent clauses of a compound sentence: joining them with a conjunction (*and*, *or*, *nor*, *but*, *for*, *so*, or *yet*), with a semicolon, or with a conjunctive adverb. To remember the coordinating conjunctions, think of the acronym **FANBOYS**: "for" "and" "nor" "but" "or" "yet" and "so".

(1) We use "*and*" to show the relation of **addition** between the clauses:

Paul left early, *and* David followed.

(2) We use "*nor*" to show **addition of a negative point**:

Lucy didn't come to class this morning, *nor* did Liz.

(3) We use "*but*" to show **contrast**:

I like pop songs, *but* my mother love folk songs.

(4) We use "*yet*" to show **concession**:

I don't eat much, *yet* I am still a extra-large size.

(5) We use "*for*" or "*so*" to show logical **consequence**:

He felt no fear, *for* he was a brave man.

He hit me, *so* I struck him back.

(6) We use "*or*" to show **alternative**:

They should leave, *or* I will.

A **conjunctive adverb**, following a semicolon or a coordinating conjunction, can also be used to build a compound sentence. And conjunctive adverbs can specify a relation between one clause and another.

Tab 1.1

Relations	Conjunctive Adverbs	Examples
addition	besides, furthermore, moreover, in addition	She saw that there was indeed a man immediately behind her; *moreover*, he was observing her strangely.
likeness	likewise, similarly, in the same way	Some people have little power to do good; likewise they have little strength to resist evil.
contrast	however, nevertheless, still, nonetheless, conversely, otherwise, instead, in contrast, on the other hand	The news may be unexpected; *nevertheless*, it is true.
cause and effect	therefore, hence, accordingly, consequently, as a result, for this reason, thus, thereby	It rained; *therefore* the football match was postponed.
reinforcement	in fact, in particular, indeed	She carries her age very well. She looks 50 *but in fact* she's more than 60.
example	for example, for instance	Public transportation will also be vastly improved; a high-speed train, *for instance*, will take passengers from Montreal to Toronto in less than two hours.
time	meanwhile, then, subsequently, afterward, earlier, later	He mended the mechanism; *meanwhile*, she watched him.

Most independent clauses are connected by coordinating conjunctions. However, the clauses can also be joined with a semicolon if the relationship between the ideas expressed in the independent clauses is very close and obvious without a conjunction. For example:

In youth we learn; in age we understand.

I love Orleans Roast Chicken wings and Beijing Chicken Roll; they are my favorite kinds of KFC food.

3. Complex sentence

A complex sentence is composed of one independent clause with one or more subordinate (dependent) clauses. Subordinate clauses cannot be sentences on their own. They depend on an independent clause to support them. A complex sentence is often used to make clear which ideas are most important, and which ideas are subordinate: the independent clause in a complex sentence carries the main meaning; subordinate clauses carry minor meanings. Either an independent clause or a subordinate clause may come first, but when the subordinate clause comes first, it is always followed by a comma. For example:

I ate the meal that you cooked.

In this sentence, "I ate the meal" is an independent clause, while "that you cooked" is a relative clause. The independent clause could stand alone as a simple sentence without the relative clause.

Before I went to work, I ate breakfast.

This sentence has "I ate breakfast" as an independent clause, and "before I went to work" as a subordinate clause. When the subordinate clause comes first, it is followed by a comma.

We can recognize subordinate clauses by the kinds of words that introduce them, making them dependent. The technical terms for these words are subordinating conjunctions and relative pronouns. Notice that each of the following dependent clauses begins with such a word:

after I reached the hotel that night

if we can speak a foreign language

because it took so long to get dressed

that I received from him yesterday

Although these clauses contain subjects and verbs, they do not express complete ideas; therefore, they are dependent. By adding an independent clause to each subordinate clause, however, we can change them into complete, grammatically correct *complex* sentences. For example:

After I reached the hotel that night, I called my mother.

If we can speak a foreign language, we will have an advantage when applying for our future jobs.

Because it took so long to get dressed, the boy was always late.

The letter that I received from him yesterday is very important.

4. Compound-complex sentence

A compound-complex sentence contains at least two independent clauses and at least one subordinate clause. For example:

The dog that you gave me barked at me, and it bit my hand.

This compound-complex sentence has two independent clauses "The dog barked at me" and "It bit my hand", and one subordinate clause "that you gave me".

More examples:

Tell the doctor how you feel, and he will decide whether you can be discharged from the hospital.

Hatred, which could destroy so much, never failed to destroy the man who hated, and this was an immutable law. (James Baldwin)

I believe entertainment can aspire to be art, and can become art, but if you set out to make art, you're an idiot. (Steve Martin)

Be who you are and say what you feel, because those who mind don't matter and those who matter don't mind. (Theodor Geisel)

Task 1.15

Identify each of the following sentences as *simple*, *compound*, *complex*, **or** *compound-complex*.

The sentences in this exercise have been adapted from poems in two books by Shel Silverstein: *Where the Sidewalk Ends* (Harper Collins, 1974) and *Falling Up* (Harper Collins, 1996). (http://grammar.about.com)

1. I made an airplane out of stone. ("Stone Airplane")
2. I put a piece of cantaloupe underneath the microscope. ("Nope")
3. Oaties stay oaty, and Wheat Chex stay floaty, and nothing can take the puff out of Puffed Rice. ("Cereal")
4. While fishing in the blue lagoon, I caught a lovely silver fish. ("The Silver Fish")
5. They say if you step on a crack, you will break your mother's back. ("Sidewalking")
6. They just had a contest for scariest mask, and I was the wild and daring one who *won* the contest for scariest mask—and (sob) I'm not even *wearing* one. ("Best Mask?")

7. My voice was raspy, rough, and cracked. ("Little Hoarse")
8. I opened my eyes and looked up at the rain, and it dripped in my head and flowed into my brain. ("Rain")
9. They say that once in Zanzibar a boy stuck out his tongue so far that it reached the heavens and touched a star, which burned him rather badly. ("The Tongue Sticker-Outer")
10. I'm going to Camp Wonderful beside Lake Paradise across from Blissful Mountain in the Valley of the Nice. ("Camp Wonderful")
11. I joke with the bats and have intimate chats with the cooties who crawl through my hair. ("The Dirtiest Man in the World")
12. The animals snarled and screeched and growled and whinnied and whimpered and hooted and howled and gobbled up the whole ice cream stand. ("Ice Cream Stop")
13. The antlers of a standing moose, as everybody knows, are just the perfect place to hang your wet and drippy clothes. ("A Use for a Moose")
14. We'll walk with a walk that is measured and slow, and we'll go where the chalk-white arrows go. ("Where the Sidewalk Ends")
15. If I had a brontosaurus, I would name him Horace or Morris. ("If I Had a Brontosaurus")
16. I am writing these poems from inside a lion, and it's rather dark in here. ("It's Dark in Here")
17. A piece of sky broke off and fell through the crack in the ceiling right into my soup. ("Sky Seasoning")
18. The grungy, grumpy, grouchy Giant grew tired of his frowny pout and hired me and Lee to lift the corners of his crumblin' mouth. ("The Smile Makers")
19. If you were only one inch tall, you'd ride a worm to school. ("One Inch Tall")
20. The traffic light simply would not turn green, so the people stopped to wait as the traffic rolled and the wind blew cold, and the hour grew dark and late. ("Traffic Light")

1.9.2 Building Sentences with Modifiers

A modifier is a word or word group that describes, limits, or qualifies another word or word group in a sentence. There are many patterns of sentence modifiers. Let's learn to build sentences with common modifiers.

1. Building sentences with adjectives and adverbs

The simplest modifiers are adjectives and adverbs. Adjectives modify nouns, while adverb modify verbs, adjectives, and other adverbs. We have the information as the following set of sentences:

The man handed me a photograph of a woman.

He did this silently.

The man was old.

The woman was beautiful.

How should we combine them into a single clear sentence without leaving out any important details?

Combination: The old man silently handed me a photograph of a beautiful woman.

Or: Silently, the old man handed me a photograph of a beautiful woman.

Task 1.16

Combine the sentences in each set into a single clear sentence. Omit words that are needlessly repeated, but don't leave out any important details.

1. Willie had a beard and a moustache.
   The beard was bushy.
   The beard was long.
   The moustache was droopy.
2. The man handed me a photograph of a woman.
   The photograph was torn.
   The photograph was faded.
   The woman was young.
3. The photograph brought back memories.
   The memories were brought back instantly.
   The memories were fine.
   The memories were old.
4. The photograph of the woman brought back memories.
   The memories were brought back instantly.

The woman was beautiful.

The woman was young.

The photograph was torn.

The photograph was faded.

The memories were fine.

The memories were old.

2. Building sentences with appositives

An appositive is a noun or noun phrase that identifies anther noun or noun phrase, or a pronoun.

Marilyn Monroe, *a famous movie star*, committed suicide.

A chronic complainer, she was never satisfied.

My brother *John* wants to be a painter.

All his best friends—*Paul, Kate, Bill and Judy*—are here.

How can we build a sentence with an appositive according to the information given below?

St. Valentine is the patron saint of lovers.

St. Valentine was never married.

Combination: St. Valentine, the patron saint of lovers, was never married.

Task 1.17

Combine the sentences in each set below into a single clear sentence with at least one appositive. Omit words that are needlessly repeated, but don't leave out any important details.

1. Monroe and I strolled through the graveyard.

   The graveyard is the most peaceful spot in town.

2. We were waiting outside the prison cells.

   The cells were a row of sheds fronted with double bars.

   The cells were like small animal cages.

3. My father was outside.

   My father was beneath the window.

   My father whistled for Reggie.

   Reggie was our English setter.

4. We arrived at a group of peasant houses.

   The group was small.

The houses were low yellow constructions.
The houses had dried-mud walls.
The houses had straw mats.
5. A great many old people came.
They knelt around us.
They prayed.
They included old women with jet-black faces.
The women had braided hair.
They included old men with work-gnarled hands.
6. I led a raid on the grocery.
It was the grocery of Barba Nikos.
The grocery was small.
The grocery was shabby.
Barba Nikos was old.
Barba Nikos was short.
Barba Nikos was sinewy.
Barba Nikos was a Greek.
Barba Nikos walked with a slight limp.
Barba Nikos sported a flaring handlebar moustache.

3. Building sentences with adjective clauses

An **adjective clause**, sometimes called a "relative clause", normally begins with a relative adverb *when*, *where*, or *why* or a relative pronoun *who*, *whom*, *whose*, *that*, or *which*. The relative pronoun relates the clause to its antecedent, which is normally the noun or noun phrase preceding the clause. For example:

That is the house *where* I grew up.

This is the dress *that I bought this morning*.

A physician *who smokes and overeats* has no right to criticize the personal habits of his patients.

I know the man *whom you are talking about*.

That is the dog *whose* big brown eyes begged me for another cookie.

I lent some money to Earl, *whose house was destroyed in the flood*.

When he was 18 years old, he went to a technical school in Shanghai, *where he studied physics*.

The English relative pronoun may be omitted and only implied if it plays the role of the object of the verb or object of a preposition in a restrictive clause. For example:

He is *the boy I saw*.

He is the boy whom I saw. (more formal)

I saw *the boy you are talking about*.

I saw the boy about whom you are talking. (more formal)

Consider how these two sentences can be combined:

My mobile phone fell apart after a few weeks.

My mobile phone cost over ¥1,000.

By substituting the relative pronoun *which* for the subject of the second sentence, we can create a single sentence containing an adjective clause:

My mobile phone, *which cost over ¥1,000*, fell apart after a few weeks.

Or we may choose to substitute *which* for the subject of the first sentence:

My mobile phone, *which fell apart after a few weeks*, cost over ¥1,000.

Put what you think is the main idea in the main clause, the secondary (or *subordinate*) idea in the adjective clause. And keep in mind that an adjective clause usually appears *after* the noun it modifies.

Task 1.18

Combine the sentences in each set into a single, clear sentence with at least one adjective clause. Subordinate the information that *you* think is of secondary importance.

1. The first alarm clock woke the sleeper by gently rubbing his feet.
   The first alarm clock was invented by Leonardo da Vinci.
2. Some children have not received flu shots.
   These children must visit the school doctor.
3. Success encourages the repetition of old behavior.
   Success is not nearly as good a teacher as failure.
4. I showed the arrowhead to Rachel.
   Rachel's mother is an archaeologist.
5. Merdine was born in a boxcar. Merdine was born somewhere in Arkansas.
   Merdine gets homesick every time she hears the cry of a train whistle.
6. The space shuttle is a rocket.
   The rocket is manned.

This rocket can be flown back to earth.

This rocket can be reused.

7. Henry Aaron played baseball.

Henry Aaron played with the Braves.

Henry Aaron played for 20 years.

Henry Aaron was voted into the Hall of Fame.

The vote was taken in 1982.

8. Oxygen is colorless.

Oxygen is tasteless.

Oxygen is odorless.

Oxygen is the chief life-supporting element of all plant life.

Oxygen is the chief life-supporting element of all animal life.

9. Bushido is the traditional code of honor of the samurai.

Bushido is based on the principle of simplicity.

Bushido is based on the principle of honesty.

Bushido is based on the principle of courage.

Bushido is based on the principle of justice.

10. Mary danced on the roof.

It was the roof of her trailer.

Mary danced during the thunderstorm.

The thunderstorm flooded the county.

The thunderstorm was last night.

4. Building sentences with adverbial clauses

An adverbial clause is a dependent clause that functions as an adverb.

Tab 1.2

Kind of Clause	Common Conjunctions	Function	Examples
Time Clauses	when, before, after, since, while, as, as long as, until, till, etc. (conjunctions that answer the question "when?"); hardly, scarcely, no sooner, etc.	These clauses are used to say when something happens by referring to a period of time or to another event.	She lived in Beijing *when she was a child*.

Continue Tab 1.2

Kind of Clause	Common Conjunctions	Function	Examples
Conditional Clauses	if, unless, suppose, given, assuming that, providing that, as (so) long as	These clauses are used to talk about a possible or counterfactual situation and its consequences.	*If the weather is fine tomorrow*, we shall go out for a picnic.
Purpose Clauses	so that, in order that	These clauses are used to indicate the purpose of an action.	She drew a plan of the street *so that he could find her house easily*.
Reason Clauses	because, since, as	These clauses are used to indicate the reason for something.	You shouldn't get angry *just because some people speak ill of you*.
Result Clauses	so that	These clauses are used to indicate the result of something.	She sat behind me *so that I couldn't see the expression on her face*.
Degree Clauses	so that, such that, as (so) far as	These clauses are used to indicate the degree of action or state.	His courage is *such that he does not know the meaning of fear*.
Concession Clauses	although, though, even though, while	These clauses are used to make two statements, one of which contrasts with the other or makes it seem surprising.	*Although I understand your point of view*, I don't share it.
Place Clauses	where, wherever, anywhere, everywhere, etc. (conjunctions that answer the question "where?")	These clauses are used to talk about the location or position of something.	He would live with his grandmother *anywhere she lived*.
Clause of Comparison	as, than	Adverb as is a clause which states comparison.	He speaks English as fluently as his teacher.

Continue Tab 1.2

Kind of Clause	Common Conjunctions	Function	Examples
Clauses of Manner	as, as if, as though, the way	These clauses are used to talk about someone's behavior or the way something is done.	Do it *the way your teacher did.*

An adverb clause, like an ordinary adverb, can be shifted to different positions in a sentence. It may be placed at the beginning, at the end, or occasionally even in the middle of a sentence.

(1) An adverb clause commonly appears *after* the main clause:

We waited inside a restaurant *until the rain stopped.*

(2) However, if the action described in the adverb clause precedes the action in the main clause, it is logical to place the adverb clause at the beginning:

When I told her the news, she stared at me in astonishment.

Placing an adverb clause at the beginning can help to create suspense as the sentence builds toward a main point:

After she eloped, she disowned her son.

(3) When working with two adverb clauses, you may want to place one in front of the main clause and the other behind it:

Whenever he ate in the restaurant, he ordered Peking noodles, *which reminded him of the hometown flavor.*

(4) An adverb clause can also be placed inside a main clause, usually between the subject and verb:

The best thing to do, *when you've got a dead body on the kitchen floor and you don't know what to do about it,* is to make yourself a good strong cup of tea.

(Anthony Burgess, *One Hand Clapping*)

Task 1.19

Combine the sentences in each set below by turning the sentence(s) in bold into an adverb clause. Begin the adverb clause with an appropriate

subordinating conjunction.

1. It is unlikely that Cleopatra actually committed suicide with an asp.

   The species is unknown in Egypt.

2. The boy hid the gerbil.

   No one would ever find it.

3. **Our neighbors installed a swimming pool.**

   The pool is in their backyard.

   They have gained many new friends.

4. My parents and I watched in awe.

   We watched on a hot August evening.

   Erratic bolts of lightning illuminated the sky.

   The bolts of lightning were from a distant storm.

5. **Benny played the violin.**

   The dog hid in the bedroom

   The dog whimpered.

6. Natural rubber is used chiefly to make tires and inner tubes.

   It is cheaper than synthetic rubber.

   It has greater resistance to tearing when wet.

7. **A Peruvian woman finds an unusually ugly potato.**

   She runs up to the nearest man.

   She smashes it in his face.

   This is done by ancient custom.

8. Credit cards are dangerous.

   They encourage people to buy things.

   These are things that people are unable to afford.

   These are things that people do not really need.

9. Some day I shall take my glasses off.

   Some day I shall go wandering.

   I shall go out into the streets.

   I shall do this deliberately.

   I shall do this when the clouds are heavy.

   I shall do this when the rain is coming down.

   I shall do this when the pressure of realities is too great.

   5. Building sentences with noun clauses

   A **Noun Clause** is a dependent clause that functions as a noun (that is, as a subject, object, predicative or appositive) within a sentence. It is also known as a *nominal clause*.

It is disappointing *that Judy can't come*. (subject)

I can prove *that he did it*. (object)

This is the story of *what a Woman's patience can endure*, and of *what a Man's resolution can achieve*. (the object of the preposition "of")

The question is *whether he will come to help us*. (predicative)

The residents ignored the report *that the area was dangerous*. (appositive)

Consider how each group of sentences should be combined into a single clear sentence by using at least one noun clause.

Troubles come.

That is not the real problem.

We don't know how to meet troubles.

That is the real problem.

Dr. Robert Harris suggests this.

Dr. Robert Harris is a water specialist at the Environmental Defense Fund.

Do something before you make a major investment in bottled water.

Check with the manufacturer as to its source.

Check with the manufacturer as to the type of processing.

Check with the manufacturer as to results of tests of its content and purity.

Combination of the first group of sentences:

The real problem is not just *that troubles come*, but *that we don't know how to meet them*.

Combination of the second group of sentences:

Dr. Robert Harris, water specialist at the Environmental Defense Fund, suggests *that before you make a major investment in bottled water, check with the manufacturer as to its source, the type of processing, and results of tests of its content and purity*.

(Jane E. Brody, "How to Make Sure Your Water Is Fit to Drink")

Task 1.20

Combine the sentences in each set into a single clear sentence with at least one noun clause. Turn all questions into declarative statements, and elim-

inate any needless repetition.

1. One either has or does not have a mathematical mind.
   This is a common myth about the nature of mathematical ability.
2. How does cross-country skiing differ most fundamentally from downhill skiing?
   It differs in the way you get yourself uphill.
3. What will radar scanning be valuable for?
   It will detect modern waterways lying near the surface in arid areas.
   Geologists believe this.
4. What does the American value?
   The American does not value the possession of money as such.
   The American values his power to make money as a proof of his manhood.
5. What should politicians be encouraged to do?
   They should stand for what they believe in.
   They should not formulate their principles on the basis of opinion polls.
6. What is the only thing a man can do for eight hours a day, day after day?
   He can work.
   That is the saddest thing.
7. Do you have what you want?
   That is not happiness.
   Do you want what you have?
   That is happiness.
8. What kind of inner resources do we have?
   What imperishable treasures of mind and heart have we deposited in the bank of the spirit against this rainy day?
   The truth is this.
   When we are in trouble we discover these things.
   We discover them swiftly.
   We discover them painfully.
9. Is work useful?
   Or is work useless?
   Is work productive?
   Or is work parasitic?
   In practice nobody cares.
   Work shall be profitable.

That is the sole thing demanded.
10. What kind of person are you?

How do you feel about others?

How will you fit into a group?

Are you assured?

Or are you anxious?

To what degree do you feel comfortable with the standards of your own culture?

Nonverbal communications signal these things to members of your own group.

6. Building sentences with participle

A **participle** is a form of a verb which is used in a sentence to modify a noun or noun phrase, and thus plays a role similar to that of an adjective or adverb. It is one of the types of non-finite forms. There are two forms of participles: the present participle and the past participle.

The girl *sitting* over there is my sister.

Not *knowing* the language and *having* no friends in this city, he found it difficult to find a job.

Having read the instructions, he snatched up the fire extinguisher.

The chicken *eaten* by the children was contaminated.

Aroused by the crash, he leapt to his feet.

Having been bitten twice, the postman refused to deliver our letters unless we chained our dog up.

How the following set of sentences can be combined by using at least one participle phrase?

He eats slowly.

He eats steadily.

He sucks the sardine oil from his fingers.

The sardine oil is rich.

He sucks the oil with slow and complete relish

The dishwasher was invented in 1889.

The dishwasher was invented by an Indiana housewife.

The first dishwasher was driven by a steam engine.

Combination of the first group of sentences:

He eats slowly, steadily, *sucking* the rich sardine oil from his fingers with slow and complete relish.

Combination of the second group of sentences:

Invented by an Indiana housewife in 1889, the first dishwasher was driven by a steam engine.

Task 1.21

Combine the sentences in each set into a single clear sentence with at least one participial phrases. Eliminate any needless repetition.

1. I took small sips from a can of Coke.

   I was sitting on the ground in a shady corner.

   I was sitting with my back against the wall.

2. I was sitting on the window ledge.

   The ledge overlooked the narrow street.

   I watched the children.

   The children were frolicking in the first snow of the season.

3. The first edition of *Infant Care* was published by the U. S. Government.

   The first edition of *Infant Care* was published in 1914.

   The first edition of *Infant Care* recommended the use of peat moss for disposable diapers.

4. The house sat stately upon a hill.

   The house was gray.

   The house was weather-worn.

   The house was surrounded by barren tobacco fields.

5. I washed the windows in a fever of fear.

   I whipped the squeegee swiftly up and down the glass.

   I feared that some member of the gang might see me.

6. Goldsmith smiled.

   He bunched his cheeks like twin rolls of toilet paper.

   His cheeks were fat.

   The toilet paper was smooth.

   The toilet paper was pink.

7. The medieval peasant was distracted by war.

   The medieval peasant was weakened by malnutrition.

   The medieval peasant was exhausted by his struggle to earn a living.

The medieval peasant was an easy prey for the dreadful Black Death.

7. Building sentences with absolutes

In linguistics, an absolute construction is a grammatical construction standing apart from a normal or usual syntactical relation with other words or sentence elements. An absolute is made up of a noun and its modifiers. It may precede, follow, or interrupt the main clause. For example:

Night falling, we hurried home.

This done, we went home.

He came into the room, *his ears red with cold*.

The meeting over, we all went home.

She came out of the library, *a large book under her arm*.

He used to sleep *with the window open*.

There being no bus or taxi, we had to go home on foot.

Task 1.22

Revise the following incorrect absolutes.

1. Being freezing cold, he put on his down jacket.
2. A young mother was going window shopping, followed her little son.
3. His compute wrong, he had to write her assignment by hand.
4. Having finished her composition, we went home.
5. My brother came home at midnight, with his clothes covering with snow.

Task 1.23

Combine the sentences in each set into a single clear sentence with an absolute construction. Eliminate any needless repetition.

1. Ed and the little man climbed the stairs together.

   Each was lost in his own strange world.

2. I sat on the highest limb of a sturdy oak tree.

   Its branches were reaching to the clouds.

   The branches were reaching as if to claim a piece of the sky.

3. The dog trots away.

   His head and tail are erect.

   His hips are slightly to one side and out of line with his shoulders.

4. The raccoon goes down on all fours and strides slowly off.
   Her slender front paws are reaching ahead of her.
   Her slender front paws are like the hands of an experienced swimmer.
5. My grandparents were holding hands in a New York City subway train.
   Their faces were old.
   Their faces were beautifully lined.
   Their gray heads were almost touching.
6. I sat huddled on the steps.
   My cheeks were resting sullenly in my palms.
   I was half listening to what the grownups were saying.
   I was half lost in a daydream.
7. One sunny morning I whipped down the Roxbury Road on my bicycle.
   The front spokes were melting into a saw blade.
   The wind was shrilling tunes.
   The tunes came through the vent holes in my helmet.
8. An elderly woman shuffles slowly to a park bench and sits down heavily.
   Her wig is slightly askew.
   Her wig is ash-blond.
   Her wig is showing tuffs of hair.
   The hair was thin.
   The hair was gray.
9. Arthur fidgets on his high-legged chair.
   A pencil is poking out from behind his ear.
   Arthur is in his box-like office.
   His office is in the old Loft's candy factory on Broome Street.
10. There were several species of turtle.
    These species took to the sea between 90 million and 100 million years ago.
    The turtles had stubby legs.
    Their legs were adapting into flippers.
    The flippers were streamlined.

Chapter 2　Punctuation and Mechanics

2.1　End Punctuation

2.1.1　The Period

(1) A period(.) is used to mark the end of a declarative sentence, a mild command, or an indirect question. For example:

She tells her little daughter a short story every night.
Please give me your telephone number.
The taxi driver asked me where I wanted to go.

(2) A period is conventionally used in abbreviations of titles and Latin words or phrases, including the time designations for morning and afternoon.

Mr.　　i.e.　　a.m. (or AM)
Ms.　　e.g.　　p.m. (or PM)
Dr.　　etc.　　R.S.V.P.

Current usage is to omit the period in abbreviations of organization names, academic degrees, and designations for eras.

NATO　UNESCO　UCLA　IBM　BS　PhD　BC

2.1.2　Question Mark

(1) A direct question should be followed by a question mark(?).

What is your favorite sport?

If a polite request is written in the form of a question, it may be followed by a period.

Would you please send me your catalog of lilies.

(2) A question mark indicates uncertainty within a statement.

She must have paid much money (2,000 Yuan?) for that dress.

Do not use a question mark after an indirect question, one that is reported rather than asked directly. Use a period instead.

He asked me who was teaching the psychology course this term.

(3) When using the Question Mark with Quotations or Dialogue, be sure to check if a question mark is part of a quotation or a piece of dialogue (whether we are quoting a question or a person is asking a question) or if we are asking a question about a quotation.

If it is part of a quotation or a piece of dialogue, the question mark goes inside the quotation marks:

She asked, "Who wrote the song?"

If we are asking a question about a quotation, the question mark comes after the closing quotation marks:

Who was it that said, "Music is the universal language"?

2.1.3 The Exclamation Point

An exclamation point(!) is used after a word group or sentence to express exceptional feeling or to provide special emphasis.

You scared me to death!

What a spectacular view!

When Donna entered the room, I switched on the lights, and we all yelled, "Surprise!"

Do not overuse the exclamation point. Too many of them will dull the effect:

We finally got there! We thought we'd never make it!! But we were there at last!!!

Revised: We finally got there. We thought we'd never make it. But we were there at last!

Task 2.1

The following paragraph has been adapted from an essay by British journalist Richard Boston. Throughout the paragraph, you'll find a number of empty paired brackets: [ ]. Replace each set of brackets with the appropriate end mark of punctuation: a period, question mark, or exclamation point. Then capitalize the first letter of the word that starts each new sentence.

Down With Skool!

I am not against all schools[ ] I am very much in favor of schools that consist of groups of porpoises or similar aquatic animals that swim together[ ] I only wish that I had been to one[ ] no, I'm thinking more of school in the dictionary sense as an institution or building at which children and young people receive education[ ] that dictionary definition tells the story[ ] what a school of porpoises do is play[ ] skool is for work[ ] it is an institution[ ] why put children in an institution[ ] the real reason is that it gets the brats out from under parents' feet[ ] the purported reason is that this is the best way to get useful information into the skulls of the little darlings[ ] how absurd[ ] children are more intelligent than adults and wiser[ ] instead of instilling into them the accepted knowledge and wisdom of the past, what we ought to be doing is learning from them[ ] that would be my idea of a good school: one run by children—or porpoises[ ]

(Adapted from "Down With Skool!" by Richard Boston. *Guardian Weekly*, April 22, 1990)

2.2 The Comma

The comma (,) is the most common form of punctuation. It serves several functions in writing and helps our readers understand our ideas and sentences. Commas clarify, make distinctions, or create the pauses that help our readers follow our sentences and ideas.

(1) Use a comma before a coordinating conjunction in order to combine two independent clauses to create a compound sentence. Use FANBOYS ("for" "and" "nor" "but" "or" "yet" and "so") after a comma to combine two independent clauses (when we use any other word, we end up with a comma splice). Always use one of the FANBOYS and a comma when joining two independent clauses.

Independent clause + , + FANBOYS + independent clause

The computer graphics course is fun, and the professor is excellent.

Many students want to take the course, but it is already full.

He felt no fear, for he was a brave man.

I am not an emotional type, so I cannot bring myself to tell him I love him.

She had to have the operation, or she would die.

I never saw her again, nor I regret it.

I have been on diet for a long time, yet I am a size 16.

Do *not* use a comma to separate coordinate word groups that are not independent clauses.

Linder took the course last semester *and* said it was great.

(2) Use a comma to separate the items in a series (a list of three or more items) or a list of coordinate adjectives.

Item + , item + , item + , and item

1) Using commas with items in a series. Commas help separate distinct items within a list of items. For example:

My uncle willed me all of his property, houses, and boats.

The activities include touring the White House, visiting the Air and Space Museum, attending a lecture about the Founding Fathers and kayaking on the Potomac River.

Maya has taken several other computer courses, including Computer Programming, Software Tools, and Web Site Development.

Although some writers view the comma between the last two items as optional, most experts advise using the comma because its omission can result in ambiguity or misreading.

I went to the movie with my cousins, Marco, and Sofia.

Without the second comma, the reader would not know whether Marco and Sofia are the names of the speaker's cousins or the names of two other people who accompanied the speaker and the speaker's cousins to the movie.

2) Use a comma between coordinate adjectives. Don't use a comma between cumulative or compound adjectives.

When two or more adjectives each modify a noun separately, they are coordinate. We use a comma between them.

Martin is a *kind, gentle, affectionate* father.

If the adjectives can be joined with *and*, the adjectives are **coordinate**, so we should use commas: *warm* and *gentle* and *affectionate* (*warm, gentle, affectionate*).

If the adjectives are working together in order to describe something or modify each other in stages, then *do not* use commas:

Two large dark shapes moved slowly toward us.

The modifiers lean on one another, with each modifying a larger word group. *Dark* modifies *shapes*, *large* modifies *dark shapes*, and *two* modifies *large dark shapes*. Cumulative adjectives cannot be joined with *and* (not *two* and *large* and *dark shapes*).

The man often wears *dirty blue* jeans.

No comma should come between *dirty* and *blue* because the words function as cumulative adjectives.

If two adjectives are used together to make one descriptor, then they become a compound adjective, and we should use a hyphen between them instead of a comma.

Coordinate adjectives: The *small*, *modern* hospital provides excellent care for patients.

Small and *modern* are two separate qualities, so use a comma.

Compound adjective: The *small-animal* hospital provides excellent care for dogs and cats.

Small-animal is one quality, so use a hyphen.

Task 2.2

Add or delete commas where necessary in the following sentences. If a sentence is correct, write "C" after it.

1. The cold impersonal atmosphere of the university was unbearable.
2. An ambulance threaded its way through police cars, fire trucks and irate citizens.
3. The 1812 *Overture* is a stirring, magnificent piece of music.
4. After two broken arms, three cracked ribs and one concussion, Ken quit the varsity football team.
5. My cat's pupils had constricted to small black shining slits.
6. NASA's rovers on Mars are equipped with special cameras that can take close-up high-resolution pictures of the terrain.
7. A baseball player achieves the triple crown by having the highest batting average, the most home runs, and the most runs batted in during the regular

season.

8. If it does not get enough sunlight, a healthy green lawn can turn into a shriveled brown mess within a matter of days.
9. Love, vengeance, greed and betrayal are common themes in Western literature.
10. Many experts believe that shark attacks on surfers are a result of the sharks' mistaking surfboards for small, injured seals.

(3) Use a comma after an introductory clause or phrase.

Dependent clause + , + remainder of sentence
Introductory phrase + , + remainder of sentence
Introductory word + , + remainder of sentence

1) Introductory dependent clause.

Use a comma between the end of an introductory dependent clause and the remainder of the sentence.

After I had finished our laundry, I discovered that one sock was missing.

2) Introductory prepositional phrase.

Use a comma after a prepositional phrase that comes at the beginning of the sentence.

Near a small stream at the bottom of the canyon, the park rangers discovered an abandoned mine.

3) Introductory participial phrase.

Use a comma after a participial phrase that comes at the beginning of the sentence.

Jogging through the park, I feel a little creaky at first.

4) Introductory word for emphasis or transition.

Use a comma after a transitional or emphatic word that comes at the beginning of the sentence.

Eventually, I hit my stride and feel totally energized.

5) Direct address.

When we begin a sentence by directly addressing someone by name or title, we use a comma after the name or title.

Daniel, have you ever been to the Great Wall?

If the direct address comes at the end of the sentence, we need a comma before the name or title. If the direct address comes in the middle of the sentence, use two commas, one before and one after the name or title.

Have you ever been to the Great Wall, *Daniel*?

I can tell you, *Daniel*, the Great Wall is an amazing place.

6) "Yes" "no" or "well" statements.

Use a comma after a *yes*, a *no*, or a *well* that begins a sentence.

Yes, I went there when I came to China for the first time.

No, I don't think so.

Well, I will think about it.

7) Tag lines for dialogue or quotations.

Use a comma after a tag word or phrase that comes before a quotation or a dialogue in your sentence.

The teacher asked, "Have you finished your composition?"

Walt Whitman wrote, "Justice is always in jeopardy."

(4) Use a comma to set off interrupters words, phrases, or clauses that interrupt a sentence between the beginning and end of an independent clause (IC).

Beginning of IC + , + interrupter + , + end of IC

1) Dependent clause interrupter.

Use commas before and after a dependent clause that interrupts an independent clause.

Tom decided, *after he heard of the high cost of housing*, to share an apartment.

The sentence should still make sense if we removed the interrupting clause.

Tom decided to share an apartment.

2) Transitional words and phrases or parenthetical interrupters.

Use commas before and after transitional words or parenthetical interrupters.

Most of his friends, *however*, had already made other housing arrangements.

Natural foods are not always salt free; celery, *for example*, contains more sodium than most people would imagine.

Evolution, *as far as we know*, doesn't work this way.

3) Nonrestrictive elements.

A nonrestrictive modifier describes a noun or pronoun whose meaning has already been clearly defined or limited. Because the modifier contains nonessential or parenthetical information, it is set off with commas. If we remove a nonrestrictive element from a sentence, the meaning does not change dramatically. Some meaning may be lost, but the defining characteristics of the person or thing described remain the same.

But we often find it difficult to tell whether a word group is restrictive or nonrestrictive without seeing it in context and considering the writer's meaning. Both of the following sentences are grammatically correct, but their meaning is slightly different.

The dessert *made with peaches* was delicious.

The dessert, *made with peaches*, was delicious.

In the first example, the phrase *made with peaches* tells readers which of two or more desserts the writer is referring to. In the example with commas, the phrase merely adds information about the dessert.

a. A nonrestrictive adjective clause starts with a relative pronoun (*who*, *whom*, *whose*, or *which*) or with a relative adverb (*where* or *when*). The information conveyed by this type of clause is not essential for identifying the subject of the sentence. We should bear in mind that nonrestrictive adjective clauses are set off with commas; restrictive adjective clauses are not.

Nonrestrictive: Water, *which is a clear liquid*, has many uses.

The adjective clause *which is a clear liquid* does not restrict the meaning of *water*; the information is nonessential and is therefore enclosed in commas.

Restrictive: The giant panda that was born at the San Diego Zoo in 2003 was sent to China in 2007.

The adjective clause *that was born at the San Diego Zoo in 2003* identifies one particular panda out of many, so the information is essential and is therefore not enclosed in commas.

b. Prepositional or verbal phrases may be restrictive or nonrestrictive. Nonrestrictive phrases are set off with commas; restrictive phrases are not.

Nonrestrictive: The helicopter, *with its million-candlepower spotlight illuminating the area*, circled above.

The *with* phrase is nonessential because its purpose is not to specify which of two or more helicopters is being discussed. The phrase is not required for readers to understand the meaning of the sentence.

Restrictive: One corner of the attic was filled with newspapers dating from the early 1900s.

Dating from the early 1900s restricts the meaning of *newspapers*, so the comma should be omitted.

  c. An appositive is a noun or noun phrase that renames a nearby noun. Nonrestrictive appositives are set off with commas; restrictive appositives are not.

  Nonrestrictive: Tom heard that David, *a friend from college*, was looking for an apartment mate.

  The appositive *a friend from college* is nonessential information, so it should be set off with commas.

  Restrictive: My friend *Li Wei* is from Beijing.

  Once they've read *my friend*, readers still don't know who he is. The appositive following *my friend* restricts its meaning, so the appositive should not be enclosed in commas.

  (5) Use a comma to set off absolute phrases.

  An absolute phrase, which modifies the whole sentence, is made up of a noun and its modifiers (which frequently, but not always, include a participle or participial phrase). Absolute phrases may appear at the beginning or at the end of a sentence. Wherever they appear, they should be set off with commas.

  The river having risen in the night, crossing is impossible.

  We redoubled our efforts, *each person working like two*.

  It rained and rained, *vehicles bogged down and bridges washed out*.

  Do not insert a comma between the noun and the participle in an absolute construction.

Task 2.3

Add or delete commas where necessary in the following sentences. If a sentence is correct, write "C" after it.

1. When Mt. St. Helens erupted in the 1980s many people in Seattle worried about the status of Mount Rainier.
2. My sister who plays center on the Sparks now lives at The Sands a beach house near Los Angeles.
3. Being written in haste the composition is full of mistakes.
4. I had the pleasure of talking to a woman who had just returned from India where she had lived for ten years.

5. I shall never forget the day when we first met in the park.
6. A member of an organization, that provides job training for teens, was also appointed to the education commission.
7. Crocodiles in fact do not particularly like human flesh.
8. All our savings gone we started looking for jobs.
9. Brian Eno who began his career as a rock musician turned to meditative compositions in the late 1970s.
10. Their room was on the third floor its window overlooking the sports-ground.

(6) Use commas according to conventions for dates, address, numbers, and titles and to avoid confusion.

1) Date.

Abraham Lincoln was born on *February 12, 1809*.

Charles Darwin was born on *February 12, 1809*, the same day Abraham Lincoln was born.

If more information follows, the comma is required to be placed also after the year, as in the second example above.

If the date is inverted or if only the month and year are given, commas are not needed.

Shenzhou 10th manned spacecraft was launched on 11 June 2013.

June 2013 was an extremely hot month.

2) Address.

The elements of an address or a place name are separated with commas.

Darwin grew up in a large, comfortable home in *Shrewsbury, England*.
Lincoln grew up in *Hardin County, Kentucky*, in a one-room log cabin.

3) Numbers.

In numbers more than four digits long, use commas to separate the numbers into groups of three, starting from the right. In numbers four digits long, a comma is optional.

2,800 (*or* 2800)
500,000
7,000,000

Do not use commas in street numbers, zip codes, telephone numbers, or years with four or fewer digits.

4) Formal titles.

If a title follows a name, separate the title from the rest of the sentence with a pair of commas.

Don Kroodsma, *PhD*, analyzes how and why birds sing.

(7) Use commas to prevent confusion.

To err is human; to forgive, divine.

The comma is used to signal the omission.

Because of bird-rescue efforts after the oil spill, some oil-coated birds that were not expected to *survive*, *survived*.

The comma is used to distinguish between repeated words.

When Not to Use a Comma

(1) Do not use a comma after the last item in a series of adjectives preceding the noun.

Nonstandard: He is a dedicated, imaginative, creative, artist.

Standard: He is a dedicated, imaginative, creative artist.

(2) Do not use a comma between two words joined by a coordinating conjunction.

Nonstandard: A good night's rest, and a healthy breakfast are the best preparation for a test.

Standard: A good night's rest and a healthy breakfast are the best preparation for a test.

(3) Do not separate a verb from a restrictive *that* clause.

Nonstandard: I know, that he has returned.

Standard: I know that he has returned.

(4) Do not use a comma to separate the subject from its verb.

Nonstandard: The American painter Whistler, is best known for his painting of his mother.

Standard: The American painter Whistler is best known for his painting of his mother.

(5) Do not use a comma to separate independent clauses unless the comma is followed by a coordinate conjunction.

Nonstandard: Honey is sweet, the bee stings.

Standard: Honey is sweet, but the bee stings.

Task 2.4

Add or delete commas where necessary. If a sentence is correct, write "C" after it.

1. Cricket which originated in England is also popular in Australia, South Africa and India.
2. At the sound of the starting pistol the horses surged forward toward the first obstacle, a sharp incline three feet high.
3. After seeing an exhibition of Western art Gerhard Richter escaped from East Berlin, and smuggled out many of his notebooks.
4. Corrie's new wet suit has an intricate, blue pattern.
5. The cookies will keep for two weeks in sturdy airtight containers.
6. On June 15, 2013 our office moved to 30 Peace Road, Mudanjiang 157099.
7. The coach having bawled us out thoroughly, we left the locker room with his harsh words ringing in our ears.
8. Ms. Carlson you are a valued customer whose satisfaction is very important to us.
9. Mr. Mundy was born on July 22, 1939 in Arkansas, where his family had lived for four generations.
10. Her board poised at the edge of the half-pipe, Nina waited her turn to drop in.

2.3 Semicolon

(1) Use a semicolon(;) between two independent clauses when the second clause has a strong connection to the first, and they are equally important.

  The moon went down; the stars grew pale.
  The law is clear; the question is whether it is fair.

(2) Use a semicolon between independent clauses linked with a conjunctive adverb or a transitional phrase, which is usually followed by a comma.

  The Bentley is an expensive automobile; *moreover*, its maintenance costs are higher than for most other cars.
  Many corals grow very gradually; *in fact*, the creation of a coral reef can

take centuries.

Common Conjunctive Adverbs:

Accordingly   furthermore   moreover   still   also   hence   nevertheless   subsequently   anyway   however   next   then   besides   incidentally   nonetheless   therefore   certainly   indeed   now   thus   Consequently   instead   otherwise   Conversely   likewise   similarly   finally   meanwhile   specifically

Common Transitional Phrases:

after all   even so   in fact   as a matter of fact   for example   for instance   in other words   as a result   in the first place   at any rate   in addition   on the contrary   at the same time   in conclusion   on the other hand

　　(3) Use a semicolon in a series between items that already contain internal punctuation.

　　In the United States, travelers can observe impressive waterfalls in Yosemite National Park, California; Colonial Peak, Washington; Glacier National Park, Montana; and Niagara Falls, New York.

　　Her children were born a year apart: Adam, 2010; Lily, 2011; and Betty, 2012.

Task 2.5

Add a semicolon or comma where needed in the following sentences, and delete any unnecessary punctuation. If a sentence is punctuated correctly, write "C" in front of it.

1. Cows will not eat hay that has a musty odor, therefore, farmers must make sure that it is dry before they bale it.
2. Professor Kgosi showed us slides of his trip to Zanzibar, Tabora, and Linga in Tanzanina, Nairob, Nakum, and Mombasa in Kenya, and Jube, Waw, and Kartoum in Sudan.
3. I will have to find a job this semester or I will have to get a loan to pay for my tuition.
4. Eddie decided to leave before dinner because the roads were becoming icy.
5. Jessica quit her job at the bakery last week, she plans to move to Cedar Rapids to take over her father's farm.
6. The music that the disc jockey played was from the 1950s so I decided to

listen instead of dance.
7. Tran speaks English at school, at home, however, he speaks Vietnamese.
8. Monaco has no famous colleges or universities, however, it has a ninety-nine percent literacy rate.
9. One moment he was friendly, even warm, the next he was coldly indifferent.
10. If an animal does something, we call it instinct, if we do the same thing, we call it intelligence.

2.4 Colon

(1) Use a colon(:) between two independent clauses when the second clause explains, summarizes, or answers the first one.

The contestants in the TV talent show all had the same dream: They wanted to become famous.

NOTE: When a colon separates two independent clauses, the second independent clause usually begins with a capital letter.

(2) Use a colon after an independent clause that is followed by a word or phrase that answers or explains the idea set up in the independent clause.

The contestants in the TV talent show all had the same dream: fame.

(3) Use a colon to introduce a list of items after an independent clause.

We also started getting in shape for the athletic meeting: taking long distance running, lifting weights, eating healthy foods, and getting enough sleep.

(4) Use a colon according to convention.

1) Salutation in a formal letter(American English).

Dear Sir or Madam:

2) Hours and minutes.

8:10 a.m.

3) Proportions.

The ratio of girls to boys was 2:1.

4) Title and subtitle.

The Glory of Hera: Greek Mythology and the Greek Family

5) Bibliographic entries.

Boston: Pearson, 2011

When Not to Use a Colon

(1) Do *not* place a colon between a verb and its objects or complements or between a preposition and its objects.

Nonstandard: Some important vitamins found in vegetables are: vitamin A, vitamin B1, niacin, and vitamin C.

Nonstandard: Charlie Chaplin was easily recognized by: his black mustache, his walk, and his black hat.

(2) Do not use a colon after *especially*, *such as*, *consisted of*, *including*, and other words or phrases that indicate a list will follow.

Nonstandard: The NCAA regulates college athletic teams, including: basketball, baseball, softball, and football.

Task 2.6

Insert a colon wherever needed in the following sentences, and delete any colons that are unnecessary or incorrect. If a sentence is correct, write "C" in front of it.

1. Although Barbara and I were in Boston for just one day, we were able to achieve our goal a tour of the city's historical sites.
2. The Boston area is home to more than fifty colleges and universities, including Harvard University, Boston College, and the Massachusetts Institute of Technology.
3. The North End and Beacon Hill possess quaint features of a bygone era cobbled streets, gaslights, and treacherous brick sidewalks.
4. At the Congress Street bridge we saw a full-scale working replica of the Boston Tea Party ship and a colorful reenactment of the dumping of tea into the harbor.
5. Barbara and I stopped for coffee at the Bull & Finch pub, whose facade and interior were featured in the television show *Cheers*.
6. I was amazed by the New England Aquarium's four-story circular glass tank, which houses the aquarium's main attractions sharks, turtles, eels, and hundreds of tropical fish.
7. We next visited the Old North Church, whose steeple contained the two lan-

terns that sparked the famous midnight ride of: Paul Revere.
8. Next we toured the 1713 Old State House to see: tea from the Boston Tea Party, one of John Hancock's coats, and the east front where the Boston Massacre occurred.
9. Handwritten documents, tape recordings, and the actual Oval Office desk these mementos at the John F. Kennedy Library touched us deeply.
10. As dusk descended on Boston, Barbara and I strolled to the Public Garden for our final treat a ride in one of the famous swan-shaped boats.

2.5　The Apostrophe

(1) Use an apostrophe(') to indicate omitted letters in a contraction.

It's a shame that Frank *can't* go on the tour.

It's stands for *it is*, *can't* for *cannot*.

Many people today confuse "it's" (the contraction for "it is") and "its" (the possessive pronoun, which never takes an apostrophe).

The car is old, but *its* paint is new.

Its shows the car's possession of paint.

The car is old, but *it's* reliable.

It's is a contraction for *it is*.

The apostrophe is also used to mark the omission of the first two digits of a year (*the class of* '12) or years (*the* '90s *generation*).

(2) Add an apostrophe plus "s" to a noun to show possession.

Mary's cat ate the *dog's* dinner.

(3) Add an apostrophe plus "s" to an indefinite pronoun to show possession.

Someone's umbrella has been left behind.

(4) Add only an apostrophe to a plural noun ending in "s" to show possession.

All *passengers'* luggage must undergo security check.

(5) To show joint possession between two people or things, you need to add an apostrophe and "-s" only to the second noun. To show separate ownership, add an apostrophe plus "-s" to both nouns.

Johnson and White's design project will be presented today.

Johnson's and *White's* design projects will be presented today.

(6) Be careful to avoid adding an apostrophe when the occasion simply calls for the plural use of a word.

Incorrect: We ordered *chip's* and dip.

Correct: We ordered *chips* and dip.

(7) In some cases you may add an apostrophe plus "s" to a singular word ending in "s" especially when the word is a proper name or for ease of pronunciation.

Doris's name was popular in the 1950s.

(8) To avoid confusion, you may use an apostrophe plus "s" to form the plurals of letters and words discussed as words. An apostrophe is not used on plural numbers (1960s, 80s, nines) or abbreviations (DVDs, CDs).

He made three "C's" last semester.

Or: He made three Cs last semester.

You use too many "and's" in your sentence.

Or: You use too many *ands* in your sentence.

Steve earned two PhDs before his thirtieth birthday.

Task 2.7

Edit the following sentences to correct errors in the use of the apostrophe. If a sentence is correct, write "C" after it.

1. Our favorite barbecue restaurant is Poor Richards Ribs.
2. This diet will improve almost anyone's health.
3. The innovative shoe fastener was inspired by the designers young son.
4. Each days menu features a different European country's dish.
5. Sue worked overtime to increase her families earnings.
6. Ms. Jacobs is unwilling to listen to students complaints about computer failures.

2.6 Quotation Marks

In the U.S., *periods* and *commas* always go *inside* the quotation marks(" " and ' '). In the U.K., periods and commas go inside the quotation marks only for a complete quoted sentence; otherwise, they go outside. In all varieties of English, *semicolons* and *colons* go *outside* the quotation marks.

(1) Use quotation marks for direct quotations; that is, use quotation marks around the exact words of a speaker.

"I'd like a soda and a hamburger, please," said the customer.

Bill's mother said to him, "I'm not satisfied with your grade."

When a quotation is interrupted, an extra set of marks should be used.

"Send me an email," Linda said, "if you decide to visit Beijing."

In dialogue, begin a new paragraph to mark a change in speaker.

"Mom, his name is Willie, not William. A thousand times I've told you, it's *Willie*."

"Willie is a derivative of William, Lester. Surely his birth certificate doesn't have Willie on it, and I like calling people by their proper names."

"Yes, it does, ma'am. My mother named me Willie K. Mason."

—Gloria Naylor

Do not use quotation marks for indirect quotations.

Bill's mother told him that she was not satisfied with his grade.

Long quotations of prose or poetry are generally set off from the text by indenting. Quotation marks are not used because the indented format tells readers that the quotation is taken word-for-word from the source.

After making an exhaustive study of the historical record, James Horan evaluates Billy the Kid like this:

The portrait that emerges of [the Kid] from the thousands of pages of affidavits, reports, trial transcripts, his letters, and his testimony is neither the mythical Robin Hood nor the stereotyped adenoidal moron and pathological killer. Rather Billy appears as a disturbed, lonely young man, honest, loyal to his friends, dedicated to his beliefs, and betrayed by our institutions and the corrupt, ambitious, and compromising politicians in his time. (158)

(2) Use quotation marks around the titles of essays, articles, chapter headings, short stories, short poems, and songs.

The first draft of my favorite E. B. White essay, "Once More to the Lake," was a letter that White wrote to his brother a week after their mother's death.

(3) Use quotation marks around definitions and words with special meanings.

The word "bigwig" meaning an important person, is derived from the large wigs worn by seventeenth-century British judges.

(4) Use quotation marks around words that are being singled out to indicate irony.

School and work leave little time for anything else: My "free time" is used for running errands and doing chores.

(5) The period and the comma go inside quotation marks; the semicolon and the colon go outside. If the quoted material is a question, the question mark goes inside; if the quoted material is a part of a whole sentence that is a question, the mark goes outside. The rules for exclamation points are the same as those for question marks.

"The contract negotiations are stalled," the airline executive told reporters, "but I am prepared to work night and day to bring both sides together."

Harold wrote, "I regret that I am unable to attend the fundraiser for AIDS research"; his letter, however, came with a substantial contribution.

"That video game is too loud!" exclaimed Ed's father.

"Which ice cream flavor is your favorite?" I asked my classmate.

Have you heard the old proverb "Do not climb the hill until you reach it"?

The word I associate with my job is "exciting"!

(6) Use single quotation marks to enclose a quotation (or words requiring quotation marks) within a quotation.

"One of my favorite songs is 'In My Life' by the Beatles," said Jane.

"Please don't call me 'Cutie-Pie' in front of my friends," the boy begged his mother.

(7) Use quotation marks to quote prose or poetry.

If you quote only part of a sentence, then don't start the quotation with a capital letter.

James Baldwin said that "the time is always now".

If you leave out part of a quotation, use an ellipsis (three spaced dots) to indicate where the omitted word or words were deleted.

Frederico García Lorca wrote, "There is nothing more poetic and terrible than the skyscrapers battle with the heavens that cover them. Snow, rain, and mist highlight, drench, or conceal the vast towers, but those towers . . . shine their three thousand swords through the soft swan of the fog."

If you quote four or more lines of poetry or prose, set the quotation off in a block by indenting 10 spaces from the left margin and omit quotation marks.

Maya Angelou wrote:
The caged bird sings with a fearful trill
Of things unknown but longed for still
And his tune is heard on the distant hill for
The caged bird sings of freedom.

Task 2.8

Add or delete quotation marks as needed and make any other necessary changes in punctuation in the following sentences. If a sentence is correct, write "C" after it.

1. Gandhi once said, An eye for an eye only ends up making the whole world blind.
2. As for the advertisement "Sailors have more fun", if you consider chipping paint and swabbing decks fun, then you will have plenty of it.
3. Even after forty minutes of discussion, our class could not agree on an interpretation of Robert Frost's poem "The Road Not Taken."
4. After winning the lottery, Juanita said that "she would give half the money to charity."
5. After the movie, Vicki said, "The reviewer called this flick "trash of the first order." I guess you can't believe everything you read."
6. "Cleaning your house while your kids are still growing," said Phyllis Diller, "is like shoveling the walk before it stops snowing."

Task 2.9

Insert *quotation marks* wherever they are needed in the sentences below.

1. For several weeks in 2009, the Black Eyed Peas held the top two spots on the music charts with their songs I Gotta Feeling and Boom Boom Pow.
2. Last week we read A Modest Proposal, an essay by Jonathan Swift.
3. Last week we read A Modest Proposal; this week we're reading Shirley Jackson's short story The Lottery.
4. In a famous *New Yorker* essay in October 1998, Toni Morrison referred to Bill Clinton as our first black president.

5. Bonnie asked, Are you going to the concert without me?
6. Bonnie asked if we were going to the concert without her.
7. In the words of comedian Steve Martin, Talking about music is like dancing about architecture.
8. The indie folk band Deer Tick sang What Kind of Fool Am I?
9. Was it Dylan Thomas who wrote the poem Fern Hill?
10. Uncle Gus said, I heard your mother singing Tutti Frutti out behind the barn at three o'clock in the morning.
11. I've memorized several poems, Merdine said, including The Road Not Taken by Robert Frost.
12. All our failures, wrote Iris Murdoch, are ultimately failures in love.

2.7 Other Punctuation Marks

2.7.1 The Dash

The dash is a forceful punctuation mark, but it must be used carefully. It often takes the place of the comma, the semicolon, the colon, or parentheses in a sentence in order to separate emphatically words or groups of words. The difference between the dash and these other marks is that it focuses attention on the items being separated.

(1) Use a dash to mark an abrupt change in the thought or structure of a sentence.

I wonder if we should—oh, let's take care of it later.

Tom took a few steps back, came running full speed, kicked a mighty kick—and missed the ball.

(2) Use a dash to set off appositives that contain commas.

An appositive is a noun or noun phrase that renames a nearby noun. Ordinarily most appositives are set off with commas, but when the appositive itself contains commas, a pair of dashes helps readers see the relative importance of all the pauses.

In my hometown, people's basic needs—food, clothing, and shelter—are less costly than in a big city like Los Angeles.

(3) Use a dash to make parenthetical or explanatory matter more prominent in the sentence.

Early autumn—when the morning air is crisp, and the first red leaves appear—is my favorite time of year.

Sandra thinks about only one thing—money.

(4) Use a dash before a statement that summarizes or amplifies the preceding thought.

Leonardo da Vinci, William the Conqueror, Alexander Hamilton, and Richard Wagner—they were all illegitimate children.

Dashes can also be used to introduce a humorous or ironic twist on the first idea in the sentence.

Aged wine, delicious food, someone else picking up the check—the dinner was perfect.

2.7.2 Parentheses

(1) Use parentheses ( ) to set off words, dates, or statements that give additional information, explain, or qualify the main thought.

Popular American author Mark Twain (Samuel Clemens) described many of his childhood experiences in *Tom Sawyer* (1876).

Nurses record patients' vital signs (temperature, pulse, and blood pressure) several times a day.

(2) The period comes inside the close parenthesis if a complete sentence is enclosed; it occurs after the close parenthesis when the enclosed matter comes at the end of the main sentence and is only a part of the main sentence.

The Colorado winters of 1978 and 1979 broke records for low temperatures. (See pages 72~73 for temperature charts.)

Jean hates Colorado winters and would prefer a warmer environment (such as Alaska, the North Pole, or a meat locker in Philadelphia).

(3) If you are confused trying to decide whether information should be set off by commas, parentheses, or dashes, here are three guidelines.

1) Use commas to set off information closely related to the rest of the sentence.

When Billy Clyde married Maybelle, his brother's young widow, the family was shocked.

The information identifies Maybelle and tells why the family was shocked.

2) Use parentheses to set off information loosely related to the rest of the sentence or material that would disturb the grammatical structure of the main sentence.

Billy Clyde married Maybelle (his fourth marriage, her second) in Las Vegas on Friday.

The information is merely additional comment not closely related to the meaning of the sentence.

Billy Clyde married Maybelle (she was previously married to his brother) in Las Vegas on Friday.

The information is an additional comment that would also disturb the grammatical structure of the main sentence were it not enclosed in parentheses.

3) Use dashes to set off information dramatically or emphatically.

Billy Clyde eloped with Maybelle—only three days after her husband's funeral—without saying a word to anyone in the family.

(4) Use parentheses to set off numbers or letters in a list or series.

Regulations stipulated that only the following equipment could be used on the survival mission: ① a knife, ② thirty feet of parachute line, ③ a book of matches, ④ two ponchos, ⑤ an E tool, and ⑥ a signal flare.

When administering CPR, remember your ABC's: (A) Airway (check the airway), (B) Breathing (provide rescue breathing), and (C) Circulation (check pulse to determine if chest compressions are needed).

(5) Parentheses may enclose the first-time use of acronyms (words formed from the initials of several words) or abbreviations.

Life is only known to exist on earth, but in 1986 National Aeronautics and Space Administration (NASA) found what they thought might be fossils of microscopic living things in a rock from Mars.

At the Center on Aging of University of California at Los Angeles (UCLA), memory-training programs are offered to older adults with memory concerns.

The Federal Drug Administration (FDA) has not yet approved the new medication.

Task 2.10

Depending on what you believe is the desired emphasis, insert parentheses or dashes in the following sentences. An "X" in the following sentences indicates that a student may insert either a parenthesis or a dash, depending on the desired emphasis.

1. Dollar my pet dog is not allowed to enter the house.
2. Law, navigation, politics, medicine, war Shakespeare wrote about all of these topics.
3. If we win the championship game and the critics say we won't it will be a tremendous victory for our athletic program.
4. My oldest brother the computer programmer who lives in Rockville Centre is unable to attend our cousin's wedding.
5. Earl claims that it was her intelligence not her wealth that attracted him.
6. The most common American slang terms according to an authority on language deal with money, sex, and drinking.
7. Only one obstacle kept Con from a career in music talent.
8. I read an article in the *Times* or maybe it was *Newsweek* describing the tornado in Kansas last week.
9. Kent's father an acupuncturist lives in San Antonio.
10. Our dinner last night salad, steak, a vegetable, and dessert cost only five dollars with a special coupon.

2.7.3 Brackets

(1) Use brackets [ ] to enclose any words or phrases that you have inserted into an otherwise word-for-word quotation.

Audubon reports that "if there are not enough young to balance deaths, the end of the species [California condor] is inevitable".

The sentence quoted from the *Audubon* article did not contain the words *California condor* (since the context of the full article made clear what species was meant), so the writer needed to add the name in brackets.

(2) The Latin word "sic" in brackets indicates that an error in a quoted sentence appears in the original source.

According to the review, Nelly Furtado's performance was brilliant, "exceeding [sic] the expectations of even her most loyal fans."

"Sic" in brackets indicates the misspelling of the word "exceeding" appeared in the original text.

The highway advertisement read as follows: "For great stakes [sic], eat at Joe's, located right behind Daisy's Glue Factory."

Here, "sic" in brackets indicates an error in word choice; the restaurant owner incorrectly advertised "stakes" instead of "steaks".

(3) If additional information needs to appear in material already enclosed in parentheses, use brackets to avoid the confusion of double parenthesis marks.

Nineteenth-century author Kate Chopin often found herself in the midst of controversy. (For example, *The Awakening* [1899] was considered so scandalous that it was banned by the St. Louis Library.)

2.7.4 Ellipsis Points

(1) Use three spaced dots.

1) To indicate that a list goes on beyond those items actually spelled out in the text:

An evil witch, a tap-dancing scarecrow, flying monkeys, an emotionally unstable lion, disturbing Munchkins... Dorothy couldn't help but wonder if, in the wonderful Land of Oz, they sold guns.

2) To show an omission in quoted material within a sentence:

Thoreau wrote, "We must learn to reawaken and keep ourselves awake... by an infinite expectation of the dawn, which does not forsake us in our soundest sleep."

The material left out should be nonessential to the meaning of what is quoted. Here, for example, the words omitted are "not by mechanical aids, but".

3) To show hesitation or halting speech in dialogue:

"I... have no idea where to go," she whispered.

(2) Use four spaced dots.

1) To show that we are omitting the end of a quoted sentence:

Lincoln wrote, "Four score and seven years ago our fathers brought forth, upon this continent, a new nation...."

The fourth dot is a period.

(2) To show that we have omitted one or more whole sentences:

"If we don't properly train, teach, or treat our growing prison population," says long-time reform advocate Luis Rodríguez, "somebody else will... This may well be the safety issue of the new century".

(3) Use an entire line of spaced dots to indicate one or more missing lines of poetry.

Failing to fetch me at first keep encouraged.

. . . .

I stop somewhere waiting for you.

—Walt Whitman, "Song of Myself"

2.7.5 The Slash

(1) Use a slash (/) between two words to indicate there is a choice of using either. Do not put a space on either side of the slash.

Bring a salad *and/or* a dessert to share at the picnic.

Be careful to avoid the *either/or* fallacy in your argument paper.

(2) Use a slash to indicate line breaks when you quote two or three lines of poetry within your own sentence. Do use a space both before and after the slash.

In this poem Shakespeare describes love as "an ever-fixed mark / That looks on tempests and is never shaken."

Task 2.11

Edit the following sentences to correct errors in punctuation, focusing especially on appropriate use of the dash, parentheses, brackets, the ellipsis mark, and the slash. If a sentence is correct, write "C" after it.

1. Social insects, bees, for example, are able to communicate complicated messages to one another.
2. A client left his/her cell phone in our conference room after the meeting.
3. The films we made of Kilauea—on our trip to Hawaii Volcanoes National Park—illustrate a typical spatter cone eruption.
4. Although he was confident in his course selections, Greg chose the pass/fail

option for Chemistry 101.
5. Masahiro poked through his backpack—laptop, digital camera, guidebook—to make sure he was ready for a day's study at the Ryoanji Temple garden.
6. Of three engineering fields, chemical, mechanical, and materials, Keegan chose materials engineering for its application to toy manufacturing.

2.7.6 The Hyphen

(1) Use a hyphen(-) to divide a long word at the end of a line.

Do not divide one-syllable words, such as *court*, and *thought*; do not put syllables of one or two letters on either side of a hyphen, as *e-lect* and *play-ed*. (In most dictionaries, dots are used to indicate the division of syllables: *trans · la · tion*.)

(2) Use a hyphen (-) to form compound words. Check your dictionary to be sure that the compound word you're using is usually hyphenated. Some are not. Here are some commonly hyphenated compound words.

Fractions such as *one-third*, *two-thirds*, *one-fourth*
Numbers that are spelled out between twenty-one and ninety-nine
Compound nouns such as *mother-in-law* or *brother-in-law*
Several words as a single grammatical unit, for example:
But they don't want a *stick-in-the-mud* either.
She prefers novels with *they-lived-wretchedly-ever-after* endings.

(3) Use a hyphen with compound modifiers, usually adjectives, which are used together as one descriptor before a noun.

a short-term loan
a well-written essay
a well-known tenor

When such compounds follow the noun, then omit the hyphens:

Keanu Reeves is *well known* for his portrayal of Neo in the action film trilogy *The Matrix*.

Do not use a hyphen when the modifier ends in "-ly".

a highly regarded worker
a beautifully landscaped yard

(4) Use a hyphen to join letters, prefixes, and suffixes to a word:

Letters before words: T-shirt, S-curve, A-frame, J-bar, C-note
self-before words: self-esteem, self-control
all-before words: all-knowing, all-wool
ex-before words: ex-wife, ex-mayor

If the second word begins with a capital letter, a hyphen is almost always used:

Post-Renaissance

Non-English

We should not use hyphen when joining a prefix to an uncapitalized word:

Postwar

nonprofit

Some words with prefixes use a hyphen; again, check your dictionary if necessary. (Hint: If the second word begins with a capital letter, a hyphen is almost always used.)

Task 2.12

Edit the following sentences to correct errors in hyphenation. If a sentence is correct, write "C" after it.

1. Zola's first readers were scandalized by his slice of life novels.
2. Gold is the seventy-ninth element in the periodic table.
3. The swiftly-moving tugboat pulled alongside the barge and directed it away from the oil spill in the harbor.
4. The Moche were a pre-Columbian people who established a sophisticated culture in ancient Peru.
5. Your dog is well-known in our neighborhood.
6. Road-blocks were set up along all the major highways leading out of the city.

2.7.7 Italics and Underlining

We usually use *italic type* for distinction and emphasis in our printed matter. But when we use pen or pencil or standard typewriter, we cannot readily produce words in italic lettering. In this case we can use *underling* instead of *italics*.

(1) Underline or italicize the title of books, plays, magazines, news-

papers, long poems, movies, works of art, television programs (but use quotation marks for individual episodes), airplanes, trains, ships, web sites, and electronic games.

BOOK	*Harry Potter and the Deathly Hallows*
	Harry Potter and the Deathly Hallows
PLAY	*Wicked*
	Wicked
MAGAZINE	*Reader's Digest*
	Reader's Digest
NEWSPAPER	*Wall Street Journal*
	Wall Street Journal
LONG POEM	*Paradise Lost*
	Paradise Lost
MOVIE	*Casablanca*
	Casablanca
WORKS OF ART	*Mona Lisa*
	Mona Lisa
TELEVISION PROGRAM	*American Idol*
	American Idol
SHIP	*Titanic*
	Titanic
AIRPLANE	*High Flyer*
	High Flyer
TRAIN	*Midnight Express*
	Midnight Express
WEB SITE	*Google*
	Google
ELECTRONIC GAME	*Call of Duty*
	Call of Duty

Note: Do not italicize or underline the names of sacred texts (Bible, Torah, Koran), the titles of legal documents (United States Constitution, Magna Carta), or the name of your own essay when it appears on your title page.

(2) Italicize or underline foreign words that are not commonly regarded as part of the English language.

One Chinese *Jin* is 500 grams.

One Chinese <u>Jin</u> is 500 grams.

(3) Italicize or underline letters, numbers, and words when referring to the letters, numbers, and words themselves.

Mary received two *B's* and three *A's* this semester.

Mary received two <u>B</u>'s and three <u>A</u>'s this semester.

Two Chinese ice-skaters received 10*s* in the Championships.

Two Chinese ice-skaters received <u>10</u>s in the Championships.

(4) Use underlining or italics sparingly to show emphasis.

He lives in Manhattan, *Kansas*, not Manhattan, *New York*.

He lives in Manhattan, <u>Kansas</u>, not Manhattan, <u>New York</u>.

Task 2.13

Edit the following sentences to correct errors in the use of italics. If a sentence is correct, write "C" after it.

1. *Rubber Duck*, designed by Florentiji Hofman, came to Hong Kong in May 2013.
2. The story of the sinking of the Titanic is the subject of the movie The Titanic.
3. I learned the Latin term ad infinitum from an old nursery rhyme about fleas: "Great fleas have little fleas upon their back to bite 'em, / Little fleas have lesser fleas and so on ad infinitum."
4. In the film The Postman the leading character wins a woman's heart by quoting from the poems "Walking Around" and "Leaning into the Afternoons" by the poet Pablo Neruda.
5. Cinema audiences once gasped at hearing the word *damn* in *Gone with the Wind*.
6. Song of Myself, Walt Whitman's famous long poem, was published in 1855.

2.8 Capitalization

(1) Capitalize the first word in every sentence, including direct quotations that are complete sentences. And Capitalize the first word after a colon if it begins an independent clause.

Many homes in China have two or more televisions.

Betty asked, "**H**as anyone seen my mobile phone?"

If a group of words following a colon could stand on its own as a complete sentence, capitalize the first word.

Clinical trials called into question the safety profile of the drug: **A** high percentage of participants reported hypertension and kidney problems.

(2) Capitalize the principal words in the titles and subtitles of articles, books, movies, plays, magazines, journals, TV shows, video games, musical compositions, and pieces of art. Capitalize the first word, the last word, and all principal words, including those that follow hyphens in compound terms. Do not capitalize the following parts of speech when they fall in the middle of a title: articles (a, an, the), short prepositions (fewer than five letters), coordinating conjunctions, and the *to* in infinitives.

Collection of **W**ell-**K**nown **C**ontemporary **W**riters' **M**asterpieces

War and **P**eace

Avatar

A Midsummer **N**ight's **D**ream

Entertainment **W**eekly

Rhapsody in **B**lue

(3) Capitalize the titles of relatives and professions when they precede the person's name or when they are used to address the person.

Happy anniversary, **A**unt Lucy and **U**ncle George!

We knew that **P**rofessor Wang was also a renowned volleyball player.

Do not capitalize titles of relatives and professions when they are preceded by possessives (such as *my*, *his*, *our*, and *their*) and when they are used alone in place of the full name.

My uncle and aunt live in Hong Kong.

We knew that our professor was also a renowned volleyball player.

When a name follows, capitalize the title.

My **U**ncle Mike lives in Toronto.

Everyone wants to take **P**rofessor Liu's class.

(4) Capitalize official titles of honor and respect when they precede personal names.

Captain John White

Congressman Haddad

Assistant Principal Webb

Do *not* capitalize titles of honor and respect when they follow personal names.

John White, a brave captain

Ali Haddad, our congressman

Susan Webb, the school's assistant principal

An exception to this rule may be made for certain national officials (the President, Vice President, and Chief Justice) and international figures (the Pope, the Secretary General of the United Nations).

(5) Capitalize the names of particular nationalities, languages, ethnic groups, religions, and adjectives derived from them.

Mexicans

Kenyan

Filipino people

African-American

the Welsh language

Buddhism

Judaism

Don't capitalize the names of academic subjects (*algebra*, *art*, *history*) unless they are languages (*English*, *Spanish*, *French*) or part of a department name (*Department of Languages and Literature*).

(6) Capitalize the names of specific places (planets, countries, counties, cities, rivers, streets, buildings, geographical features, and schools and other institutions).

Mars

Canada

Canberra

Sunset Boulevard

Powell Library

Westminster Abbey

Mississippi River

Rocky Mountains

Bethune Cookman College

Yellowstone National Park

Capitalize common nouns—such as *road*, *river*, and *republic*—only when they're part of the full name of a place. Don't capitalize these common nouns when they stand alone in follow-up references. Also, when two or more geographical names are linked in a single expression, the usual practice is to put the generic part of the names in lower case: *the Atlantic and Pacific oceans*. Don't capitalize *sun* and *moon*.

(7) Capitalize the formal names of government units, agencies, and divisions.

>**W**hite **H**ouse
>**H**ouse of **R**epresentatives
>**H**ouse of **C**ommons
>**S**upreme **C**ourt
>**D**epartment of **E**ducation

(8) Capitalize the formal names of acts, treaties, and government programs.

>**D**eclaration of **I**ndependence
>the **A**ct of **U**nion
>the **M**arshall **P**lan
>the **T**reaty of **V**ersailles

(9) Capitalize directions when they refer to specific regions or are part of a proper name.

>**S**outh **C**arolina
>the **N**orthwest
>immigrants from the **M**iddle **E**ast
>friends from the **S**outh
>the **W**est **C**oast
>winds from the **N**orth

Do not capitalize these words when they merely indicate a direction or general location.

>in an easterly direction
>northern Alabama
>the west side of the street
>the south of Italy

(10) Capitalize the days of the week, months of the year, and names of holidays and religious seasons.

>**M**onday

October
the **F**ourth of **J**uly
Mother's **D**ay
Christmas
Easter
Ramadan

(11) Capitalize the names of particular historical events, periods, and special events.

Operation **D**esert **S**torm
the **M**iddle **A**ges
the **I**nformation **A**ge
the **C**ivil **W**ar
the **H**arlem **R**enaissance
Cannes **I**nternational **F**ilm **F**estival
World **S**eries

(12) Capitalize all references to a supreme being holy books.

God
a **S**upreme **B**eing
Allah
the **B**uddha
the **L**ord
Shiva
the **H**oly **S**pirit
the **B**ible

(13) Capitalize the names of awards, prizes, and scholarships.

the **N**obel **P**rizes
the **A**cademy **A**ward (and the **O**scar)
National **M**erit **S**cholarship

(14) Capitalize each letter in an acronym or initialism.

NATO
CNN
BBC
LA (*or* L. A.)
DVD
AWOL

(15) Capitalize the names of particular businesses and legally protected brand names and trademarks.

Google
General **M**otors
Kit **K**at
Coca **C**ola
Adidas
Range **R**over

The obvious exceptions are trademarks that begin with a lowercase letter: *eBay*, *iPhone*, *iPad*. Also, don't capitalize a brand name that has been transformed into a common noun through popular usage: *aspirin*, *thermos*, *escalator*.

Task 2.14

Circle every letter or word that should be capitalized. If a sentence is correct, write "C" in front of it.

1. Marion Cotillard, the French film actress, won an academy award for best actress in the movie *La Vie en Rose* in 2008.
2. The 1964 civil rights act established as law equal rights for all citizens in voting, education, public accommodations, and federally assisted programs.
3. Applicants for the sales position were required to pass written examinations in english, spanish, and japanese.
4. Sara Gruen is the author of the novel *Water for Elephants*.
5. The oldest university in the united states is harvard, which was founded in 1636.
6. Happy birthday, aunt mary.
7. The commencement speaker was chief justice souter of the supreme court.
8. Colin Powell, a retired general in the united states army, was born in New York.
9. For many years the irish, italians, and jews were the dominant ethnic groups in new york city.
10. My uncle Dan told me many stories about fishing along the banks of the Mississippi river.

11. Many african americans celebrate the festival called kwanzaa, which means "first fruits of the harvest" in the african language Swahili.
12. Munich is the capital of bavaria in southern Germany and is located on the Isar river.

Chapter 3 The Process of Writing an Essay

> **Thinking over the Questions before Starting Your Writing**
> **Subject**
> ➤ Has the subject (or a range of possible subjects) been given to you, or are you free to choose your own?
> ➤ What interests you about your subject? What questions would you like to explore?
> ➤ Why is your subject worth writing about? How might readers benefit from reading about it?
> ➤ Do you need to narrow your subject to a more specific topic (because of length restrictions, for instance)?
>
> **Purpose**
> ➤ Why are you writing: To inform readers? To persuade them? To call them to action? To entertain them? Some combination of these?
>
> **Audience**
> ➤ Who are your readers? How well informed are they about the subject? What do you want them to learn?
> ➤ How interested and attentive are they likely to be? Will they resist any of your ideas?
> ➤ What is your relationship to your readers: Student to instructor? Employee to supervisor? Citizen to citizen? Expert to novice?

Writing is a process of figuring out what we think, not a matter of recording already developed thoughts. Since it's not possible to think about everything all at once, most experienced writers handle a piece of writing in stages. Different writers choose writing process suitable for themselves. Do you have your effective steps of writing?

Let's look at how three students have described the steps they typically follow when writing a composition.

"Before doing anything, I make sure I've got a quiet room and a clear head. When I feel ready to work, I sit in front of my laptop and begin tapping out whatever comes to mind. Then, after taking a short walk, I read over what I've written and pick out the things that strike me as worth keeping—key ideas and interesting details. After this, I usually go on to compose a rough draft pretty quickly. Then (maybe in a day or two, if I've gotten an early start) I read the draft and add explanations and ideas and make some grammatical changes. Then I write it over again, making more changes as I go. Sometimes I complete the whole process in an hour or two. Sometimes it takes a week or more."

"I like to do my first draft on paper—that is, after I've daydreamed for an hour or two, raided the refrigerator, and made a fresh pot of coffee. I specialize in procrastination. After running out of ways to distract myself, I start to scribble down everything I can think of. And I mean *scribble*—write fast, make a mess. When I figure out what I've scrawled, I try to fix it up into an orderly, halfway-decent essay. Then I put it aside (after making another trip to the refrigerator) and start all over again. When I'm done, I compare both papers and combine them by taking some things out and putting other things in. Then I read my draft out loud. If it sounds okay, I go to the computer and type it up."

"In trying to put together a paper, I go through four phases. First, there's the *idea phase*, where I get this bright idea. Then there is the *productive phase*, where I'm really smoking, and I start thinking about the Pulitzer Prize. After that, of course, comes the *block phase*, and all those prize-winning dreams turn into nightmares of this big, six-foot guy jammed into a first-grader's desk and being made to print the alphabet over and over again. Eventually (hours, sometimes days later), I hit the *deadline phase*: I realize that this sucker has *got* to be written, and so I start burning it out again. This phase often doesn't start until ten minutes before a paper is due, which doesn't leave a lot of time to *proofread*—a phase I never seem to get around to."

As these examples show, no single method of writing is followed by all writers in all circumstances. Each of us has to discover the approach that works best on any particular occasion. We can, however, try this traditional approach to the five stages of the writing process: **prewriting**, **organizing**, **drafting**, **revising**, and **editing.**

(1) Prewriting: Generate ideas and our paper's purpose.

(2) Organizing: Develop a plan for presenting our purpose and ideas.

(3) Drafting: Create a first draft of our essay based on our plan and the pattern(s) of organization we have chosen; develop support for our essay's purpose.

(4) Revising: Reassess the draft for content, development, organization, and support (examples and details).

(5) Editing: Check for sentence-level effectiveness, style, diction, grammar, and spelling errors.

3.1 Prewriting

Prewriting refers to any activity that helps a writer think about a topic, determine a purpose, analyze an audience, and prepare to write. The most common techniques include: listing, clustering, free-writing, and so on.

3.1.1 Listing

Listing ideas (a technique sometimes known as *brainstorming*) is a good way to figure out what we know and what questions we have. It provides a nearly guaranteed solution to writer's block. It's actually a very easy process.

(1) Begin with a blank piece of paper or computer screen.

(2) Write your paper's topic, such as "The Ethics of Cigarette Advertising" at the top.

(3) Write down everything you can about the topic; omit nothing, no matter how bizarre, and don't stop until you are completely out of ideas. Don't worry about grammar or editing. Here's an example:

Paper Topic: The Ethics of Cigarette Advertising

    a. Cigarettes & cancer

    b. Cigarette ads not on TV

    c. Teenagers & cigarettes

    d. Government subsidizes tobacco farmers

    e. Macho image of Marlboro Man

    f. Camel "Hard Pack?"

    g. Anti-smoking groups

h. Surgeon General's warnings
i. Why don't we see pipe and cigar ads?
j. Nicotine is addictive
k. Cigarettes still very popular

(4) Look at the list above, and reconsider the paper's topic. Ideas (d) and (i) stray from the topic, so cut them.

(5) Organize the remaining points. Idea (a) provides a decent place to start a draft, since it touches on a central truth about smoking.

(6) Next, try to logically arrange the other points in the order that you would use in your essay. It helps to think about patterns into which ideas would fall, such as "Appeal of Ads" "Limits on Ads" "Future of Ads". You could write down these categories and then categorize your ideas from the brainstorming list. You'll end up with a working outline for the paper.

(7) New ideas may occur to you as you organize the material. That's okay as long as these ideas relate to the topic.

Listing questions and ideas helped the writers narrow their subject and identify her position. In other words, they should treat their early list as a record of their thoughts and a springboard to new ideas, not as an outline.

3.1.2 Clustering

To cluster ideas, we should write our subject in the center of a sheet of paper, draw a circle around it, and surround the circle with related ideas connected to it with lines. If some of the satellite ideas lead to more specific clusters, write them down as well. Look at the following example:

Environmental issues

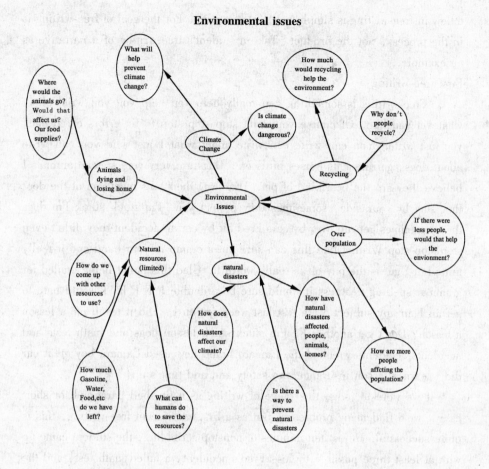

3.1.3 Free-writing

By jotting down the first thoughts that come to our mind, free-writing is useful for searching for the topic of our writing. Free-writing means writing without rules. When free-writing, we set the clock for five to ten minutes and put pen to paper or fingers to keyboard and go at it. We should never stop to look back, to cross something out, to worry about transitions or connecting the ideas or paragraphing or subject-verb agreement or even commas. The only point of free-writing is to keep writing. If we can't think of anything to write, we write about how that feels or repeat over and over "I have nothing to write" or "Non-sense" or something like: "I'm stuck but I'll think of something soon." If we get stuck in the middle of a sentence or thought, just repeat the last word or phrase till something comes along. We should bear in mind that the only rule to follow in free-writing is simply not to stop writing. For the goal of free-writing is in the process, not the product. Take a student's free-writing of a narrative as an example.

First free-writing:

"Free-writing is something can really help you help you you write about whatever you like. Of course you don't stop stop stop to fix errors or go back you just write. You can write can write about what I just said you can write about dogs, gorillas cats horses birds etc. Dogs are very very special animals I believe they are the best kind of pet. They wag their tails meet you at the door they stay by your side, sometimes they protect you. I'm stuck stuck I'm dogs they sometimes get run over by cars Fred hit by car an accident they didn't even stop stop stop Writing like this can sure put a cramp in your hand and it really hurts but I guess the pay off is really worth it. Glad this is not being graded for grammar spelling neatness it would sure be a double F F F F. I would hate to get an F in any subject Math test last week got an F. Did it teach me a lesson a lesson? Don't get another F! I'm stuck stuck lesson dogs and math tests and accidents accidents wrecked the Camaro brand new used Camara boy great car did I learn a lesson insurance and safety and and time's up!"

If we were to judge this piece of writing as a finished paragraph or short essay, we'd find many problems. But as a first exercise in free-writing, this is quite successful. In just ten minutes of nonstop scribbling, the student came up with at least three possible topics: Fred's accident, a failed math test, and the wreck of the Camaro.

Through first free-writing, the student chooses "Wrecking My Camaro" as his topic. The following is his second free-writing.

Wrecking My Camaro

It happened so fast I can hardly remember what really happened now but I'll try anyhow. Riding down Ferguson Ave. in my new used car a Camaro I was faced with a situation unlike any situation that I did had ever been in before. There in the oncoming lane was a Caddie that was about to kiss the front of my car or the other way around. Anyway before I could even react we hit. All I remember then all I remember was asking my girlfriend if she was all right and then getting out of the car and walking in all the glass that was on the road. A witness who saw the accident walked up to my car and looked in and saw what happened and that I had nothing to worry about because it wasn't my fault she thought. I was still worried sick. The police came and the ambulance and then and then all the confusion started. The cop's first question was have you been drinking and I said no. He then wanted me to put me in his car but understood the situation and was very understanding. The crowd broke up and the ambulance left and the confusion seemed to be over this night even though it had just started what would soon turn out to be one of the worst Christmas eves in my entire life. This would not be the last time I would have to discuss this terrible incident because court was right down the road and so was a huge lawsuit where I learned a lesson about the importance of safe driving and also the importance of extra liability coverage because you never know how much someone and I mean anyone might sue you for. The amount is limitless and it all comes down to what a judge says.

This second free-writing has produced a rough draft. Though it should be improved in many aspects, the writer has identified a number of key details related to the car accident. In successive revisions he will have opportunities to clarify, supplement, and rearrange these details. Free-writing, then, has not only helped the writer discover a topic but has also allowed him to *explore* that topic.

3.2 Organizing

After deciding the topic, we shall start to organize the materials we have already produced in the pre-writing stage, and arrange them in an appropriate order. The most common arrangement are as follows.

3.2.1 Time Order

This arrangement of points follows the order of events in time. Time order is also called chronological order. It is the best order to use in explaining a process, such as cooking or cleaning, and is also commonly used in narrating.
Process example:
Making Egg Rolls
Many Americans like to eat Chinese egg rolls, but how can you make egg rolls? I think most people do not know; they maybe think it is difficult. In

fact, making egg rolls is very easy. If you follow the steps below, you can do it.

First, go to store and buy two packages of egg roll dough, one head of cabbage, one head of celery, one bundle of green onion, one pound of ground beef (or pork), and a little ginger. If at home you do not have eggs, you can buy a dozen eggs, but you do not need this much. You should also add a bottle of soy sauce.

Second, you need to take half a head of cabbage, half a head of celery, half a bundle of green onion, and one half ounce of ginger. Wash and use the blender to cut them up small; after you put one pound raw ground beef and two eggs in that all of raw vegetables. Then, add a little soy sauce, a litter sugar, and a little salt. Mix everything together.

Then, open the package of the egg roll dough, and take one piece of dough and put the mixture in the center and wrap up; you wrap up all the dough. After you boil the oil, put raw egg rolls in pan, but don't make heat too high; waiting 6 to 8 minutes. Take the egg rolls out of the pan when light golden brown.

When you follow this information, you can make egg rolls by yourself. If sometime you want eat egg rolls, you don't need to go to a restaurant and you can choose the taste that you like. Homemade egg rolls are very good, and you can also have fun!

(by Guoying Gao)

Narration example:

Yesterday, I bought a story book for my little daughter at Xinhua bookstore. When I read the book for her at night, I found two pages missing. So this morning, I returned to the bookstore where I had purchased it and filed a complaint directly to the general manager about the problem.

3.2.2 Spatial Order

Spatial arrangement follows the order of objects in space. Spatial order is used when we are describing a place, such as a town, city, or room in your house. Using spatial order helps us describe what something looks like: a messy room, a float in a parade, a neighbor's garden. Spatial order helps create a mental picture for our reader of the space we are describing. For instance, if we were describing our room, we could start from front to back, top to bottom, or side to side. One part at a time, describe the space to give the whole picture.

Example 1:

The house is set back about 200 feet from the road, and as we saunter up the narrow dirt pathway, lined with neat rows of flamboyant orange gladiolas on each side, the tidy appearance of the small, unpainted frame house entices us to enter. Up the steps and onto the porch, we can't help but notice a high-backed rocker on one side and a bench worn smooth by age on the other. Both remind us of the many vesper hours spent here in the absence of modern-day entertainment.

(by Mary White)

Example 2:

Gill's garden was beautiful. Front and center was a pool with a fountain in the shape of a little boy in the middle surrounded by water lilies. Immediately behind the pool was a dark green hedge with a wooden bench in front of it. Rising behind the hedge was a line of graceful willow trees whose long drooping branches brushed the top of the bench.

3.2.3　Climatic Order

When we order our writing climactically, we arrange points in order of ascending importance, rising from least important to most important. An effective essay will almost always present the least important evidence first and the most important last, becoming more convincing and emphatic as it moves along. When arranging the body paragraphs sometimes we can use this rule of thumb: **Unless logic dictates some other order, arrange your essay's body paragraphs in climactic order; save the best, most vivid, most interesting, or most emphatic point for last.**

Example 1:

There are several important things to keep in mind when buying a house. First, find a real estate agent you like. Also, set up tours of the houses you like the look of from the real estate website. It's very important to set up an inspection of the house you are interested in to make sure it is safe and in the condition the seller says it is. Finally, and most important, check that the houses are in your price range by figuring out your finances and loan possibilities before you start looking seriously for a new home.

Example 2:

Consider the potential effect of just a small increase in the earth's atmospheric temperature. A rise of only a few degrees could melt the polar ice caps. Rainfall patterns would change. Some deserts might bloom, but lands now fertile might turn to desert, and many hot climates could become uninhabitable. If the sea level rose only a few feet, dozens of coastal cities would be destroyed, and life as we know it would be changed utterly.

(by Fulwiler and Alan Hayakawa, *The Blair Handbook*. Prentice Hall, 2003)

3.2.4 Cause and Effect Order

Cause and effect order is to explain one point as the reason for another, or one point as the result or consequence of another. Either way, this kind of order generates strong continuity in the treatment of any topic because it is based on a logical connection.

Example 1:

Why Do We Exercise?

These days, just about everyone, from toddler to retiree, seems to be running, pedaling, lifting weights, or performing aerobics. Why are so many people exercising? There are several reasons. Some people, the ones in designer jump suits, exercise simply because keeping in shape is trendy. The same people who a few years ago thought doing drugs was cool are now just as seriously involved in self-conditioning. Other people exercise to lose weight and appear more attractive. The paunchy crowd is willing to undergo extreme self-torture in the name of beauty: thin is in. Finally, there are those who exercise for their health. Regular, intensive exercise can strengthen the heart and lungs, build endurance, and improve the body's immunity system. In fact, judging from my observations, most people who exercise probably do so for a combination of these reasons.

Example 2:

Effects of Automobiles

I worry about the private automobile. It is a dirty, noisy, wasteful, and lonely means of travel. It pollutes the air, ruins the safety and sociability of the street, and exercises upon the individual a discipline which takes away far more freedom than it gives him. It causes an enormous amount of land to be unnecessarily abstracted from nature and from plant life and to become devoid of any natural function. It explodes cities, grievously impairs the whole institution of neighborliness, fragmentizes and destroys communities. It has already spelled the end of our cities as real cultural and social communities, and has made impossible the construction of any others in their place. Together with the airplane, it has crowded out other, more civilized and more convenient means of transport, leaving older people, infirm people, poor people and children in a worse situation than they were a hundred years ago.

(by George F. Kennan, *Democracy and the Student Left*, 1968)

3.2.5 Oppositional Order

Oppositional order opposes one point to another. It is often used in contrast essay and persuasive essay.

Example 1:

Sloppy people can't bear to part with anything. They give loving attention to every detail. When sloppy people say they're going to tackle the surface of a desk, they really mean it. Not a paper will go unturned; not a rubber band will go unboxed. Four hours or two weeks into the excavation, the desk looks exactly the same, primarily because the sloppy person is meticulously creating new piles of papers with new headings and scrupulously stopping to read all the old book catalogs before he throws them away. A neat person would just bulldoze the desk.

Neat people are bums and clods at heart. They have cavalier attitudes toward possessions, including family heirlooms. Everything is just another dust-catcher to them. If anything collects dust, it's got to go and that's that. Neat people will toy with the idea of throwing the children out of the house just to cut down on the clutter.

Neat people don't care about process. They like results. What they want to do is get the whole thing over with so they can sit down and watch the rasslin' on TV. Neat people operate on two unvarying principles: Never handle any item twice, and throw everything away.

(by Suzanne Britt, "Neat People vs. Sloppy People" *Show and Tell*. Morning Owl Press, 1983)

Example 2:

Differences in posture, like differences in eating utensils (knife and fork, chopsticks or fingers, for example), divide the world as profoundly as political boundaries. Regarding posture there are two camps: the sitters-up (the so-called western world) and the squatters (everyone else). Although there is no Iron Curtain separating the two sides, neither feels comfortable in the position of the other. When I eat with oriental friends I soon feel awkward sitting on the floor, my back unsupported, my legs numb. But squatters don't like sitting up either. An Indian household may have a dining room with table and chairs, but when the family relaxes during the hot afternoon, parents and children sit together on the floor. The driver of a three-wheeled motor scooter in Delhi has to sit on a seat, but instead of doing so in a western manner he squats cross-legged, his feet on the bench instead of on the floor (precariously to my eyes, comfortably to his). A Canadian carpenter works standing up, at a bench. My Gujarati friend Vikram, given the choice, prefers to work sitting down, on the floor.

(by Witold Rybczynsk, published by *Viking Penguin* in 1986.)

3.2.6 Making an Outline

Some writers don't like making an outline at all. They think it's a waste of time. But an outline, even a sketchy one, can be a helpful tool in the creative process. Creating outlines, whether formal or informal, can help us make sure our writing is credible and logical and can help us identify any gaps in our support.

1. Informal outline

We can sketch an informal outline to see how we will support our thesis and to figure out a tentative structure for our ideas. Informal outlines can take many forms. Perhaps the most common is simply the thesis followed by a list of major ideas. For example:

Working thesis: Television advertising should be regulated to help prevent childhood obesity.

(1) Children watch more television than ever.

(2) Snacks marketed to children are often unhealthy and fattening.

(3) Childhood obesity can cause sleep disorders and other problems.

(4) Addressing these health problems costs taxpayers billions of dollars.

(5) Therefore, these ads are actually costing the public money.

(6) If advertising is free speech, do we have the right to regulate it?

(7) We regulate alcohol and cigarette ads on television, so why not advertisements for soda and junk food?

2. Formal outline

Guidelines to formal outline:

(1) Put the thesis at the top.

(2) Make items at the same level parallel grammatically.

(3) Use sentences unless phrases are clear.

(4) Use the conventional system of numbers, letters, and indents:

I.
    A.
    B.
        1.
        2.
            a.
            b.

II.
    A.
    B.
        1.
        2.
            a.
            b.

(5) Always include at least two items at each level.

(6) Limit the number of major sections in the outline; if the list of roman numerals (at the first level) gets too long, try clustering the items into fewer major categories with more subcategories.

Modern Technology

Thesis: The most significant discoveries to benefit humankind in modern times are in the fields of television and computer technology.

I. Introduction with thesis statement

II. Body

A. A popular form of instant communication all over the world is television.
   1. Witnessing important events
      a. Destruction of the Berlin Wall
      b. Launching of spacecraft
   2. Long-distance medicine using video-conferencing
      a. Patient and doctor conferences
      b. Special equipment to monitor patients

B. Great progress computer technology has made in the world of communication to benefit humankind in the last few decades.
   1. Long-distance communication
   2. Global computer networks
   3. Electronic mail

C. Advances in computer medicine benefiting both doctors and patients.
   1. Rural doctors and medical information
      a. Less access in the past
      b. Immediate access today
   2. Rural doctors and urban medical centers Use of computers to prescribe treatment
   3. X-ray pictures of body parts
      a. Diagnoses of diseases and illnesses
      b. Necessary treatments
   4. Computer-aided diagnosis Example of woman with headaches

III. Conclusion

To conclude, scientific research and experiments have certainly opened the doors to faster, more easily accessible information worldwide on television and the computer. Many of these discoveries have changed our lives for the better and have made the peoples of the world closer.

3.3 Drafting

Before writing, we should gather all the materials we've already prepared, such as lists, clusters, outlines, and so on, to help us get started and keep us moving. With these materials close by, we don't need to search for ideas. Many experienced authors believe that writing tends to flow better when it is drafted relatively quickly, without many stops and starts.

3.3.1 The Introduction

The introduction, at the beginning of the essay, is where we introduce our general topic, specific thesis statement, and approach. For most essays, the introduction only needs to be a single, well-written paragraph. Introductions should be captivating, short, and to the point. A great introduction makes the reader want to learn more and gives them a roadmap for reading our essay.

1. Opening statements

In standard academic essays, introductory paragraphs usually consist of four or five sentences. The first sentence in the introductory paragraph is called the Opening Statement. It is a very important sentence because, after the title, it is the first contact the readers have with the essay itself. This sentence is viewed as an invitation. We need to capture the readers' attention and invite them to read the essay. Our opening statement usually determines if the readers will be interested in reading the rest of the essay. In this sentence, we should use catchy words to spark the readers' interest and curiosity into reading what we wrote. Typically, there are seven different types of opening statements that we can use to our advantage.

(1) General to specific.

Begin with a broad, general statement of your topic and narrow it down to your thesis statement. Broad general statements ease the reader into your thesis statement by providing a background for it. Look at the following example:

Consuming Fresh Foods Instead of Canned Foods

Eating is an activity that we as humans do at least two times a day. We live in a world where the variety of food is immense, and we are responsible for what we eat. We decide what we are about to eat and how it will affect our bodies. Considering flavor, cost, and health benefits, we should consume fresh food instead of canned foods.

(2) Quotations.

A quotation can grab your reader's attention. Quoting a respected person can add credibility to your argument. Sometimes, though, a quotation will simply add a bit of interest to your opening. Using a quotation in your introductory paragraph lets you add someone else's voice to your own.

Helping Your Country

Former U. S. President J. F. Kennedy once said: "It is not what the country can do for you, but what you can do for your country." Most of the people around us are always complaining about the problems in their community and the country in general. However, they do little to help or to provide alternatives for those problems. If you want to help, there are many things you could do! Cleaning your neighborhood, participating in civil organizations, and acting as a role model are just some examples of how you can help your country.

(3) Question.

A question easily sparks the readers' attention and curiosity by inviting them to read the essay to find possible answers to the question. By using this type of technique, you may simply want the reader to think about possible answers, or you may plan to answer the questions yourself later in the paper.

Stressful Waiting Rooms

Do you remember the last time you visited a dentist? Ouch! Yes, indeed it was a torture chamber resembling ancient medieval times. But if you remember well, the worst part of the visit was the waiting room itself. There are many waiting rooms that can really fill your existence with distress and anguish. If you are in need of experiencing a lot of stress and anxiety lately, all you have to do is visit your local dentist office, the emergency room at a hospital, or a court hearing session at your nearest judicial center.

(4) Opposite.

This approach works because your readers will be surprised, and then intrigued, by the contrast between the opening idea and the thesis statement that follows it.

Max

Max was a cute dog, a Tibetan Terrier with a "winning smile", but he had annoying habit of "lifting his leg" on my furniture if I left him alone for more than a couple of hours. Also, half-way through our walks, he would roll on his back indicating he had had enough. I would have to carry him home. Just when I decided to give him up for adoption, he used his amazing talent as a "chick magnet" to find me the love of my life.

(5) Short anecdote/ brief story.

Stories are naturally interesting. They appeal to a reader's curiosity. In your introduction, an anecdote will grab the reader's attention right away. The story should be brief and related to your main idea. The incident can be something that happened to you, to someone else, or something you have heard about or read about in a newspaper.

Fighting at Schools

I remember my first fight at school. It was a terrible experience and so were the consequences. I had to fight one of my best friends just because both of us wanted to grab a ball while playing baseball. At the end, everybody laughed and enjoyed the fight, while we were being punished. Fighting at schools is not a good business. The physical and emotional damage, the loss of school privileges, and the loss of one's reputation are some of the negative consequences of fighting at school.

(6) Warning (importance of topic).

If you can convince your readers that the subject in some way applies to them, or is something they should know more about; they will want to keep reading.

Accidents on the Roads of Puerto Rico

Turn that cell-phone off and concentrate on your driving, please! Nowadays, most of the accidents are caused by negligent drivers who are usually talking on their cell-phones. These people never take a second to think about the possible consequences of their actions. But the handy cell-phones alone are not the only source of reckless driving in Puerto Rico. Along with the talking on cell-phones, not obeying traffic laws and compulsive speeding are the three major contributors to the many accidents on this island.

(7) A startling information (a statistic or an unusual fact).

This information must be true and verifiable, and it doesn't need to be totally new to your readers. It could simply be a pertinent fact that explicitly illustrates the point you wish to make. If you use a piece of startling information, follow it with a sentence or two of elaboration.

Life Is Happy and Meaningful

Not long ago, a poll was conducted among students in a middle school. They were asked to make a choice between two statements— "Life is happy and meaningful", and "Life is bitter and meaningless". Shockingly enough, about 20 percent of the students agreed to the former. I have been thinking of the question ever since. The more I think, the more I am convinced that if we have a right attitude toward life, it can surely be happy and meaningful.

Task 3.1

Read the following statements written for comparison and contrast essays and select the most appropriate opening statement from the list of options given according to the technique and the title of the essay presented.

1. Title: Nothing is Better than a Mercedes

   Opening technique: GENERAL TO SPECIFIC

   a. Do you own a Mercedes Benz car?

   b. I want a Mercedes Benz with all the luxury!

   c. Mercedes Benz vehicles are famous and recognized worldwide!

2. Title: Basketball is the King of Sports

   Opening technique: QUOTATIONS

   a. "I really love this game!" It's the classic NBA slogan to promote basketball around the world.

   b. If you don't like basketball, you're missing the fun!

   c. The famous chant goes like this: "Take me out to the ball game." Everybody sings along during the seventh inning.

3. Title: Love

   Opening technique: QUESTION

   a. Have you ever kissed somebody? Have you ever been kissed?

   b. What is love? How do we know that we are really in love?

   c. Love is the most beautiful feeling that human beings can possess.

   d. I remember the first time I fell in love with my girlfriend!

4. Title: The Best Moments of my Life

   Opening technique: ANECDOTE/ BRIEF STORY

   a. I want to enjoy my life as much as I can by having good moments.

   b. The best moments of my life have been very special for me.

   c. When I was in high school, I had the greatest times of my life.

   d. You have to enjoy the good moments that life offers you!

2. Thesis

Generally the most common strategy is to open the paragraph with a few sentences that engage the reader and establish our purpose for writing and then to state our main point. The statement of our main point is called the **thesis**. Thesis statement is usually **the last sentence** of the introduction. For example:

Failures are inevitable in one's life. One may fail to go to his ideal university; one may lose his job with which to make a living; one may even be reduced to a beggar overnight as a result of mistakes in business. **But failure is not always a bad thing and success, more often than not, comes after many failures.**

Although the thesis frequently appears at the end of the introduction, it can just as easily appear. For example:

If I were to leave my home for a year, there is one thing I definitely would take with me: my cell phone. With my cell phone, I could call my friends or family if I ever was lonely needed advice, or just wanted to talk.

The thesis statement, written in a single declarative sentence, declares the main point or controlling idea of your entire essay. Frequently located near the beginning of a short essay, the thesis answers these questions: "What is the subject of this essay?" "What is the writer's opinion on this subject?" "What is the writer's purpose in this essay?" (to explain something? to argue a position? to move people to action? to entertain?). Consider the example:

China has a lot of interesting festivals.

The statement is too broad, for the writer can't discuss all Chinese festivals in a short essay. Even though it does state the writer's opinion, the statement is not clear: it doesn't explain why the festivals are interesting. A better one could be:

The Dragon Boat Festival is an important festival for Chinese because they celebrate, remember traditional legends, and enjoy time with their families.

The topic is specific enough, and it clearly gives the writer's opinion. In addition, it lists the supporting ideas.

(1) Types of thesis statement.

In fact, thesis statement in different types of essay has its own characteristics. There are a few different types of thesis statement, the content of which will be accordance with the type of essay we're writing. In other words, our thesis statement offers the reader a preview of our paper's content, but the message differs a little depending on the essay type.

(2) Argument thesis statement.

If we write an argument essay, our thesis statement should express the stance we are taking and may give the reader a preview or a hint at our evidence. The thesis in an argument essay could look something like the following.

Not only will banning smoking improve people's health, it will also increase worker productivity and reduce conflicts.

The popular practice of lashing a child can lead to risky behavior in adolescence.

Street cameras and street-view maps have led to a total loss of privacy in the United States.

(3) Expository essay thesis statement.

An expository essay "exposes" the reader to a new topic; it informs the reader with details, descriptions, or explanations of a subject. If we are writing an expository essay, our thesis statement should explain to the reader what he or she will learn in our essay.

Eggs contain many of the ingredients that your body needs for good health.

The rewarding process of photographing a lunar eclipse requires careful preparation and sound equipment.

The Spanish Inquisition is characterized by religious persecution that was often carried out with extreme cruelty.

You can see how the statements above provide a statement of fact about topic (not just opinion), but this statement leaves the door open for you to elaborate with lots of details. The good thesis statement in an expository essay leaves the reader wanting more details!

(4) Analytical essay thesis statements.

In an analytical essay assignment we will be expected to break down a topic, process, or object in order to observe and analyze our subject piece by piece. Our goal is to clarify the object of our discussion by breaking it down. A thesis statement might contain the following format:

A careful examination of the way that our fat cells store and release calories will shed light on the difficulties of losing weight.

Ultimately, the crime scene did yield sufficient evidence for solving the crime, but the clues were only discovered after a meticulous investigation.

It is easy to see why school mornings are so chaotic when you examine every task we try to accomplish in this short amount of time.

3. Guidelines on writing effective thesis statements

An effective thesis statement is a central idea that requires supporting evidence; its scope is appropriate for the required length of the essay; and it is sharply focused. It should answer a question you have posed, resolve a problem you have identified, or take a position in a debate. Generally, the guidelines on thesis statement are as follows:

(1) A strong thesis takes some sort of stand.

Remember that your thesis needs to show your conclusions about a subject. For example, if you are writing a paper for a class on fitness, you might be asked to choose a popular weight-loss product to evaluate. Here are two thesis statements:

There are some negative and positive aspects to the Banana Herb Tea Supplement.

This is a weak thesis. First, it fails to take a stand. Second, the phrase "negative and positive aspects" are vague.

Because Banana Herb Tea Supplement promotes rapid weight loss that results in the loss of muscle and lean body mass, it poses a potential danger to customers.

This is a strong thesis because it takes a stand.

(2) A strong thesis justifies discussion.

Your thesis should indicate the point of the discussion. If your assignment is to write a paper on kinship systems, using your own family as an example, you might come up with either of these two thesis statements:

My family is an extended family.

This is a weak thesis because it states an observation. Your reader won't be able to tell the point of the statement, and will probably stop reading.

While most American families would view consanguineal marriage as a threat to the nuclear family structure, many Iranian families, like my own, believe that these marriages help reinforce kinship ties in an extended family.

This is a strong thesis because it shows how your experience contradicts a widely accepted view. A good strategy for creating a strong thesis is to show that the topic is controversial. Readers will be interested in reading the rest of the essay to see how you support your point.

(3) A strong thesis expresses one main idea.

Readers need to be able to see that your paper has one main point. If your thesis expresses more than one idea, then you might confuse your readers about the subject of your paper. For example:

Companies need to exploit the marketing potential of the Internet, and web pages can provide both advertising and customer support.

This is a weak thesis statement because the reader can't decide whether the paper is about marketing on the Internet or web pages. To revise the thesis, the relationship between the two ideas needs to become clearer. One way to revise the thesis would be to write:

Because the Internet is filled with tremendous marketing potential, companies should exploit this potential by using web pages that offer both advertising and customer support.

This is a strong thesis because it shows that the two ideas are related. Hint: a great many clear and engaging thesis statements contain words like "because" "since" "so" "although" "unless" and "however".

(4) A strong thesis statement is specific.

A thesis statement should show exactly what your paper will be about, and will help you keep your paper to a manageable topic. For example, if you write a paper on hunger, you might say:

World hunger has many causes and effects.

This is a weak thesis statement for two major reasons. First, "world hunger" can't be discussed thoroughly in five or ten pages. Second, "many causes and effects" is vague. You should be able to identify specific causes and effects. A revised thesis might look like this:

Hunger persists in Appalachia because jobs are scarce and farming in the infertile soil is rarely profitable.

This is a strong thesis because it narrows the subject to a more specific and manageable topic and it also identifies the specific causes for the existence of hunger.

Because the role of the thesis statement is to state the central message of your entire paper, it is important to re-visit (and maybe rewrite) your thesis statement after the paper is written. It is quite normal for your message to change as you construct your paper!

Task 3.2

For each pair of sentences below, select the one that you think would make the more effective thesis in the introductory paragraph of a short essay. Keep in mind that an effective thesis statement should be sharply focused and specific, not just a general statement of fact.

1. (a) *The Hunger Games* is a science fiction adventure film based on the novel of the same name by Suzanne Collins.
   (b) *The Hunger Games* is a morality tale about the dangers of a political system that is dominated by the wealthy.
2. (a) There is no question that cell phones have changed our lives in a very big way.
   (b) While cell phones provide freedom and mobility, they can also become a leash, compelling users to answer them anywhere and at any time.
3. (a) Finding a job is never easy, but it can be especially hard when the economy is still feeling the effects of a recession and employers are reluctant to hire new workers.
   (b) College students looking for part-time work should begin their search by taking advantage of job-finding resources on campus.
4. (a) For the past three decades, coconut oil has been unjustly criticized as an artery-clogging saturated fat.
   (b) Cooking oil is plant, animal, or synthetic fat that is used in frying, baking, and other types of cooking.
5. (a) There have been over 200 movies about Count Dracula, most of them only very loosely based on the novel published by Bram Stoker in 1897.
   (b) Despite its title, *Bram Stoker's Dracula*, a film directed by Francis Ford Coppola, takes considerable liberties with Stoker's novel.
6. (a) There are several steps that teachers can take to encourage academic integrity and curtail cheating in their classes.
   (b) There is an epidemic of cheating in America's schools and colleges, and there are no easy solutions to this problem.
7. (a) J. Robert Oppenheimer, the American physicist who directed the building of the first atomic bombs during World War II, had technical, moral, and political reasons for opposing the development of the hydrogen bomb.

(b) J. Robert Oppenheimer, often referred to as "the father of the atomic bomb," was born in New York City in 1904.
8. (a) The iPad has revolutionized the mobile-computing landscape and created a huge profit stream for Apple.
(b) The iPad, with its relatively large high-definition screen, has helped to revitalize the comic book industry.
9. (a) Like other addictive behaviors, Internet addiction may have serious negative consequences, including academic failure, job loss, and a breakdown in personal relationships.
(b) Drug and alcohol addiction is a major problem in the world today, and many people suffer from it.
10. (a) When I was a child I used to visit my grandmother in Moline every Sunday.
(b) Every Sunday we visited my grandmother, who lived in a tiny house that was undeniably haunted.

3.3.2 Build Effective Body Paragraphs

The body is the bulk of your essay; this is where we present our details that support the thesis statement. After having conducted research and thought at length about our topic, we should have several points to make. We will therefore use the body to present our ideas in as clear and organized a fashion as possible.

Most of the body paragraphs in our essay will profit from a focused *topic sentence*. In addition, body paragraphs should have adequate *development*, *unity*, and *coherence*.

1. The topic sentence

Before writing a paragraph, it is important to think, first about the **topic** and then what we want to say about the topic. Most often, the topic is easy, but the question then turns to *what you want to say about the topic* which is the **controlling idea.** Topic sentences should always contain both a **topic** and a **controlling idea.** When our introduction contains a clearly stated topic sentence, our reader will know what to expect and, therefore, understand our ideas better. For example:

Topic sentence: Industrial waste poured into Lake Michigan has led to dramatic changes in its ability to support marine life.

Topic: Industrial waste poured into Lake Michigan

Controlling idea: dramatic changes in its ability to support marine life

Topic sentence: There are several advantages to growing up in a small town.

Topic: growing up in a small town

Controlling idea: several advantages

The **topic sentence** establishes the paragraph's topic and purpose. Think of a body paragraph (or a single paragraph) as a kind of mini-essay in itself. The topic sentence is, in a sense, a smaller thesis. It too asserts one main idea on a limited subject that the writer can explain or argue in the rest of the paragraph. It is the sentence that alerts the reader to the central idea. It also reminds the writer of that central idea so that he or she does not include sentences that wander off the topic. For this reason, the topic sentence is frequently placed at the beginning of the paragraph, although it can appear in other parts of the paragraph. Regardless of its location, the topic sentence is usually the most general sentence in the paragraph, and it is developed and supported by the specifics in the sentences that follow or precede it.

In our reading we occasionally notice paragraphs by experienced writers that do not include a topic sentence. In such instances the topic sentence is implicit—that is, the controlling or central idea is implied because the details in the paragraph are clear and well organized. But until we become an adept writer and are certain that our paragraphs stick to one idea, we should provide each paragraph with a topic sentence.

(1) Location of the topic sentence.

Usually the topic sentence comes *first* in the paragraph:

Internet has become our chief means of obtaining information. Without going out, we can know what the weather will be like tomorrow, what is going on at home and abroad, and whether the current prices of stocks are going up of down. Because of Internet, the world has become much smaller and things and people that used to be strangers are now familiar to us. Because of Internet, we are thousands of times more informed than our ancestors. *Now, we depend so much on Internet for information that we will feel stupid if we do not surf the Internet for only a few days.*

This paragraph with a topic sentence at the beginning also contains a concluding sentence that makes a final general comment based on the supporting details. The last sentence of the paragraph reemphasizes the main point.

Sometimes the topic sentence is placed in the **middle** of the paragraph:

There are many different types of toys on the market today. There are still many action figures that let children use their imagination to play roles. For instance, superhero figures still spark the imagination. Spiderman is an example of an action figure that many children like to use to save the day. Also, many puzzle games and strategy board games are still popular and help children build their math and logic skills. For example, the classic game Battleship is available in peg form and electronic form: Both forms build prediction and math skills. **In fact, there are many toys on today's market that help build children's imagination and physical and intellectual skills.** Another popular type of toy is one that lets children construct shapes and objects. For instance, Legos are more popular than ever. They even have Star Wars based Legos that allow children to make stories from the Star Wars stories and also help them to build their analytical and hand eye coordination skills.

In the following example, the writer places the topic sentence *last* to sum up the information in the paragraph.

Rumors certainly fly around Washington's Capitol Building—but ghosts too? According to legend, the building was cursed in 1808 by construction superintendent John Lenthall, who was crushed by a falling ceiling following a feud with his architect over the wisdom of ceiling braces. Some workers in the building swear they have heard both the ghostly footsteps of James Garfield, who was assassinated after only four months as president, and the spooky last murmurings of John Quincy Adams, who died mid-speech on the House floor. Others claim to have seen a demon cat, so large and terrifying that it caused a guard to suffer a fatal heart attack. Perhaps the most cheerful ghosts appear on the night of a new president's swearing-in ceremony when the statues in Statuary Hall are said to leave their pedestals and dance at their own Inaugural Ball. **Whether these stories are true or merely the products of rich imaginations, the U. S. Capitol Building boasts the reputation as one of the most haunted buildings in America.**

(2) Focusing the topic sentence.

A topic sentence must be focused and limited enough to be discussed fully within a single paragraph. A topic sentence is *too broad* if it is too generalized or too large in scope to develop and support in one paragraph.

Too Broad: Ping-pong is a popular sport.

Focused: Ping-pong is a sport that requires both physical and mental training.

Another requirement of the topic sentence is that it must be capable of being developed. If the main idea is merely factual, it does not permit development. A topic sentence is *too narrow* if it is just a fact or detail and not an opinion that can be supported and developed.

Too Narrow: Some school systems in United States do not have music appreciation courses in their grade schools.

Revised: Students should be introduced to the pleasures of music while still in the lower grades.

Task 3.3

Underline the topic sentence in each of the following paragraphs. Be ready to explain your choice.

1. Before humans learned to farm, they were nomads, moving from place to place in search of game and vegetation. Each group consisted of about thirty to fifty people. Once farming was developed, the beginnings of cities appeared. Farming provided steady sustenance, which allowed people to live in larger groups and in permanent settlements. Each group had to make rules for civil coexistence, for divisions of labor, and for trade. People began to base their identities less on family ties than on geographical or cultural ties, and they placed growing value on the interests of the larger community.

2. My mother is neither tall nor heavy, but she's the biggest person in my life. There has been no other person with a greater influence on me. Most mothers feed, wash, and clothe their children, and my mother is no exception. But more than this, she made sure that I received the finest education possible. This education was not at expensive schools or famous universities, but at home, by her knee, patiently. My mother explained to me the difference between right and wrong; the virtues of generosity, honesty, and hard work; and the importance of family and social ties. From her I understood who I was, where I belonged, and how I should spend my energies. No matter how big I might grow to be, I hope to be as great as my mother.

3. Reasons for the popularity of fast-food chains appear obvious enough. For one thing, the food is generally cheap as restaurant food goes. A hamburger, French fries, and a shake at McDonald's, for example, cost about one-half as much as a similar meal at a regular "sit-down" restaurant. Another advantage of the chains is their convenience. For busy working couples who don't want to spend the time or effort cooking, the fast food restaurants offer an attractive alternative. And, judging by the fact that customers return in increasing numbers, many Americans like the taste of the food.

Task 3.4

Creating topic sentences that will attract the interest of your readers.
The passage below contains a series of sentences with specific examples of a single character trait: patience. Please complete the paragraph by creating an imaginative topic sentence that both identifies the particular character trait and creates enough interest to keep readers reading.

For example, recently I began taking my two-year-old dog to obedience school. After four weeks of lessons and practice, she has learned to follow only three commands—sit, stand, and lie down—and even those she often gets confused. Frustrating (and costly) as this is, I continue to work with her every day. After dog school, my grandmother and I sometimes go grocery shopping. Inching along those aisles, elbowed by hundreds of fellow customers, backtracking to pick up forgotten items, and standing in the endless line at the checkout, I could easily grow frustrated and cranky. But through years of trying times I have learned to keep my temper in check. Finally, after putting away the groceries, I might go out to a movie with my fiance, to whom I have been engaged for three years. Layoffs, extra jobs, and problems at home have forced us to postpone our wedding date several times. Still, my patience has enabled me to cancel and reschedule our wedding plans again and again without fuss, fights, or tears.

2. Unity

Unity means that each sentence included in our essay helps develop the point we have set out to make. In order to achieve unity, each paragraph must support and develop our essay's thesis statement. Also, within the paragraphs, each sentence must develop or support the topic sentence or controlling idea of that paragraph.

Every supporting sentence in a paragraph must relate to the main idea stated in the topic sentence. A sentence that does not support the main idea does not belong in the paragraph, thus such a sentence should be omitted. When a sentence does not belong in a paragraph, it is called an **irrelevant sentence.** For example:

The students in the class come from many different party of the world. Some are from European countries, such s France, Spain, and Italy. Others are from Middle Eastern countries like Saudi Arabia and Israel. Still other students were born in Asian countries, including Japan and Korea. **Korean food is delicious.** The largest number of students is from Latin American countries like Mexico, Venezuela and Peru. The class is an interesting mix of people from many different countries.

Unity is the essential quality of a paragraph. A paragraph may not have a topic sentence, but it must have unity. A paragraph is supposed to have a central idea, and everything in the paragraph relates to and develops that idea. In the following paragraph, is there any irrelative information upsetting the unity of the paragraph?

①The capital city of a country is usually a very important city. ②The government offices are located in the capital city and political leaders usually live there nearby. ③There are many different types of governments in the world. ④The capital may also be the centre of culture. ⑤There are often museums, libraries, and universities in the capital. ⑥Finally, the capital city can serve as a centre of trade, industry and commerce, so it is often the financial centre of the country.

Sentence ③ in the paragraph ("There are many different types of governments in the world.") is the odd one out: the information about governments is not directly relevant to the central idea of the passage. To restore the unity of the paragraph, delete this sentence.

Not all unity errors will be easy to spot. Sometimes, we will find we have changed direction or switched focus in a very subtle way during the process of writing our first draft. In order to stick to the focus, we should bear in mind these **Rules of Thumb for Writing Unified Paragraphs**:

➤ Be sure your paragraphs focus on one idea and state that idea in a topic sentence.

- Place your topic sentence effectively within your paragraph. Let the purpose of your paragraph and the nature of your evidence guide you.
- Let your paragraph's evidence—the selected details, the examples—illustrate or clarify the idea expressed in your topic sentence.
- Make sure you explain the relationship between your evidence and your idea so that it is clear to readers.
- Think about unity among paragraphs when writing essays. Be sure your paragraphs are related, that they fit together and clarify your essay's idea.

Task 3.5

Point out the topic sentences in the following paragraphs. Cross out any irrelevant sentences.

Paragraph 1

Almost every wedding tradition has a symbolic meaning that originated centuries ago. For example, couples have been exchanging rings to symbolize unending love for over a thousand years. Most often, the rings are worn on the third finger of the left hand, which was thought to contain a vein that ran directly to the heart. The rings in ancient times were sometimes made of braided grass, rope, or leather, giving rise to the expression "tying the knot." Another tradition, the bridal veil, began when marriages were arranged by the families and the groom was not allowed to see his bride until the wedding. The tossing of rice at newlyweds has long signified fertility blessings, and the sweet smell of the bride's bouquet was intended to drive away evil spirits, who were also diverted by the surrounding bridal attendants. Weddings may vary enormously today, but many couples still include ancient traditions to signify their new life together.

Paragraph 2

Adlai Stevenson, American statesman and twice an unsuccessful presidential candidate against Eisenhower, was well known for his intelligence and wit. Once on the campaign trail, after he had spoken eloquently and at length about several complex ideas, a woman in the audience was moved to stand and cheer, "That's great! Every thinking person in America will vote for you!" Stevenson immediately retorted, "That's not enough. I need a majority!" Frequently a reluctant candidate but never at a loss for words, Stevenson once defined a politician as a person who "approaches every question with an open mouth." Stevenson was also admired for his work as the Governor of Illinois and, later, as Ambassador to the United Nations.

Task 3.6

Support a topic sentence with specific details.
Here is an effective topic sentence for a descriptive paragraph:
My most valuable possession is an old, slightly warped, blond guitar—the first instrument that I ever taught myself how to play.
Some of the sentences below support this topic sentence with specific descriptive details. Others, however, offer information that would be inappropriate in a unified descriptive paragraph. Read the sentences carefully, and then pick out only those that support the topic sentence with precise descriptive details.

1. It is a Madeira folk guitar, all scuffed and scratched and finger-printed.
2. My grandparents gave it to me on my thirteenth birthday.
3. I think they bought it at the Music Lovers Shop in Rochester where they used to live.
4. At the top is a bramble of copper-wound strings, each one hooked through the eye of a silver tuning key.
5. Although copper strings are much harder on the fingers than nylon strings, they sound much better than the nylon ones.
6. The strings are stretched down a long slim neck.
7. The frets on the neck are tarnished, and the wood has been worn down by years of fingers pressing chords.
8. It was three months before I could even tune the guitar properly, and another few months before I could manage the basic chords.
9. You have to be very patient when first learning how to play the guitar.
10. You should set aside a certain time each day for practice.
11. The body of the Madeira is shaped like an enormous yellow pear, one that has been slightly damaged in shipping.
12. A guitar can be awkward to hold, particularly if it seems bigger than you are, but you need to learn how to hold it properly if you're ever going to play it right.

13. I usually play sitting down because it's more comfortable that way.
14. The blond wood has been chipped and gouged to gray, particularly where the pick guard fell off years ago.
15. I have a Gibson now and hardly ever play the Madeira any more.

3. Coherence

Coherence means that all the sentences and ideas in our paragraph flow together to make a clear, logical point about our topic. But a good paragraph is more than just a *collection* of ideas set down in random order. The readers should be able to follow what we have written and see easily and quickly how one detail leads to the next. To achieve coherence, we should have a smooth connection or transition between the sentences in our paragraphs. In general, there are four common means of achieving coherence in our paragraphs:

➤ Organizing paragraphs in easily recognized order
➤ Using transitional words and phrases
➤ Repeating key words and sentence structures
➤ Using pronouns effectively

(1) A recognizable order of information.

Without consciously thinking about the process, we usually organize paragraphs in easily recognized patterns that give the reader a sense of logical movement and order. There are five common types of order: **time order, spatial order, climatic order, cause and effect order, and oppositional order.** (refer to "Organizing" section)

(2) Transitional words and phrases.

Some paragraphs may need internal transitional words to help the reader move smoothly from one thought to the next so that the ideas do not appear disconnected or choppy. The following paragraph is unified and coherent. Notice how the transitional words and phrases (italicized) guide us along, helping us see how one detail leads to the next.

Why I Don't Make My Bed

Ever since I moved into my own apartment last fall, I have gotten out of the habit of making my bed—except on Fridays, of course, when I change the sheets. Although some people may think that I am a slob, I have some sound reasons for breaking the bed-making habit. ***In the first place***, I am not concerned about maintaining a tidy bedroom because no one except me ever ventures in there. If there is ever a fire inspection or a surprise date, I suppose I can dash in there to fluff up the pillow and slap on a spread. ***Otherwise***, I am not bothered. ***In addition***, I find nothing uncomfortable about crawling into a rumpled mass of sheets and blankets. ***On the contrary***, I enjoy poking out a cozy space for myself before drifting off to sleep. ***Also***, I think that a tightly made bed is downright uncomfortable: entering one makes me feel like a loaf of bread being wrapped and sealed. ***Finally***, and ***most importantly***, I think bed-making is an awful way to waste time in the morning. I would rather spend those precious minutes checking my email or feeding the cat than tucking in corners or snapping the spread.

Transitional words and phrases guide readers from one sentence to the next. Although they most often appear at the beginning of a sentence, they may also show up *after* the subject. Here are the common transitional expressions, grouped according to the type of relationship shown by each.

1) Addition transitions:

and

also

besides

first, second, third

in addition

in the first place, in the second place, in the third place

furthermore

moreover

to begin with, next, finally

Example:

In the first place, no "burning" in the sense of combustion, as in the burning of wood, occurs in a volcano; ***moreover***, volcanoes are not necessarily mountains; ***furthermore***, the activity takes place not always at the summit but more commonly on the sides or flanks; ***and finally***, the "smoke" is not smoke but condensed steam.

(Fred Bullard, *Volcanoes in History*)

2) Cause-effect transitions:

accordingly

and so

as a result

consequently

for this reason
hence
so
then
therefore
thus

Example:

The ideologue is often brilliant. **Consequently** some of us distrust brilliance when we should distrust the ideologue.

(Clifton Fadiman)

3) Comparison transitions:
by the same token
in like manner
in the same way
in similar fashion
likewise
similarly

Example:

When you start with a portrait and search for a pure form, a clear volume, through successive eliminations, you arrive inevitably at the egg. *Likewise*, starting with the egg and following the same process in reverse, one finishes with the portrait.

(Pablo Picasso)

4) Contrast transitions:
but
however
in contrast
instead
nevertheless
on the contrary
on the other hand
still
yet

Example:

Every American, to the last man, lays claim to a "sense" of humor and guards it as his most significant spiritual trait, *yet* rejects humor as a contaminating element wherever found. America is a nation of comics and comedians; *nevertheless*, humor has no stature and is accepted only after the death of the perpetrator.

(E. B. White)

5) Conclusion and summary transitions:
and so
after all
at last
finally
in brief
in closing
in conclusion
on the whole
to conclude
to summarize

Example:

Reporters are not paid to operate in retrospect. Because when news begins to solidify into current events and *finally* harden into history, it is the stories we didn't write, the questions we didn't ask that prove far, far more damaging than the ones we did.

(Anna Quindlen)

6) Example transitions:
as an example
for example
for instance
specifically
thus
to illustrate

Example:

With all the ingenuity involved in hiding delicacies on the body, this process automatically excludes certain foods. *For example*, a turkey sandwich is welcome, but the cumbersome cantaloupe is not.

(Steve Martin, "How to Fold Soup")

7) Insistence transitions:
in fact
indeed
no
yes

Example:

The joy of giving is ***indeed*** a pleasure, especially when you get rid of something you don't want.

(Frank Butler, *Going My Way*)

8) Place transitions:
above
alongside
beneath
beyond
farther along
in back
in front
nearby
on top of
to the left
to the right
under
upon

Example:

What did it matter where you lay once you were dead? In a dirty sump or in a marble tower ***on top of*** a high hill? You were dead, you were sleeping the big sleep, you were not bothered by things like that.

(Raymond Chandler, *The Big Sleep*)

9) Restatement transitions:
in other words
in short
in simpler terms
that is
to put it differently
to repeat

Example:

Anthropologist Geoffrey Gorer studied the few peaceful human tribes and discovered one common characteristic: sex roles were not polarized. Differences of dress and occupation were at a minimum. Society *in other words*, was not using sexual blackmail as a way of getting women to do cheap labor, or men to be aggressive.

(Gloria Steinem, "What It Would Be Like If Women Win")

10) Time transitions:

afterward
at the same time
currently
earlier
formerly
immediately
in the future
in the meantime
in the past
later
meanwhile
previously
simultaneously
subsequently
then
until now

Example:

At first a toy, then a mode of transportation for the rich, the automobile was designed as man's mechanical servant. *Later* it became part of the pattern of living.

Task 3.7

Combine and Connect Sentences by Using Transitional Words and Phrases.

Instructions: Combine the sentences in each set into *two* clear and concise sentences, eliminating any needless repetition. As you do so, add a transitional word or phrase (in italics at the head of each set) to the beginning of the second sentence to show how it relates to the first. Keep in mind that many combinations are possible, and in some cases you may prefer your own sentences to the original versions.

1. *Instead*

Retirement should be the reward for a lifetime of work.

It is widely viewed as a sort of punishment.

It is a punishment for growing old.

2. *Therefore*

In recent years viruses have been shown to cause cancer in chickens.

Viruses have also been shown to cause cancer in mice, cats, and even in some primates.

Viruses might cause cancer in humans.

This is a reasonable hypothesis.

3. *In fact*

We do not seek solitude.

If we find ourselves alone for once, we flick a switch.

We invite the whole world in.

The world comes in through the television screen.

4. *On the contrary*

We were not irresponsible.

Each of us should do something.

This thing would be of genuine usefulness to the world.

We were trained to think that.

5. *However*

Little girls, of course, don't take toy guns out of their hip pockets.

They do not say "Pow, pow" to all their neighbors and friends.

The average well-adjusted little boy does this.

If we gave little girls the six-shooters, we would soon have double the pretend body count.

6. *Next*

We drove the wagon close to a corner post.

We twisted the end of the wire around it.

We twisted the wire one foot above the ground.

We stapled it fast.

We drove along the line of posts.

We drove for about 200 yards.

We unreeled the wire on the ground behind us.

7. *Indeed*

We know very little about pain.

What we don't know makes it hurt all the more.

There is ignorance about pain.

No form of illiteracy in the United States is so widespread.

No form of illiteracy in the United States is so costly.

8. *Moreover*

Many of our street girls can be as vicious as any corporation president.

Many of our street girls can be as money mad as any corporation president.

They can be less emotional than men.

They can be less emotional in conducting acts of personal violence.

9. *For this reason*

The historical sciences have made us very conscious of our past.

They have made us conscious of the world as a machine.

The machine generates successive events out of foregoing ones.

Some scholars tend to look totally backward.

They look backward in their interpretation of the human future.

10. *However*

Rewriting is something that most writers find they have to do.

They rewrite to discover what they have to say.

They rewrite to discover how to say it.

There are a few writers who do little formal rewriting.

They have capacity and experience.

They create and review a large number of invisible drafts.

They create and review in their minds.

They do this before they approach the page.

(3) Repetition of key words and sentence structures.

Careful repetition of key words and sentence structures can help to make our writing clear and coherent. Repeating **key words** in a paragraph is an important technique for achieving coherence. Of course, careless or excessive repetition is boring—and a source of clutter. But used skillfully and selectively, as in the paragraph below, this technique can help to hold sentences together and focus the reader's attention on a central idea.

We Americans are a charitable and humane people: we have institutions devoted to every good cause from rescuing homeless cats to preventing World War III. But what have we done to promote the art of **thinking**? Certainly we make no room for **thought** in our daily lives. Suppose a man were to say to his friends, "I'm not going to PTA tonight (or choir practice or the baseball game) because I need some time to myself, some time to **think**?" Such a man would be shunned by his neighbors; his family would be ashamed of him. What if a teenager were to say, "I'm not going to the dance tonight because I need some time to **think**?" His parents would immediately start looking in the Yellow Pages for a psychiatrist. We are all too much like Julius Caesar: we fear and distrust people who **think** too much. We believe that almost anything is more important than **thinking**.

(Carolyn Kane, from "Thinking: A Neglected Art", in *Newsweek*, 14 December 1981)

Notice that the author uses various forms of the same word—*think*, *thinking*, *thought*—to link the different examples and reinforce the main idea of the paragraph.

A similar way to achieve cohesion in our writing is to repeat a particular **sentence structure** along with a key word or phrase. Although we usually try to vary the length and shape of our sentences, now and then we may choose to repeat a construction to emphasize connections between related ideas.

Here's a short example of structural repetition from the play *Getting Married*, by George Bernard Shaw:

There are couples who dislike one another furiously for several hours at a time; there are couples who dislike one another permanently; and there are couples who never dislike one another; but these last are people who are incapable of disliking anybody.

Notice how author's reliance on semicolon (rather than periods) reinforces the sense of unity and cohesion in this passage.

On rare occasions, emphatic repetitions may extend beyond just two or three main clauses. Recently, the Turkish novelist Orhan Pamuk provided an example of **extended repetition** in his Nobel Prize Lecture, "My Father's Suitcase":

The question we writers are asked most often, the favorite question, is: Why do you write? I write because I have an innate need to write. I write because I can't do normal work as other people do. I write because I want to read books like the ones I write. I write because I am angry at everyone. I write because I love sitting in a room all day writing. I write because I can partake of real life only by changing it. I write because I want others, the whole world, to know what sort of life we lived, and continue to live, in Istanbul, in Turkey. I write because I love the smell of paper, pen, and ink. I write because I believe in literature, in the art of the novel, more than I believe in anything else. I write because it is a habit, a passion. I write because I am afraid of being forgotten. I write because I like the glory and interest that writing brings. I write to be alone. Perhaps I write because I hope to understand why I am so very, very angry at everyone. I write because I like to be read. I write because once I have begun a novel, an essay, a page I want to finish it. I write because everyone expects me to write. I write because I have a childish belief in the immortality of libraries, and in the way my books sit on the shelf. I write because it is exciting to turn all life's beauties and riches into words. I write not to tell a story but to compose a story. I write because I wish to escape from the foreboding that there is a place I must go but—as in a dream—can't quite get to. I write because I have never managed to be happy. I write to be happy.

(The Nobel Lecture, 7 December 2006. Translated from the Turkish, by Maureen Freely. THE NOBEL FOUNDATION 2006)

(4) Using pronouns effectively.

The repetition of key words and structures is an effective coherence technique as long as it's not overworked. Carried on for too long, repetitions gets tedious, as shown in the paragraph below:

A characteristic human reaction to flies is to eradicate *flies*. *Eradicating flies* is deemed a meritorious action. *Eradicating flies* may be an innate tendency. I have already alluded to the propensity of children for amputating the appendages of flies. Ants *amputate the appendages of flies* if a fly is unfortunate enough to fall into *the ants'* clutches. I venture to predict, however, that the fly is in no danger of extinction. *The fly* has no sociological impediments to reproduction; *the fly's* food supply is unlimited; *the fly's* basic requirements, few.

We can maintain the coherence of this paragraph while eliminating the excessive repetition by substituting pronouns for some of the repeated nouns. Consider this revised and more concise version of the paragraph:

A characteristic human reaction to flies is to eradicate *them*. *This* is deemed a meritorious action. *It* may be an innate tendency. I have already alluded to the propensity of children for amputating the appendages of flies. Ants do the *same thing* if a fly is unfortunate enough to fall into *their* clutches. I venture to predict, however, that the fly is in no danger of extinction. *It* has no sociological impediments to reproduction; *its* food supply is unlimited; *its* basic requirements, few.

(Vincent Dethier, *To Know a Fly*. Holden-Day, 1962)

When using pronouns to enforce coherence, keep this principle in mind: each pronoun should refer clearly to an appropriate noun.

Task 3.8

Rewrite the two passages below, replacing the words and phrases in italics with appropriate pronouns.

Passage 1

A society that has no heroes will soon grow enfeebled. *That society's* purposes will be less elevated; *that society's* aspirations less challenging; *that society's* endeavors less strenuous. *That society's* individual members will "hang loose" and "lay back" and, so mellowed out, the last thing of which *that society's individual members* wish to hear is heroism. *That society's individual members* do not want to be told of men and women whose example might disturb *that society's individual members*, calling *that society's individual members* to effort and duty and sacrifice or even the chance of glory.

Passage 2

The Fortune Teller

The fortune teller moved *the fortune teller's* dry, shriveled hands over the glass ball that *the fortune teller* had bought at a dollar store a long time ago. The *fortune teller* could hear the laughter and the occasional shouts of the children as *the children* ran outside from ride to ride and from tent to tent. *The children* never came in to see *the fortune teller*. Instead it was always the face of a laid-off dock worker or a romantic teenager that peered through the entrance way *of the fortune teller's* tent. The unemployed dock workers wanted to hear about winning lottery tickets and new job opportunities. The teenagers were eager to hear stories about far away places and dark, mysterious strangers. And so the fortune teller always told *the dock workers and the teenagers* what *the dock workers and the teenagers* wanted to hear. *The fortune teller* liked giving *the dock workers and the teenagers* something to dream about. *The fortune teller* tried to fill the minds *of the dock workers and the teenagers* with great expectations. Just then, a young man appeared in the entrance way. *The young man* was nervous, and the smile *of the young man* was timid. *The young man* shuffled into the dark tent, *the young man's* head full of dreams and yet, at the same time, innocently empty. The fortune teller took the trembling hands *of the young man* into *the fortune teller's* own hands, and peered at the revealing lines etched on the palms *of the young man*. Then, slowly, in the cracked, ancient voice *of the fortune teller*, *the fortune teller* began to speak of new job opportunities, far away places, and dark, mysterious strangers.

3.3.3 The Conclusion

After reading the body and all the evidence we've presented in support of the thesis, the reader should now view the thesis statement not as conjecture but as a claim that is supported. That's exactly what we express in the conclusion.

The conclusion is essentially the mirror image of the introduction, but one that stresses the fact that the thesis has now been proven. The conclusion should therefore refer to the thesis statement in some form, and affirm that it has been proven and supported. We should also recap the major points we've made in the paper to establish our argument.

Like the introduction, the conclusion for most essays only needs to be one paragraph and it should primarily represent our own words and ideas. This is also not a place to quote or paraphrase extensively from secondary sources.

While the introduction contributes to the reader's first impression of our essay, the conclusion will influence the reader's final impression. We want to end with a bang—with some of our most powerful and dramatic writing—that leaves the reader absolutely convinced of the validity of our argument.

The most basic conclusion inverts the structure of the introduction, starting off with a restatement of the thesis statement, followed by more general statements that sum up the essay's main ideas. The final sentence is a broad remark about the subject or topic.

We can vary from this standard format in some instances. Many writers, for example, choose to introduce some new point or question in the conclusion that emerges from the thesis. After establishing the validity of the thesis statement, they then address its consequences or implications. No matter the form of the conclusion, the same general rule applies: The conclusion should bring the essay to a formal close and affirm that the thesis statement has been proven.

A concluding paragraph is our chance to remind the reader of our thesis. Also, the conclusion brings the paper to a natural and graceful end, sometimes leaving the reader with a final thought on the subject. There are four common methods of conclusion.

(1) Summary and final thought.

Paraphrase our thesis statement and remind the readers about our main points. This is the most common method used. We should not use the exact wording we used before. Look at the following example.

The Advantages of Video Rentals

Watching movies at home, definitely, has several advantages over going to the theater. This way you don't spend so much money, you can use your time more effectively, and you can enjoy the comfort of your house. There's nothing better than staying at home on a rainy day while enjoying a good movie on your TV screen.

(2) Thought provoking question or short series of questions.

Like we have said earlier, a question always grabs the reader's attention. It is a direct appeal to our reader to think further about what we have written. A question should follow logically from the points we have already made in the paper. A question must deal with one of these areas:

▶ why the subject of your paper is important?
▶ what might happen in the future?
▶ what should be done about this subject?

▶ which choice should be made?

Look at the following example.

Helping Your Country

You can help your country by contributing in many ways. Are you going to sit around waiting for the government to do everything? What will happen in the future, when the government can no longer sustain your needs? What will happen to your children and their future generations? Do they have to pay for your laziness? Stand up and do something!

(3) Recommendations.

A recommendation suggests what should be done about a situation or problem. For example:

Women Exploitation on TV

Nowadays, women are being more exploited than ever on TV commercials and other propaganda. These commercials are denigrating the feminine figure to the extremes. It's time for women and society in general to stop this pattern of abuse. Consumers should boycott companies and products whose advertising continues to exploit women in such way.

(4) Predictions.

A prediction states what will happen in the future. For example:

Animal Cruelty

If people stopped to think before acquiring pets, there would be fewer instances of cruelty to animals. Many times, it is the people who adopt pets without considering the expenses and responsibility involved who mistreat and neglect their animals. Pets are living creatures. If people continue being negligent and irresponsible with their pets, animal cruelty will exist forever!

Task 3.9

Read the three concluding paragraphs that follow. Then, in the space provided, identify the kind of conclusion used in each case (final thought, question, prediction, or recommendation).

1. A pet cannot be thrown onto a trash heap when it is no longer wanted or tossed into a closet if it begins to bore its owner. A pet, like us, is a living thing that needs physical care, affection, and respect. Would-be owners, therefore, should think seriously about their responsibilities before they acquire

a pet.

---

2. Neither letters, phone calls, nor conversations guarantee perfect communication. With all our sophisticated skills, we human beings often communicate less effectively than howling wolves or chattering monkeys. Even if we were able to read each other's mind, we'd probably still find some way to foul up the message.

---

3. Although our looks, talents, and accomplishments were constantly compared, Shelley and I have somehow managed not to turn into deadly enemies. Feeling like the outcast of the family, in fact, helped me to develop a drive to succeed and a sense of humor. In our sibling rivalry, we both managed to win.

3.4 Revising

Revision is the process of improving what we have written. Revising is more than correcting spelling errors; it is finding clarity of thought.

Revising is an opportunity to reconsider our topic, our readers, even our purpose for writing. Taking the time to rethink our approach may encourage us to make major changes in the content and structure of our work.

We should keep in mind that revising involves much more than just correcting errors in grammar, spelling, and punctuation. Those will be the focus of later editing.

As a general rule, the best time to revise is not right after we've completed a draft (although at times this is unavoidable). Instead, wait a few hours—even a day or two, if possible—in order to gain some distance from our work. This way we'll be less protective of our writing and better prepared to make changes.

Besides, we'd better read our work *aloud* when we revise. We may *hear* problems in our writing that we can't see.

3.4.1 Revision Checklist

▶ Does the essay have a clear and concise main idea? Is this idea made clear to the reader in a thesis statement early in the essay (usually in the introduction)?

▶ Does the essay have a specific purpose (such as to inform, entertain, evaluate, or persuade)? Have you made this purpose clear to the reader?

▶ Does the introduction create interest in the topic and make your audience want to read on?

▶ Is there a clear plan and sense of organization to the essay? Does each paragraph develop logically from the previous one?

▶ Is each paragraph clearly related to the main idea of the essay? Is there enough information in the essay to support the main idea?

▶ Is the main point of each paragraph clear? Is each point adequately and clearly defined in a topic sentence and supported with specific details?

▶ Are there clear transitions from one paragraph to the next? Have key words and ideas been given proper emphasis in the sentences and paragraphs?

▶ Are the sentences clear and direct? Can they be understood on the first reading? Are the sentences varied in length and structure? Could any sentences be improved by combining or restructuring them?

▶ Are the words in the essay clear and precise? Does the essay maintain a consistent tone?

▶ Does the essay have an effective conclusion—one that emphasizes the main idea and provides a sense of completeness?

3.4.2 Peer Revision

Peer revision has added benefits over revising by ourselves. Other people can notice things in our essay that we didn't. Some instructors set aside class time for peer review, but even if our instructor doesn't, it's a good idea to seek out feedback from a classmate, roommate, or anyone at all who can offer a fresh perspective.

As a writer, we should tell our peer what our biggest concern with the essay is. If we need help writing a conclusion, we don't want our peer to spend time circling grammatical mistakes in a paragraph we were thinking about deleting anyway. Remember, our peer isn't just there to catch our mistakes; he/she might have some ideas about new material we can add to make our writing more exciting.

On the other hand, when we review our peer's essay, we should think about what we would want in his/her place. We should ask if there is anything he/she is having trouble with. Be nice, of course, but we shouldn't be so nice that we aren't helpful. He/she may like to hear "Good job," but we should explain what we like about the paper and where we think it could be even better. We should remember that peer reviewing isn't about whether the essay is good or bad, it is about how the essay can be improved. We have a responsibility to the student whose essay we are reading. We should be familiar with the qualities and requirements of the assignment. By considering the merits and shortcomings of the essay, we do our best to provide a complete evaluation.

3.4.3 Checklist for Peer Revision

- What is the writer's purpose?
- Does the writing include all the necessary characteristics of its particular type (cause-and-effect, narrative, research, etc.)?
- Is the writing organized logically?
- Has the writer used language that enhances her/his message?
- Is the writing unified/coherent?
- Did we point out the strength(s) or part(s) we found interesting?
- Is there any part that required more information?
- Is there any part that was irrelevant?

Talking with someone else about our paper will always help us re-evaluate our content. Sometimes it reassures us that we've got it right; sometimes it reveals to us the places that need work. It is always a good idea to share our work before submitting the final draft.

3.5 Editing

After revising an essay until we're satisfied with its basic content and structure, we still need to edit our work. In other words, we need to improve our draft by correcting errors and by making words and sentences clearer, more precise, and more effective.

Checklist for Editing:
- Is each sentence clear and complete?
- Can any short, choppy sentences be improved by combining them?
- Can any long, awkward sentences be improved by breaking them down into shorter units and recombining them?
- Can any wordy sentences be made more concise?
- Can any run-on sentences be more effectively coordinated or subordinated?
- Does each verb agree with its subject?
- Are all verb forms correct and consistent?
- Do pronouns refer clearly to the appropriate nouns?
- Do all modifying refer clearly to the words they are intended to modify?
- Is each word in the essay appropriate and effective?
- Is each word spelled correctly?
- Is the punctuation correct?

Make sure to save enough time to proofread carefully. Don't let surface errors distract the reader and undermine our hard work.

Task 3.10

Compare the following two versions of an essay (a draft and a revised version). See if you can identify the numerous changes that have been made in this revision, and consider the extent to which the essay has been improved as a result.

Types of Shoppers
(a draft)

Working at a supermarket has given me a chance to observe the different ways human beings behave. I like to think of the shoppers as rats in a lab experiment, and the aisles are a maze designed by a psychologist. Most of the customers follow a dependable route, walking up and down the aisles, checking through my counter, and then escaping through the exit door. But not everybody is so dependable.

   The first type of unusual shopper is one that I call the amnesiac. He always seems to be going down the aisles against the normal flow of traffic. He mutters things to himself because he left his shopping list at home. When he finally makes it to my register and starts unloading the cart, he suddenly remembers the one item of food that brought him here in the first place. He then resumes his trip around the store while the customers waiting in line start to grumble impatiently. Inevitably, when it comes time to pay for the goods, the amnesiac discovers that he has left his wallet at home. I don't say a word. I just void his receipt and tell him to have a nice day.

   Senior citizens mean well, I guess, but they can also try my patience. One man stops by several times a week, more to pay a visit than to shop. He wanders around the aisles slowly, pausing now and then to read a box of cereal or squeeze a roll or sniff one of those lemon-scented blobs of room freshener. But he never buys very much. When he finally comes up to the checkout, this type likes to chat with me—about my hair, his bunions, or that pretty tune tinkling out of the ceiling speakers. Although the people waiting behind him in line are usually fuming, I try to be friendly. I really don't think this man has anywhere else to go.

   Even more annoying is someone I call the hot shopper. You can tell that she plans her shopping trip days in advance. She enters the store with a pocketbook on her arm and a calculator in her hip pocket, and she carries a shopping list that makes the Dewey Decimal System look chaotic. Like a soldier marching in a parade, she struts from one sale item to another, carefully organizing things in her basket by size, weight, and shape. Of course, she is the biggest complainer: something she wants always seems to be missing or mispriced or out of stock. Often the manager has to be called in to settle her down and set her back on course. Then, when she reaches my lane, she begins barking orders at me, like "Don't put the grapes in with the Nutty Ho Hos!" In the meantime, she stares at the prices on the register, just waiting to jump on me for making a mistake. If my total doesn't match the one on her calculator, she insists on a complete recount. Sometimes I make up the difference myself just to get her out of the store.

These are the three main types of unusual shoppers I have encountered while working as a cashier at the Piggly Wiggly. At least they help to keep things interesting!

Shopping at the Pig
(a revised version)

Working part-time as a cashier at the Piggly Wiggly has given me a great opportunity to observe human behavior. Sometimes I think of the shoppers as white rats in a lab experiment, and the aisles as a maze designed by a psychologist. Most of the rats—customers, I mean—follow a routine pattern, strolling up and down the aisles, checking through my chute, and then escaping through the exit hatch. But not everyone is so dependable. My research has revealed three distinct types of abnormal customer: the amnesiac, the super shopper, and the dawdler.

The amnesiac stops his car in the loading zone, leaves the engine running with the keys locked inside, and tries to enter the store by crashing into the exit door. After dusting himself off and slipping through the entrance, he grabs a cart and begins hurtling down the aisles against the normal flow of traffic. "Peaches or potatoes?" he mutters to himself. "Doughnuts or Ding Dongs?" He has, of course, left his shopping list at home. When he finally makes it to my register and starts unloading the cart, he suddenly remembers the jug of milk or the loaf of bread that brought him here in the first place. He then resumes his race around the store while the customers waiting in line begin to grumble, tap their feet, and rattle the rack of *Stars* and *National Enquirers*. Inevitably, of course, when it comes time to pay for the goods, the amnesiac discovers that he has left his wallet at home. Without saying a word, I void his receipt and lend him a coat hanger.

The super shopper has been planning her assault for days. She enters the store with a pocketbook on her arm, a coupon purse around her neck, a calculator in her pocket, and in her hand a shopping list that makes the Dewey Decimal System look downright chaotic. With military-like efficiency, she trundles her cart from one sale item to another, carefully organizing them in her basket by size, weight, and shape. Rarely, however, does she make it through the store without a breakdown: either the Charmin has been moved to a different shelf or else some poor stock clerk has forgotten to replenish a supply of Cool Ranch Doritos. Usually the manager has to be called in to settle her down and set her back on course. Then, when she reaches my lane, she begins barking orders: "Double bag the Creamsicles! Twelve-cents off on Jell-O! Don't put the grapes in with the Nutty Ho Hos!" In the meantime, she glares at the prices blinking on the register, just waiting to pounce on me for making an error. If my total doesn't match the one on her calculator, she insists on a complete recount. Sometimes I make up the difference myself just to get her out of the store.

The dawdler wanders in as if he had been looking for the library and arrived here by mistake. He tours the aisles slowly, pausing often to read a box of Froot Loops, squeeze a dinner roll, or sniff one of those lemon-scented rubber blobs of room freshener. However, he seldom ends up buying many of the things he picks up. When he finally strolls up to the checkout, the dawdler likes to settle in for a chat—about my hair style, his bunions, or that nice Yanni tune tinkling out of the ceiling speakers. Although the people waiting behind him in line are fuming, I try to be friendly, knowing that this must be the major social event of the dawdler's week.

To be truthful, most of the people who pass through my checkout are quietly efficient and polite—and a little boring. Though the abnormal ones may try my patience, they also help to make a dull job more interesting. So, for your own amusement keep an eye out for these characters the next time you pull into the parking lot of the Piggly Wiggly: a fellow trying to unlock his car with a coat hanger, a woman fussing at the bag boy for squashing a grape, and a sweet old man who may try to tell you about the arthritis in his knees or the expiration date on his buttermilk.

Chapter 4 Modes of Essays

There are four modes of writing: narration (the author intends to tell a story or recount an event); description (the author intends to create in words a picture of a person, place, object, or feeling); exposition (the author intends to explain or inform in many ways, for instance by process, illustration, comparison and contrast, classification and/or division, or an analysis of their causes and/or effects); and argumentation (the author intends to convince or persuade). In this chapter we will learn to write these modes of essays listed below.

A narrative essay: Telling a story using narrative details and description.

A descriptive essay: The art of using vivid details to paint a picture with words.

A process essay: Describing a step-by-step process or a series of steps one must take to accomplish a task.

An illustration essay: Providing examples in order to illustrate an idea or set of ideas.

A cause and effect essay: The relationship between causes (reasons) and effects.

A comparison and contrast essay: Similarities and differences between two subjects or among several subjects.

A classification and/or division essay: Categorizing people, things, or concepts into particular groups in order to draw conclusions about them.

An argumentative essay: Persuading an audience to agree with a particular viewpoint or arguing for a change in the status quo.

4.1 A Narrative Essay

Thinking over the Questions before Writing

▶ What did I learn from the experience?

➤ What do I want my readers to learn or understand after reading about the event I experienced or witnessed?
➤ How can I re-create the event vividly in my readers heads? What examples and details should I use to re-create the story?
➤ How should I organize my paragraphs after my introduction and thesis, and how can I move smoothly from one event or detail to the next?
➤ What's the best way to conclude my essay?

Narrative writing is very important in the English writing class. The narrative offers several important benefits.

➤ It can help us "loosen up" and write naturally. Telling or listening to stories is so enjoyable that learning to write them down is a good way to gain a sense of comfort as a writer.
➤ We can use narrative as a brainstorming technique to generate ideas for future essays, regardless of the type of essay we are writing.
➤ We can employ narrative writing, in expository and argumentative contexts, to introduce our essays and to provide supporting evidence for the body paragraphs.
➤ Because stories happen in time, we can begin to learn how to pace our writing and provide transitions to enhance the way it flows.
➤ Furthermore, the natural pauses in the flow of most narratives give us the chance to practice describing people, scenery, and emotions.

In a **narrative essay**, we recount an event, story, or series of events in order to explain some insight or truth gained from an experience. Although some narrative essays are less formal and involve a straightforward telling of a story or event, most narrative essays include a more analytical purpose: They have a point, a plot, a lesson, or a message to impart to the reader through telling a story or recounting an event and framing it with analysis. So someone briefly describes a narrative essay as **a story told for a reason.**

Generally, the events in a narrative essay are arranged in **chronological order**—the order in which they happened. Read the following narrative paragraph, and pay attention to the arrangement of the events.

Sample 1

Fishing Fun

Fishing at Horning's Hideout proved to be an enjoyable outing for Jeff and his family. All family members rose early in the morning excited to prepare for the trip. Mother packed food for the family as well as her books and needlework. Father checked the car to make certain it was ready for the drive. Then with Father's help, Jeff and his brother readied their fishing poles along with the books and toys which would entertain them on the hour's drive. When the family arrived at their destination, they stopped by the office to purchase some worms to use as bait. Cheerfully walking along the narrow path, the family transported their gear all the way around the small pond looking for just the right place to cast their lines. In hopes that fish would be lurking in the shadows, Jeff and his brother decided to fish from a shady area along one side of the pond. Though it seemed like the perfect fishing spot, overhead branches interfered with casting. Undaunted after snagging lines several times, the avid fishermen decided it would be best to move to the other side of the pond. Here, the boys began to get bites. Before long, Jeff's older brother caught the first fish. Jeff caught one soon after. Suddenly the fish were biting and Father became very active helping the two excited boys keep their hooks baited, and reel in their catch. Just before noon, Jeff hooked what turned out to be the largest trout of the day which he hung in the water near the shore with the other captured fish. While Father and the boys fished, Mother enjoyed sitting at the picnic table and reading quietly or doing her needlework. After several hours of fishing, and a total catch of seven fish, Father showed the boys how to clean the fish before packing up for the trip home. **The outing was great fun for the whole family.** Jeff and his brother found much excitement in catching the fish. Father enjoyed helping the boys and spending a day in the woods. Mother expressed her pleasure in being with her family and seeing everyone having an agreeable time. Most of all, everyone's taste buds were delighted with the dinner that evening. All the family is hoping for a return trip before too long.

Now look at the arrangement of the events in sample 1:

    A. Topic sentence—trip was enjoyable.
       1. Preparations

  a. Mother—food, books, needlework
  b. Father—car
  c. Boys—fishing poles, toys, books
 2. Reach destination—Purchase bait
 3. Finding fishing spot
  a. Finding first place
  b. Moving to second place
 4. Real fishing began
  a. Brother caught fish
  b. Father busy
   (1) His pole
   (2) Helping boys cast
   (3) Helping keep hooks baited
   (4) Helping reel in catch
  c. Jeff caught fish
  d. Caught seven fish
  e. Cleaned fish before leaving
B. Concluding sentence—It was fun for all
 1. Jeff and brother were excited to catch fish
 2. Father enjoyed time with sons
 3. Mother enjoyed quiet time

  A narrative is usually arranged chronologically, but there are sometimes **flash forwards** and **flash backs.** Consider the following example:

Sample 2

  In June 1964... two Italian fishing boats, working in tandem with (同时地) a crew of 18, were dragging their nets along the bottom of the Adriatic (亚得里亚海). Toward dawn, as they pulled up the nets after a long trawl (拖网捕鱼), the fishermen realized their catch was unusually heavy.... When they finally swung the nets inboard they saw an ungainly, prehistoric-looking figure missing both feet. It was, in fact, a 500-pound Greek statue covered with nearly 2,000 years of sea encrustations (硬壳,沉积物).

  In November 1977, this life-size bronze fetched the highest known price ever paid for a statue— $3.9 million. The work is attributed to the fourth century B. C. Greek artist Lysippus.... Professor Paolo Moreno of Rome University, author of two books on Lysippus, identifies the statue as the portrait of a young athlete after victory and suggests that it may have been plundered (掠夺) by ancient Romans from Mount Olympus. The ship bearing the statue was probably sunk in a storm and there may well have been other treasures on board. Pliny the Elder tells us Lysippus made more than 1,500 works, all of them bronze, but it was doubted that any of the originals had survived—until this one surfaced.

The fishermen stealthily unloaded the barnacle-covered (布满藤壶的) masterpiece in Fano, near Rimini, and took it to the captain's house, where it was put on a kitchen table and propped up (支撑) against a wall.

—Bryan Rosten, "Smuggled!"

The first paragraph tells readers how a statue was discovered in June 1964. At the beginning of the second paragraph, the writer flashes forward to 1977, when the statue was sold for a large sum of money. Then the writer flashes back to ancient times, when the statue was lost. And in the third paragraph, the writer comes back to continue the original story.

The details in the paragraph should answer the 5 W-How questions: who? what? when? where? why? and how? Look at the following example of a narrative paragraph. Can you find the answers?

Sample 3

Discovering Solitude

Last Saturday morning I discovered a new best friend: me. I have always hated being alone. I'm a real people person. I also like to sleep late whenever I can. But for some reason, I woke up at five o'clock last Saturday morning. I tried and I tried to go back to sleep. Finally, I gave up. I got out of bed and went to the kitchen. I made myself a cup of cocoa. Then I went out to our back porch. Even though it was summer, the morning was cool. I sat down on the back steps. The sun was coming up. The sky turned from blue to orange to pink. I had never noticed just how clear the colors of sunrise could be. They changed right before my eyes. The changing colors reminded me of a kaleidoscope I'd had as a child. A slight breeze lifted my hair off my neck. I could smell the honeysuckle flowers from the garden fence in the slight wind. The birds began to sing as the sky grew lighter. As I watched the world come to life, I felt at peace. I thought of all the good things in my life. I thought of all my good friends and my wonderful family. For the first time in my life, I was happy being alone. I wasn't bored. Instead, I felt refreshed, as if I'd just had another nap. <u>I gained a new appreciation for myself.</u>

4.1.1 Important Elements in an Effective Narrative Essay

All narrative essays have characters, setting, climax, and most importantly, a plot. When creating a narrative, authors must determine their purpose, consider their audience, establish their point of view, use dialogue realistically, and organize the narrative. The following aspects are essential for writing an effective narrative essay.

4.1.2 Writing Purpose

When planning a narrative essay, we should determine what we are trying to accomplish by writing this narrative essay. We should have a definite writing purpose. Our purpose may be to inform the readers some historical facts, or to tell a story persuasively from a clearly defined point of view, or to share a lesson with our audience, etc. Whatever our choice—an objective, factual retelling or a subjective interpretation—our narrative's purpose should be clear to our readers, who should never reach the end of the story wondering "What was that all about?" Bearing our writing purpose in mind will help us select the information and language best suited to meet our audience's needs.

4.1.3 Context

When writing a narrative essay, we should at first make clear **when**, **where** and **to whom** the action in an event happened at the beginning of the essay. The context will help the readers understand the whole passage.

4.1.4 Thesis Statement

To ensure that the audience easily understand our writing purpose, we can first state a thesis claim followed by a narrative that supports it. Sometimes we choose to begin with our narrative and state or sum up the point or "lesson" of our story in our concluding paragraph. Still some skilled authors choose to imply a main point or attitude through the unfolding action and choice of descriptive details. But an implied thesis is always riskier than a stated one, so unless we are absolutely convinced that our readers could not possibly fail to see our point, we had better work on finding a smooth way to incorporate a statement of our main idea into our essay.

4.1.5 Relevant, Vivid Details

We should select concrete and sensory details to explain, support, or embellish the story. All of the details should **relate to the main point** we are attempting to make. These details should create a unified, forceful effect, a dominant impression. For example, if the setting plays an important role in our story, we should describe it in vivid terms so that our readers can imagine the scene easily and be attracted. Effective narration often depends on effective description, and effective description depends on **vivid, specific detail**.

4.1.6 Logical Time Sequence

Narrative essays usually follow a **chronological order**, presenting actions as they naturally occur in the story. Occasionally, however, some writers use the technique of **flashback** or **flash-forward**, which takes the readers back or forward in time to reveal an event that occurred before or after the present scene of the essay. When we choose to use shifts in time, we had better use transitional phrases or other signals to ensure that the readers don't become confused or lost.

4.1.7 Organization

In the introductory paragraph we should **set up background** for the event or story; and state a thesis to tell the audience what we are trying to explain, show, prove, or argue in our narrative essay and what we learned from the experience.

In the body paragraphs we should **develop the narrative of the event in chronological order**, or sometimes we can use **flashback** or **flash-forward** to highlight something; **use transitions** within and between paragraphs to emphasize time changes and/or significant turns in the narrative; **provide concrete details** and description; **use senses** such as sight, sound, smell, touch, and taste in the description; **add dialogue** when appropriate; **add commentary and analysis** about the details and descriptions to help develop the thesis statement.

In the concluding paragraph, we should **sum up** the essay and **re-emphasize** the thesis.

4.1.8 Narrative Point of View

Narrative point of view describes the narrator's position in relation to the story being told.

The first-person narrator is always a character within his/her own story. This **viewpoint character "I"** (or, when plural, "we") takes actions, makes judgments and expresses opinions, thereby not always allowing the audience to be able to comprehend some of the other characters' thoughts, feelings, or perceptions as much as the narrator's own. We become aware of the events and characters of story through the narrator's views and knowledge. The first-person narrator also may or may not be the focal character in the story.

The second-person narrative is the rarest mode we choose to tell a story. In this mode the narrator **refers to the reader as "you"**, therefore making the audience member feel as if he or she is a character within the story. But in children literature, it is common for writers to use second-person point of view. For example:

"You have brains in your head. You have feet in your shoes. You can steer yourself any direction you choose. You're on your own. And you know what you know. And YOU are the guy who'll decide where to go." (Dr. Seuss, *Oh! The Places You'll Go!* 1990)

Third-person narration is the most commonly used narrative mode in literature, for it provides the greatest flexibility to the author. In the third-person narrative mode, each and every character is referred to by the narrator as "**he**", "**she**", "**it**", or "**they**". Third-person narrative may be more objective.

4.1.9 Realistic Dialogue

Writers often use dialogue, their characters' spoken words, to reveal action or personality traits of the speakers. By presenting conversations, writers show rather than tell, often creating emphasis or a more dramatic effect. Dialogue may also help readers identify with or feel closer to the characters or action by creating a sense of "you are there". If your narrative would profit from dialogue, be certain the word choice and the manner of speaking are in keeping with each character's education, background, age, location, and so forth. Also, make sure that your dialogue doesn't sound wooden or phony. The right dialogue can help make your story more realistic and interesting, provided that the conversations are essential to the narrative and are not merely padding the plot. Use dialogue as a supporting detail in your essay, not as the main vehicle for imparting your story and your story's message. Be sure to frame your dialogue with analysis, the realizations you came to and what you were feeling and thinking as the words were said during the incident always re-emphasize your analytical purpose. For example:

She screamed, "No, I refuse to leave. I can't. I won't!"

Until that moment, I hadn't realized how hard it was for her to leave the house in which she had spent her entire life.

Sample 4

Attitude Is Everything

Jerry was the kind of guy you love to hate. He was always in a good mood and always had something positive to say. When someone would ask him how he was doing, he would reply, "If I were any better, I would be twins!"

He was a unique manager because he had several waiters who had followed him around from restaurant to restaurant. The reason the waiters followed Jerry was because of his attitude. He was a natural motivator. If an employee was having a bad day, Jerry was there telling the employee how to look on the positive side of the situation.

Seeing this style really made me curious, so one day I went up to Jerry and asked him, "I don't get it! You can't be a positive person all of the time. How do you do it?"

Jerry replied, "Each morning I wake up and say to myself, 'Jerry, you have two choices today. You can choose to be in a good mood or you can choose to be in a bad mood.' I choose to be in a good mood. Each time something bad happens, I can choose to be a victim or I can choose to learn from it. I choose to learn from it. Every time someone comes to me complaining, I can choose to accept their complaining or I can point out the positive side of life. I choose the positive side of life."

"Yeah, right, it's not that easy," I protested.

"Yes, it is," Jerry said. "Life is all about choices. When you cut away all the junk, every situation is a choice. You choose how you react to situations. You choose how people will affect your mood. You choose to be in a good mood or bad mood. The bottom line: It's your choice how you live life."

I reflected on what Jerry said. Soon thereafter, I left the restaurant industry to start my own business. We lost touch, but I often thought about him when I made a choice about life instead of reacting to it.

Several years later, I heard that Jerry did something you are never supposed to do in a restaurant business: he left the back door open one morning and was held up at gunpoint by three armed robbers. While trying to open the safe, his hand, shaking from nervousness, slipped off the combination. The robbers panicked and shot him.

Luckily, Jerry was found relatively quickly and rushed to the local trauma center. After 18 hours of surgery and weeks of intensive care, Jerry was released from the hospital with fragments of the bullets still in his body.

I saw Jerry about six months after the accident. When I asked him how he was, he replied, "If I were any better, I'd be twins. Wanna see my scars?" I declined to see his wounds, but did ask him what had gone through his mind as the robbery took place.

"The first thing that went through my mind was that I should have locked the back door," Jerry replied. "Then, as I lay on the floor, I remembered that I had two choices: I could choose to live, or I could choose to die. I chose to live."

Jerry continued, "The paramedics were great. They kept telling me I was going to be fine. But when they wheeled me into the emergency room and I saw the expressions on the faces of the doctors and nurses, I got really scared. In their eyes, I read, "He's a dead man." "I knew I needed to take action."

"What did you do?" I asked.

"Well, there was a big, burly nurse shouting questions at me," said Jerry. She asked if I was allergic to anything. "Yes," I replied. The doctors and nurses stopped working as they waited for my reply. I took a deep breath and yelled, "Bullets!"

Over their laughter, I told them. "I am choosing to live. Operate on me as if I am alive, not dead."

Jerry lived thanks to the skill of his doctors, but also because of his amazing attitude. I learned from him that every day we have the choice to live fully.

Attitude, after all, is everything.

Task 4.1

Consider these questions after you read the essay carefully.

1. What do you learn from the essay?
2. How can the author create the event vividly in the audience's heads? What examples and details does the author use to create the story?
3. How does the author organize the paragraphs, and how did the author move smoothly from one event or detail to the next?
4. What is the point of view in the essay?
5. How does the author conclude the essay?

Sample 5

Only Daughter

Once, several years ago, when I was just starting out my writing career, I was asked to write my own contributor's note for an anthology. I wrote: "I am the only daughter in a family of six sons. That explains everything."

Well, I've thought that ever since, and yes, it explains a lot to me, but for the reader's sake I should have written: "I am the only daughter in a Mexican family of six sons." Or even: "I am the only daughter of a Mexican father and a Mexican-American mother." Or: "I am the only daughter of a working-class family of nine." All of these had everything to do with who I am today.

I was/am the only daughter and only a daughter. Being an only daughter in a family of six sons forced me by circumstance to spend a lot of time by myself because my brothers felt it beneath them to play with a girl in public. But that aloneness, that loneliness, was good for a would-be writer—it allowed me time to think and think, to imagine, to read and prepare myself.

Being only a daughter for my father meant my destiny would lead me to become someone's wife. That's what he believed. But when I was in the fifth grade and shared my plans for college with him, I was sure he understood. I remember my father saying, "*Que bueno, mi'ja*, that's good." That meant a lot to me, especially since my brothers thought the idea hilarious. What I didn't realize was that my father thought college was good for girls—good for finding a husband. After four years in college and two more in graduate school, and still no husband, my father shakes his head even now and says I wasted all that education.

In retrospect, I'm lucky my father believed daughters were meant for husbands. It meant it didn't matter if I majored in something silly like English. Alter all, I'd find a nice professional eventually, right? This allowed me the liberty to putter about embroidering my little poems and stories without my father interrupting with so much as a "What's that you're writing?"

But the truth is, I wanted him to interrupt. I wanted my father to understand what it was I was scribbling, to introduce me as "My only daughter, the writer." Not as "This is my only daughter. She teaches. *Es maestra*—teacher. Not even *profesora*."

In a sense, everything I have ever written has been for him, to win his approval even though I know my father can't read English words, even though my father's only reading includes the brown-ink *Esto* sports magazines from Mexico City and the bloody ? *Alarma*! magazines that feature yet another sighting of *La Virgen de Gaudalupe* on a tortilla or a wife's revenge on her philandering husband by bashing his skull in with a *molcajete* (a kitchen mortar made of volcanic rock). Or the *fotonovelas*, the little picture paperbacks with tragedy and trauma erupting from the characters mouths in bubbles.

A father represents, then, the public majority. A public who's disinterested in reading, and yet one whom I am writing about and for, and privately trying to woo.

When we were growing up in Chicago, we moved a lot because of my father. He suffered bouts of nostalgia. Then we'd have to let go of our flat, store the furniture with my mother's relatives, load the station wagon with baggage and bologna sandwiches and head south. To Mexico City.

We came back, of course. To yet another Chicago flat, another Chicago neighborhood, another Catholic school. Each time, my father would seek out the parish priest in order to get a tuition break, and complain or boast: "I have seven sons."

He meant *siete hijos*, seven children, but he translated it "sons". "I have seven sons." To anyone who would listen. The Sears Roebuck employee who sold us the washing machine. The short-order cook where my father ate his ham-and-eggs breakfasts. "I have seven sons." As if he deserved a medal from the state.

My papa. He didn't mean anything by the mistranslation, I'm sure. But somehow I could feel myself being erased. I'd tug my father's sleeve and whisper: "Not seven sons. Six! and one daughter."

When my oldest brother graduated from medical school, he fulfilled my father's dream that we study hard and use this— our heads— instead of this— our hands. Even now my father's hands are thick and yellow, stubbed by a history of hammer and nails and twine and coils and springs. "Use this," my father said, tapping his head, "and not this," showing us those hands. He always looked tired when he said it.

Wasn't college an investment? And hadn't I spent all those years in college? And if I didn't marry, what was it all for? Why would anyone go to college and then choose to be poor? Especially someone who has always been poor.

Last year, after ten years of writing professionally, the financial rewards started to trickle in. My second National Endowment for the Arts Fellowship. A guest professorship at the University of California, Berkeley. My book, which sold to a major New York publishing house.

At Christmas, I flew home to Chicago. The house was throbbing, same as always; hot tamales and sweet tamales hissing in my mother's pressure cooker, and everybody—my mother, six brothers, wives, babies, aunts, cousins—talking too loud and at the same time, like in a Fellini film, because that's just how we are.

I went upstairs to my father's room. One of my stories had just been translated into Spanish and published in an anthology of Chicano writing, and I wanted to show it to him. Ever since he recovered from a stroke two years ago, my father likes to spend his leisure hours horizontally. And that's how I found him, watching a Pedro Infante movie on Galavision and eating rice pudding.

There was a glass filled with milk on the bedside table. There were several vials of pills and balled Kleenex. And on the floor, one black sock and a plastic urinal that I didn't want to look at but looked at anyway. Pedro Infante was about to burst into song, and my father was laughing.

I'm not sure if it was because my story was translated into Spanish, or because it was published in Mexico, or perhaps because the story dealt with Tepeyac, the *colonia* my father was raised in and the house he grew up in, but at any rate, my father punched the mute button on his remote control and read my story.

I sat on the bed next to my father and waited. He read it very slowly. As if he were reading each line over and over. He laughed at all the right places and read lines he liked out loud. He pointed and asked questions: "Is this So and so?" "Yes," I said. He kept reading.

When he was finally finished, after what seemed like hours, my father looked up and asked: "Where can we get more copies of this for the relatives?"

(Sandra Cisneros)

Task 4.2

Answer the following questions according to the essay.

1. What is the purpose of this piece of writing? Is it clear?

2. What ideas and background information are provided to support the purpose of this piece of writing?

3. In paragraph 2, the author adds details to her self-description of being one daughter among six sons. Name one of the details. What effect does her including these details have on you as a reader?

4. Was the author successful in accomplishing the purpose? Why, or why not?

Transitions in Narrative Essays

| after | before | in the meantime |
| not long after | afterwards | between |

later	soon	at last
first	meanwhile	then
at length	immediately	next
while		

Task 4.3

Write a Narrative Essay on One of the Topics.

1. First Day at College
2. The Moment of Success
3. A Memorable Journey
4. The Biggest Misunderstanding
5. The Difficult Decision
6. The Day I Decided to Change My Life
7. An Unforgettable Childhood Experience
8. An Experience That Helped Me Grow Up

Task 4.4

Choose your own topic to write a narrative essay, paying attention to your writing purpose, selection of details, context, organization, and point of view.

Use the following revision form to check for the basics in your narrative essay draft.

Overall

1. Does the essay tell a story using description that has a clear purpose (lesson (s) learned from the experience)?
  (Yes/No)
2. Does the essay use time order in the body paragraphs?
  (Yes/No)
3. Are the paragraphs broken up well, and are they about the right length?
  (Yes/No)

Introduction

4. Is the title interesting and in the correct format?
  (Yes/No)
5. Is there a general introduction that gives the background for the story (the events that led up to the event/day described)?
  (Yes/No)
6. Is there a clear thesis statement that explains the message of the story being told the lesson learned or expository purpose?
  (Yes/No)

Body

7. Do the ideas in the body paragraphs develop the story logically and flow smoothly?
  (Yes/No)
8. Are transitions used between and, when needed, within the paragraphs?
  (Yes/No)
9. Do the body paragraphs include support and descriptive details that enhance the story?
  (Yes/No)
10. Does the writer use as many sensory details as possible in the description of what happened and how it made the writer feel?
  (Yes/No)
11. Does the body of the paper include some dialogue to bring the action to life?
  (Yes/No)
12. Is analysis woven throughout the body to emphasize the significance of the story and develop the thesis of the lesson(s) learned from the event?
  (Yes/No)

Conclusion

13. Does the concluding paragraph sum up the story with an analytical method that re-emphasizes the introductory paragraph and thesis, without adding new ideas?
(Yes/No)

Editing

14. Circle the following errors you think you see in this draft: spelling errors, fragments, run-ons/comma splices, errors in comma and semicolon/colon use, pronoun disagreement, reference fault errors, and errors in parallelism, apostrophe use, verb use/tense, and passive voice construction.
15. Other types of grammar or sentence-level errors:
_____
_____
_____

Comments

_____
_____
_____

4.2 Descriptive Essays

> **Thinking over the Questions before Writing**
>
> ➤ What exactly am I describing?
> ➤ What kind of language and details should I include to best describe the object, place, or person I am describing?
> ➤ How should I organize my paragraphs after my introduction and thesis, and how can I move smoothly from one descriptive detail to the next?
> ➤ Why am I writing this description? What is my purpose for describing this person, place, or thing? What do I want my readers to learn or understand from reading this description?
> ➤ How should I conclude this essay?

Descriptive essays describe people, places and settings, things, or whole narrative scenes using as many of the senses as possible *sight*, *sound*, *touch*, *smell*, *and taste* and as many concrete, descriptive words as possible. Following are some sensory details the author use to describe his hospital life.

Sight: The clean white corridors of the hospital resembled the set of a sci-fi movie, with everyone scurrying around in identical starched uniforms.

Hearing: At night, the only sounds I heard were the quiet squeaking of sensible white shoes as the nurses made their rounds.

Smell: The green beans on the hospital cafeteria tray smelled stale and waxy, like crayons.

Touch: The hospital bed sheet felt as rough and heavy as a feed sack.

Taste: Every four hours they gave me an enormous gray pill whose aftertaste reminded me of the stale licorice my great-aunt kept in candy dishes around her house.

Description is writing about the way persons, animals, or things appear. It is the fiction-writing mode for transmitting a mental image of the particulars of a story. It is more than piling up details; it is creating something alive by carefully choosing and arranging words and phrases to produce the desired effect. For example, we could say, "I got sleepy" or describe it like this, "As I was waiting for Santa, my eyelids began to get heavy, the lights on the tree began to blur with the green branches, and my head started to drop." The second sentence gives vivid details to make the reader feel like he is there.

Basic Steps to Writing an Effective Descriptive Essay

(1) Select a Subject

Observation is the key to writing a good description. For example, if you are writing about a place, go there and take notes on the sights, sounds, and smells. A descriptive essay paints a picture for the reader, using descriptive devices and the senses. Create a thesis statement that informs the reader who or what you are describing. For example:

The wooden roller coaster in Coney Island is a work of art.

My bedroom is an ocean sanctuary.

(2) Select Dominant Details

Select only the details that support the dominant impression (your thesis statement).

(3) Organize Details

The paragraphs in a descriptive essay can be structured spatially (from top to bottom or from near to far) or chronologically (time order) or from general to specific. Descriptive essays can also use other patterns of organization such as narrative or exemplification.

(4) Use Descriptive Words

Do not use vague words or generalities (such as good, nice, bad, or beautiful). **Be specific** and **use sensory, descriptive words** (adjectives). For example:

I ate a good dinner.

I devoured a steaming hot, cheese-filled pepperoni pizza for dinner.

Provide **sensory details**:

Smells that are in the air: the aroma of freshly brewed coffee

Sounds: traffic, honking horns

Sights: The sun scattered tiny diamonds across dew-covered grass as it peeked out from beyond the horizon.

Touch: The texture of the adobe hut's walls resembled coarse sandpaper.

Taste: sweet, sour, salty, bitter, tart

Giant goose bumps formed on my tongue when I accidentally bit into a sliver of lemon.

(5) Use Figurative Language When Appropriate

Figurative language produces images or pictures in the readers' minds, helping them to understand unfamiliar or abstract subjects. Here are some devices you might use to clarify or spice up your essay.

Simile: a comparison between two things using the words "like" or "as"

e.g. Seeing exactly the video game he wanted, he moved as quickly as a starving teenager spotting pie in a refrigerator full of leftover vegetables.

Metaphor: a direct comparison between two things that does not use "like" or "as"

e.g. I was a puppet with my father controlling all the financial strings.

Personification: the attribution of human characteristics and emotions to inanimate objects, animals, or abstract ideas

e.g. The truck, covered with mud and love bugs, cried out for a wash.

Hyperbole: intentional exaggeration or overstatement for emphasis or humor

e.g. The cockroaches in my kitchen had now grown to the size of carry-on luggage.

Used sparingly and with careful crafting, figures of speech can make your essay enjoyable and memorable.

(6) Draw a Logical Conclusion

Make certain the conclusion is logical and relevant. And remind your readers what the purpose of your description was—why you described this person, place, or object in the first place.

Sample 1

Summer Escape

My family has always looked forward to leaving Florida during the torrid summer months. It is a tremendous relief to get out of the heated hustle and bustle of summer living in Florida. Each summer, we follow the yellow brick road to our hometown in upstate New York.

As we drive through state after state, it becomes apparent that the world around us is changing. In South Carolina, we already begin to notice changes. The trees appear to be touchable, offering soft, plush leaves which sway in the breeze, and the grass actually invites us to share its place rather than scaring us away with mounds of intruding fire ants. As each state brings new surroundings, our anticipation builds, and home seems closer all the time.

Leaving the flatlands and entering an area where we are suddenly surrounded by hills of purple and blue are by far the most awakening moments. Virginia and Pennsylvania offer brilliant scenery with majestic hills and checkerboard farmlands. As we descend through the curves and winds of the northern region of the United States, home is now very close: we are almost there. Suddenly, we have driven from wide-open flatlands to a narrow, winding road surrounded by hillsides of stone and trees. Around every curve, orange and black tiger lilies claim their place in the world as they push themselves out toward the car, waving hello and flashing their mysterious black spots toward us as we drive by.

The journey home is almost complete. As we begin our final descent through the state of Pennsylvania into upstate New York, the surroundings become comfortably familiar. Before long, we are welcomed by a sign that reads "Waverly, 18 miles" and the familiar fields of grazing cattle. Through the last stretch of Pennsylvania, the bursting foliage seems to envelop us and carry us over the hills like a carriage created by nature.

It is at this point that our family, even the youngest member, knows that our vacation in New York is about to begin. Our eldest son has joked for years that he can "smell" Grandma's apple pie already. Approximately fifteen minutes pass and as our vehicle takes us over the final crest, we see the smoke stack from the local factory as we cross the border of Pennsylvania and New York and are aware of our surroundings. A couple of turns later, we are there. We have reached our destination; we are home.

(Arin B. Terwilliger)

The following paragraph is an example of **describing a person**. Pay attention to the descriptive words used in the narrative paragraph.

Sample 2

Nicholas is an old man, chubby and soft. His belly shakes like a bowl full of jelly when he laughs, and he laughs a lot. His hair is snow-white, and so is his beard. When you see him, and hear his loud "Ho, ho, ho!" you feel happy, as if you are with the world's most loving grandfather. His life's goal is giving gifts to children all over the world. Most of his time is spent making the gifts, although nobody really knows where his workshop really is or what goes on there! It's all a little mysterious, but somehow he manages to give every child something once a year. Nicholas has a very positive attitude, and is usually in a good mood, although he can be quite firm if he thinks that you have been naughty. He smells exactly like Christmas should smell, and whenever you smell peppermint and evergreens, you think of him.

Task 4.5

Answer the following questions:

1. Can you find any sensory details in the paragraph?
2. Can you find details about Nicholas' personality, behavior, or interests?

Depending on the subject or assignment, we could describe the person's physical appearance, behavior, inner thoughts or the influence the person had on us or others.

A person's appearance can be described in many ways. It is possible to tell about the person's style of clothing, manner of walking, color and style of hair, facial appearance, body shape, and expression or even the person's way of talking. Just what a writer selects to describe depends on the writer's chosen topic and purpose. No matter what the topic, however, the writer is a painter with words, so the description must be vivid but also coherent—logically arranged—so that the reader can clearly envision who is being described. The following paragraph describes a person's face with a spatial organization. Look at the following description and see if you can get a good image of what Mary looks like.

Sample 3

Mary is as beautiful as a Hollywood star. Her thick, wavy, long black hair gracefully falls down to her shoulders and encircles her diamond-shaped face. A golden suntan usually brings out her smooth, clear complexion and high cheek bones. Her slightly arched chestnut brown eyebrows highlight her emotions by moving up and down as she reacts to her world around her. Her large deep blue eyes, remind me of a lake on a stormy day. Her curved nose gives her a little girl look that makes me want to smile when she talks. And her mouth is a small mouth outlined by puffy lips that she often accentuates with glossy pink lipstick. When she smiles, which is often, her well formed and even, white teeth brighten up her whole face. I guess you can tell that I am head over heals in love with Mary.

In this paragraph the reader can not only tell what Mary looks like but also what the author's attitude about her outer appearance is. A good/clear topic sentence not only states the topic (in this case Mary) but also supplies a strong controlling idea which states "how the writer feels about the topic".

More often though than simply describing a person's out appearance because one loves the person, there is a deeper reason. The following essay describes a person but the descriptions are only a support for an underlying political standpoint the author wants to make.

Sample 4

Jane Goodall had long been an idol of mine before I had the opportunity to meet her personally. I have been a member of one of her international Jane-Goodall-Institutes (JGI) for a couple of years now. I have read some of her books and like her idea of teaching children all over the world about environmental conservation and wild animal care so much that I hope to do it personally one day, too. As the greatest and most popular scientist of chimpanzees in the world and today also an active member of the UN Security Council and close friend of Kofi Anan, she is very busy and always travelling, so the chance to see her is quite rare.

It was two years ago, that Jane Goodall came to the German JG—Institute in Munich to give a lecture, and so I took a flight to Munich to see her. She did not look like what I had expected a popular world-renowned scientist would look like. In spite of having been born in Britain in April 1934, she had nothing of a typical British behaviour about her. She wore blue jeans, trainers and a cotton blouse. She looked like a normal and modest woman, one that you would meet in a supermarket. And she did not even look like a woman over 50, though her long hair tied in a ponytail was grey. Her face was smooth and in a very mysterious way looked carefree like a child's face does.

There was a very lively as well as wise expression in her eyes, but most impressible was the deep love and peace they transmitted to everybody when she spoke to the audience. She had lived over 30 years next to chimpanzees in the rainforest, studying and learning from them as she said. You could see the marks of that life, as her whole body seemed to talk with peace and wisdom and was as fit as that of a young woman in her mid-twenties. And even though she has been back to the civilized world for many years now, where she has taught at many universities and fought battles against politicians, businesses and other strong opponents to get protection for chimpanzees and other apes, she must have done this with those very calm gestures that are more convincing than any powerful and eloquent talk. I guess that has made her so successful, because when you watch her you cannot help but agree with her. And her most important message to us was that the love of creatures can be more powerful than all the weapons in the world, if we will just let it.

Judith Burgdorfer

Sample 5 and sample 6 are examples **describing a place.** Read the passages carefully and pay attention to the details and different tense the authors use effectively.

Sample 5

The Laundry Room

The windows at either end of the laundry room were open, but no breeze washed through to carry off the stale odors of fabric softener, detergent, and bleach. In the small ponds of soapy water that stained the concrete floor were stray balls of multicolored lint and fuzz. Along the left wall of the room stood ten rasping dryers, their round windows offering glimpses of jumping socks, underwear, and fatigues. Down the center of the room were a dozen washing machines, set back to back in two rows. Some were chugging like steamboats; others were whining and whistling and dribbling suds. Two stood forlorn and empty, their lids flung open, with crudely drawn signs that said "Broke!" A long shelf partially covered in blue paper ran the length of the wall, interrupted only by a locked door. Alone, at the far end of the shelf, sat one empty laundry basket and an open box of Tide. Above the shelf at the other end was a small bulletin board decorated with yellowed business cards and torn slips of paper: scrawled requests for rides, reward offers for lost dogs, and phone numbers without names or explanations. On and on the machines hummed and wheezed, gurgled and gushed, washed, rinsed, and spun.

Sample 6

La Caleta

Near my house exists a beautiful and unique beach called La Caleta. It's a balcony to the Bay of Cadiz. Daily, large boats visit its waters and say hello to the green trees that surround it. When the wind blows strongly, you can see the fish trying to reach its bank; nevertheless, they can't do it, because the waters reclaim them like a treasure. I feel good there because I can relax. It's my favorite place.

When I was a child, I used to go there every afternoon after school. I liked to lay on a big stone, to see the sunset and hear the quiet waves' sound near me. Then I could imagine all the marine creatures singing from the deep sea. Sometimes, the sun seemed angry, boldly turning red and yellow. Perhaps it didn't want to leave that amazing place. When the darkness covered the sky, I walked on the bank and looked at the moon reflected on the water. On one occasion I tried to touch it, but I just got my hand full of salt water. I saw the clouds reflected in my hand, and when I breathed, I felt the pure air in my lungs. A sweet flavor filled my whole body.

The sky over this beach is also different from others. A white and bright light crosses it like a ray. The fishermen love this light, but the fish can't rest quietly, because it disturbs their dreams. What's this light in the middle of the night? It's the lighthouse light. Wherever you stand, you may see it. It's the beach's guardian.

Therefore, when I'm far from this place, I'm sad, because I miss it. I miss its clear waters, I miss its white sand, I miss its blue sky, and I miss its wonderful lighthouse. Someday I'll be there again, and I'll be able to feel the same things I felt when I was a child.

(by Francisco Rebollo)

The following essay is an example **describing an object.** Read it carefully and then answer the questions according to the essay.

Sample 7

My Husband's Guitar

My husband plays guitar everyday. I have gotten used to hearing its music move through our house, especially in the early morning and late evening. My husband's guitar is a beautiful and important part of our lives together. His guitar is a beautiful object in and of itself; however, it is more than a thing: it is also an extension of my husband himself, and the music it makes reflects his moods and serves as a tribute to our lives together.

My husband's guitar is a classically styled acoustic guitar. It is made of wood and has six metal strings. The front of the guitar is a lovely honey-amber color, with fine-lined grain and a high-polish shine. The surface feels smooth, slick, and cool to the touch. There is a black plastic, kidney-shaped back plate where he strums the strings. The sides, back, and neck of the guitar are a darker colored wood, the color of strong coffee. Also, the long neck has six metal strings, four of them copper colored and two of them the color of steel. Besides the strings, the neck has 20 fret lines and six mother-of-pearl inset dots. Both of these features help him play correct chords and guide his fingers to the right places on the strings when he plays. Finally, six knobs that look a little like keys or small handles sit at the top of the neck that the strings are wrapped around. When he turns these knobs, the stings are adjusted, and he can get his guitar in perfect tune. As you can imagine, the guitar is a beautiful object, and even if I never heard my husband play, I would still find it admirable.

However, it is when my husband plays that the life and beauty of his guitar really shine. His music is rich and comforting. The sound is like a comforting humming. His songs and chords reflect the moods and best moments of his personality and of our marriage. He plays happy songs with faster, more upbeat chords, and he plays slower songs with more somber chords for the sadder or more serious times of our lives. In fact, I can usually guess my husband's mood by the type of song or the chords he is playing on his guitar.

My husband's guitar is like an extension of himself and our relationship. It is a beautiful object with a lovely message to convey to anyone who takes the time to listen. I cherish its presence in our home and the music my husband makes with it.

(By Lynne Hill from *The Write Stuff*)

Task 4.6

Answer the following questions according to the essay.
1. Is the descriptive essay's purpose clear to the reader?
2. Are there enough specific details in the description to make the subject matter distinct to readers who are unfamiliar with the object?
3. Are the details arranged in an order that's easy to follow?
4. Does this essay end with an appropriate conclusion?

Task 4.7

Write a descriptive essay on one of the following topics, using concrete, specific nouns and adjectives and including as many of the senses as possible. Try to create a vivid picture of the subject described by developing a portrait with a description in words. Be sure to include a thesis statement that puts forth a purpose to develop: what you want to show a reader or a conclusion you have reached about this subject.
1. My Mother (father, best friend, grandmother, grandfather, or a sibling)
2. A Campus (or a local building) I admire
3. The Ugliest/Most Beautiful Place on My Campus
4. A Holiday (celebration, or ritual) in My Family
5. My Favorite Recreation Area (beach, hiking trail, park, etc.)
6. A Shopping Mall (student cafeteria, or other crowded public place)
7. My Most Precious Material Possession
8. A Common Object with Uncommon Beauty

    Use the following **revision form** to check for the basics in your descriptive essay draft.

Overall

1. Does the essay tell a story using description that has a clear purpose (lesson(s) learned from the experience)?
   (Yes/No)
2. Does the essay use a logical order in the body paragraphs (with an analytical setup and concluding paragraph)?
   (Yes/No)
3. Are the paragraphs broken up well, and are they about the right length?
   (Yes/No)

Introduction

4. Is the title interesting and in the correct format?
   (Yes/No)
5. Is there a general introduction that sets up the thesis?
   (Yes/No)
6. Is there a clear thesis statement that explains the significance of the person, place, or thing being described?
   (Yes/No)

Body

7. Do the ideas in the body paragraphs develop logically and flow smoothly?
   (Yes/No)
8. Are transitions used between and, when needed, within the paragraphs?
   (Yes/No)
9. Do the body paragraphs include support and descriptive details and concrete images?
   (Yes/No)
10. Does the writer use as many senses as possible in the description?
    (Yes/No)
11. If figurative language is used, are they fresh and effective?
    (Yes/No)

Conclusion

12. Does the concluding paragraph sum up the purpose and analysis of the description?
    (Yes/No)

Editing

13. Circle the following errors you think you see in this draft: spelling errors, fragments, run-ons/comma splices, errors in comma and semicolon/colon use, pronoun disagreement, reference fault errors, and errors in parallelism, apostrophe use, verb use/tense, and passive voice construction.
14. Other types of grammar or sentence-level errors:
    _____
    _____
    _____

Comments

_____
_____
_____

4.3 A Process Essay

> **Thinking over the Questions before Writing**
>
> ➤ What process am I describing?
> ➤ What specific steps, examples, and details should I use to describe the process?
> ➤ How should I organize my paragraphs after my introduction and thesis statement, and how can I move smoothly from one step or detail to the next?
> ➤ What is my purpose for writing this process description (to describe how something works, to tell someone how to accomplish a task, other)?
> ➤ What do I want my readers to learn and understand after reading about this process? Who is my intended audience, and how much will they already know about my topic?

Process essays tell people how things work, how to do something, or how to analyze a process to see how efficient it is. Process writing is very common in business, in science and math classes, and in careers that involve many process-related tasks.

The organization of a process essay is usually based on **chronological order**, describing one step at a time, in the order it happens. For example, if you were telling your readers how to write an essay, you might describe it like this:

Sample 1

(1) The writing process has four distinct phases. (2) The first is invention, which is aided by any number of techniques, including free-writing, mind-mapping and outlining. (3) In this first stage, it's important for a writer not to edit but to let ideas flow and to simply get them down on paper. (4) After invention, comes the first draft—the stage where the ideas start to take shape. (5) Many writers use a sentence outline at this stage to see where they need to cut

and where they need to add material. The first draft is also where writers should develop a tentative thesis to guide the structure of their essay. (6) The next stage of the process is when both the second and third drafts are done. (7) Here, ideas and structure are refined, and the thesis is revised until it becomes the unifying idea of the paper. (8) Finally, comes the last stage, that of editing. (9) Writers should take care at this stage that all sentence structure and punctuation is correct, and they should make corrections to documentation format as needed. (10) Writers often repeat these four phases more than once, or skip a phase and go back to it, making the writing process more cyclical than linear.

In this process paragraph, the topic sentence (1) introduces the number of steps in the process. Then, the next two sentences, (3) and (4), name and comment on the first step. The next series of sentences—(4) to (7)—go on to enumerate and comment on the next two steps, and sentences (8) and (9) complete the description of the process. The paragraph ends with a general statement (10) about the writing process that characterizes it and sums it up.

A process essay can also be organized by **order of importance** of the individual steps if the process doesn't require a particular sequence of steps. For example, if we were describing the process of choosing a major after entering a university , we might choose order of importance to list the steps involved and include paragraphs on knowing ourself, finding the equilibrium between the interests and abilities, and being well informed of job market.

Decide what our *writing purpose* is for writing a process description (to evaluate a process, to teach or instruct, to propose an alternative process, other). Be sure to describe the steps in chronological order or order of importance and to include *descriptive details* that explain and illustrate each one. Then make sure that our essay's conclusion reiterates the purpose of our process description or analysis. The following chart provides a brief overview of the structure of a process essay.

Basic Structure for a Process Essay

(1) Introduction.

Begin the introductory paragraph by setting up **background** for the process and why we are describing it.

End the introductory paragraph with our **thesis statement**, which describes what we are trying to explain, show, prove, or argue through describing a process.

1) Instructing how to do a task step by step:

e. g. In order to make a perfect cup of tea, complete each of the following steps in order, and you will succeed.

2) Explaining how a process works:

e. g. The three major steps involved in the digestive process are ingestion, digestion, and absorption.

(2) Body.

1) **Develop** the process of the event in time order or order of importance with the **topic sentence in each paragraph** clarifying the type of order and the categories or major stages of the process.

2) **Use transitions** within and between paragraphs to make coherence of the process.

3) **Provide concrete details** and description.

4) **Add commentary and analysis** about the steps, details, and descriptions to help develop the expository purpose/thesis statement.

(3) Conclusion.

Sum up and restate the thesis to **emphasize the purpose** for describing this process.

Sample 2

A Process of Digestion

The digestive process is important in maintaining the lives of living organisms and in providing them with needed energy. Groups of organs, such as the mouth, esophagus, stomach, and intestines, work together to perform this complex task. Digestion is the process of breaking down food from large molecules into small ones to make it easier for absorption. The three major steps involved in the digestive process are ingestion, digestion, and absorption.

Ingestion, which occurs in the mouth, is the first step of the digestive process. After food enters the mouth, the teeth chew it. Saliva, which is produced by the salivary glands, plays a major role in breaking down the food into smaller pieces. These small pieces travel to the stomach through the esophagus.

In the stomach, the second step of the digestive process begins. When the chewed food reaches the bottom of the esophagus, a valve lets the food enter the stomach. Contraction of the stomach wall mixes the food. Acidic gastric juices, which are secreted by the gastric glands in the stomach, help in mixing the food and in turning it into a partial liquid so it will have the ability to move into the small intestine. In the small intestine, enzymes are secreted, and digestion is completed.

The last step in the digestive process is absorption. Absorption takes place in the small intestine. The wall of the small intestine is lined with small, finger like projections called villi. Small molecules of food are absorbed by the huge number of villi. Some of these absorbed molecules enter the bloodstream to be distributed throughout the whole body.

In conclusion, the digestive process involves three major steps: ingestion, digestion, and absorption. Ingestion, which occurs in the mouth, helps to increase the surface are of the food particles and prepares them for digestion. In the stomach, digestion begins, and it continues until it reaches the small intestine, where absorption takes place. The digestive process maintains organisms' lives by providing them with energy needed for different functions.

Below is the outline of the essay. It will help you to understand the organization of the process better.

I. Introduction

   Thesis: Ingestion, digestion, and absorption are the three major steps involved in the digestive process.

II. Food is ingested.

   A. Food enters the mouth.

   B. Food is chewed.

   C. Food is ready to travel to the stomach.

III. Food is digested.

   A. Food is mixed with acidic gastric juices in the stomach.

   B. The partially liquid food moves from the stomach to the small intestine.

   C. Enzymes are secreted.

IV. Absorption

   A. The digested food passes through the walls of the small intestine.

   B. The digested food is absorbed into the bloodstream.

V. Conclusion

   Paraphrased Thesis: The digestion process involves three major steps: ingestion, digestion, and absorption.

Sample 3

How to Buy a Diamond

Every year many couples become engaged and find themselves shopping around for a diamond engagement ring. Many times this search turns into a confusing task. One simply cannot look to a Consumer Report to find specifics on a diamond ring. However, this process can be made quite simple if the prospective buyer follows a few simple guidelines: First, he should know the three C's of a diamond; secondly, find a respectable jeweler; and thirdly, choose a style that his fiancée will be happy with for many years to come.

First, the prospective buyer should familiarize himself with the three C's of a diamond. Every diamond has its own characteristics which determine its value. Most important is color. Every diamond possesses color, but it is the absence of color that increases the value of this gem. Second, only to color is the cut. How the fifty-eight facets are cut in relation to the weight determines the value of the diamond. On an ideally cut diamond, 53% of the weight is at the girdle or middle part of the diamond. Clarity is less important than cut and color. Clarity is a value based on the number of inclusions that a diamond contains. An ideal diamond, sometimes called a "perfect diamond", would be one without any inclusions. The least important characteristic of a diamond is its weight; that is, the number of carats it contains. A diamond that ranks high in color, cut, and clarity but weighs only. 50 carats is worth more than a 1 carat stone with poor color, cut, and clarity.

After the buyer has become familiar with the three C's of a diamond, he should find a reputable jeweler to do business with. The majority of jewelers in business today are reputable. The buyer should find out if the jeweler offers a bond that states exactly what the customer is buying. The buyer should request an appraisal and have the jeweler sign it. The customer should also find out if the jeweler offers some sort of guarantee in case the diamond comes out of the mounting. In addition, the buyer should inquire about whether the salesperson or someone within the store is a graduate of the Gemology Institute of America or certified by the Diamond Council of America. If any doubt remains, he can check with the Better Business Bureau.

Third, and equally important, is finding a style the buyer's fiancé will be happy with for many years to come. Today, diamond rings come in such a variety of styles that the buyer can easily be confused. He should always consider the type of hand on which the ring will be worn. If his fiancé's fingers are short and stubby, he should avoid styles that have wide bands. Not only do wide bands accentuate short fingers, but also they often detract from a pretty diamond. Furthermore, the buyer should keep in mind that simplicity is elegance in fine jewelry. Traditional mountings are always in style, and the wearer won't likely become bored with them. In general, the buyer should choose a band that will complement his fiancé's engagement ring since both rings are frequently worn on the same finger.

If the above process is followed, buying a diamond ring need not be a confusing task after all. If the buyer knows the three C's of a diamond, finds a reputable jeweler, and considers the style of the ring, he more than likely will choose—with the help of his fiancé, of course—a beautiful ring that will last a lifetime. Such a ring will definitely enhance a couple's engagement.

(4) Introductory paragraph.

We should begin our process essay with a general introduction that sets up the background of the process we are going to describe. And end the introductory paragraph with our thesis statement.

(5) Body paragraphs.

The body paragraphs in a process essay can be arranged in time order or order of importance, depending on the purpose of writing our essay. Topic sentences should clarify the type of order and the categories or major stages of the process. We can describe one step in each paragraph, and provide specific examples and definitions as needed. Enough transitions should be used within and between paragraphs to make coherence of the process.

Common Transition Words for Process Essay			
first(ly)	next	lastly	as soon as
then	until	as	at this point
once	after	when	at the same time
besides	moreover	furthermore	in addition
before	while	finally	equally important

(6) Concluding paragraph.

The concluding paragraph in a process essay should restate both the process being described and the purpose for describing it: to instruct the reader on how to do something; to describe how a machine, experiment, or system works; to critique the way something works and propose an alternative; and so on.

Sample 4

How to Entertain

I have always enjoyed entertaining people in my home. Over the years I have discovered three requirements to make entertaining successful: creating a relaxing atmosphere, providing lots of good food, and having many amusing things to do.

As far as creating a relaxing atmosphere is concerned, there are many ways to accomplish this. One way is by inviting guests that are compatible. Another way to provide a relaxing atmosphere is to make sure that guests have something in common. Pleasant conversation is always a must, and it leads to a most relaxing atmosphere. Depending on the particular occasion, it is also possible to add atmosphere with decorations such as hats and horns at a birthday party or ghosts and Jack O'lanterns at a Halloween party. If I can create an atmosphere that is both friendly and relaxing, my entertaining is off to a good start.

I find my favorite part of entertaining is preparing a bounty of good food. I love to cook and experiment with different types of foods for many different occasions. One of the easiest types of food preparation for a party is the buffet, a dining arrangement featuring a table laden with plenty of food, organized so that the guests can walk around the table from both sides and fill their plates. I can set up a simple buffet with turkey and roast beef slices, salads, hot vegetables, and succulent desserts. Coffee and tea or soft drinks are the common beverages that are served with a buffet. If I decide to, I can also serve mixed drinks. I find it quite a challenge to try different styles of cooking for parties. It gives me the opportunity to create new and different dishes. One of my specialties is a Mexican meal of enchiladas, tacos, and refried beans, served with cold iced tea. Another of my specialties is an Italian meal of spaghetti, accompanied with piping hot garlic bread fresh from the oven. This meal can be highlighted by serving a chilled red wine. I've found that good food is a complement to any type of entertaining.

After I have created a relaxing atmosphere and filled my guests' stomachs with good food, the last item on the agenda is amusement. I can amuse my guests in a variety of ways. When I entertain, several card tables are set up with many different games on them: card games such as pinochle, euchre, and rook and party games like Aggravation and Yachtzee. Of course, there are always some guests who do not enjoy playing games. They can be entertained with pleasant conversation. Also, it is always fun to gather around a piano or organ to sing songs like "Yankee Doodle" "Down In The Valley" and "The Yellow Rose of Texas". Generally, if there is a variety of amusements provided, the guests will entertain themselves by joining in whatever they find enjoyable.

There are two ways to determine the success of my party. One guaranteed way is checking to see if I have provided my guests with the three necessities I have mentioned: a relaxing atmosphere, plenty of food, and a variety of entertainment. Another method of judging the success of my party is watching my guests to see if they are enjoying themselves as the evening progresses.

Sample 5

How to Care for a Blind Dog

"Did you hear that? It sounded like someone entered the house, it's a burglar!" "Take it easy; it's Ruffo, my blind dog, bumping into all sorts of things!"

If you have ever had a blind dog, you might know all the daily problems it has to deal with. But don't worry, it isn't condemned yet. You can make your dog's life a lot easier by removing dangerous obstacles in your house, establishing reference points for your pet inside your home and introducing it to its new environment.

The first thing you have to do is to clear your dog's normal walking path from dangerous objects, like pulled-out chairs or toys that children leave on the floor. Also, it's a good idea to put baby gates around secure areas to prevent your dog from falling down the stairs or getting lost in the closets.

Establishing reference points for your dog in your house is the next thing to do. These can be tactile or olfactory traces. Use tactile pathways in strategic places, you can use carpet runners on wood or tile floors, and plastic mats on carpeted areas. It's useful to put oil-based scents on permanent obstacles to help your dog avoid them. Once the dog has learned where the obstacles are, you might stop using them, but remember to apply a new scent to any piece of furniture you add to your home.

Last but not less important; introduce your blind dog to its new environment. Practice with your dog on a leash; apply gentle backward pressure on the leash when it starts to walk, meanwhile, give the command "e-e-easy". If it slows down say "good easy" and give the dog a snack or lots of praise. Repeat the command to warn it whenever it's about to bump into something. Don't punish or treat your dog badly because that can cause your dog to become more depressed.

Now you know, removing dangerous objects, establishing reference points, and introducing the dog to the new environment is what you have to do in order to help your blind dog overcome its difficult life. Dogs are good friends, so we can thank their loyalty with small things such as these.

Task 4.8

Answer the questions about sample 4 and sample 5.
1. What is the writing purpose of the essay?
2. What is the thesis statement of the essay?
3. Can you find the topic sentence in each body paragraph?
4. Does the author reiterate the thesis in the concluding paragraph?

Task 4.9

Write an essay on one of the following topics.
1. How to Wash a Sweater
2. How to Make Your Favorite Dish (or sandwich)
3. How to Plan the Perfect Class Schedule
4. How to Stop Smoking (or break some other bad habit)
5. How to Develop Self-confidence
6. How to Plan the Perfect Party (wedding, holiday, birthday, or date)

Task 4.10

Choose your own topic and write a process essay in time order or order of importance.

Use the following revision form to check for the basics in your process essay draft.

Overall

1. Does the essay have a clear writing purpose (e.g., to inform, instruct, etc.)?
   (Yes/No)
2. Does the essay use time order or order of importance in the body paragraphs?
   (Yes/No)
3. Are the paragraphs broken up well and about the right length?
   (Yes/No)

Introduction

4. Is the title interesting and in the correct format?
   (Yes/No)
5. Is there a general introduction that sets up the thesis?
   (Yes/No)
6. Is there a clear thesis statement that explains the purpose of the process being described?
   (Yes/No)

Body

7. Do the body paragraphs develop the process logically and flow smoothly?
(Yes/No)
8. Are transitions used between and, when needed, within the paragraphs?
(Yes/No)
9. Do the ideas in the body paragraphs include support descriptive details to show the process?
(Yes/No)

Conclusion

10. Does the concluding paragraph sum up the process and re-emphasize the purpose set up in the introductory paragraph and thesis, without adding new ideas?
(Yes/No)

Editing

11. Circle the following errors you think you see in this draft: spelling errors, fragments, run-ons/comma splices, errors in comma and semicolon/colon use, pronoun disagreement, reference fault errors, and errors in parallelism, apostrophe use, verb use/tense, and passive voice construction.
12. Other types of grammar or sentence-level errors:

_____
_____

Comments

_____
_____

4.4　An Illustration Essay

> **Thinking over the Questions before Writing**
>
> ▶ What point am I trying to make?
> ▶ Which examples can I include to illustrate my purpose clearly?
> ▶ What facts, testimony, and experiences can I use to develop my purpose in this essay?
> ▶ What details should I provide to further illustrate my examples?
> ▶ How should I organize this essay, and how should I conclude it?

An illustrative essay is probably one of the easiest types of essays to write; and once we have mastered this type of writing, just about all other types of essays will become easier as well. That's because no matter what type of writing we're doing, if we're trying to make a point, illustrations make it much easier to accomplish our goal.

There are two types of illustration essays—**single (extended) example** type and **multiple examples** type.

For example, let's say we want to write a paper on friendship and family, and we decide our thesis "Sometimes friendship ties are stronger than family ties." Then, our task is to support that assertion through the use of examples. We may want to do a **single or extended example**, which is simply using one longer example to support our thesis. For example, we might highlight our relationship with our best friend and show how he or she has been like family to us. Another approach would be to use multiple examples, which rely on several examples to support the thesis. In this case, we might want to write about two or three of our friendships that would support the idea that friendship ties are sometimes stronger than family ties.

Look at the following paragraph. Which type does the author use—**single (extended) example** type or **multiple examples** type? Can the example(s) support the thesis effectively?

Sample 1

Wearing seat belts can protect people from injury, even in serious accidents. I know because seat belts saved me and my dad two years ago when we were driving to see my grandparents who live in California. Because of the distance, we had to travel late on a rainy, foggy Saturday night. My dad was driving, but what he didn't know was that there was a car a short way behind us driven by a drunk who was following our car's taillights in order to keep himself on the road. About midnight, my dad decided to check the map to make sure we were headed in the right direction, so he signaled, pulled over to the shoulder, and began to stop. Unfortunately for us, the drunk didn't see the signal and moved his car over to the shoulder thinking that the main road must have curved slightly since our car had gone that way. As Dad slowed our car, the other car plowed into us at a speed estimated later by the police as over eighty miles an hour. The car hit us like Babe Ruth's bat hitting a slow pitch; the force of the speeding car slammed us hard into the dashboard but not through the windshield and out onto the rocky shoulder, because, lucky for us, we were wearing our seat belts. The highway patrol, who arrived quickly on the scene, testified later at the other driver's trial that without question my dad and I would have been seriously injured, if not killed, had it not been for our seat belts restraining us in the front seat.

The story of the accident illustrates the writer's claim that seat belts can save lives; without such an example, the writer's statement would be only an unsupported generalization.

Organization of an Illustration Essay

(1) Introductory paragraph.

We should begin our illustration essay with a general introduction to the topic for which we are providing examples to illustrate our opinion. End with the thesis statement to set up the purpose of your example essay.

(2) Body paragraphs.

The body paragraphs in an example/illustration essay provide specific details and examples organized to illustrate your purpose. We can organize the examples chronologically. Or we choose to organize our body paragraphs on the basis of the relevance of each example: least to most important, or vice versa. Our topic sentences should set up each specific example and its relevance to our thesis statement's purpose. Body paragraphs can be divided into separate examples or can be parts of an extended example. For instance, the following brief outline focuses on growing up to mature during the college life, and the topic sentences would need specific examples and our analysis to illustrate it.

    I. Thesis: I truly started to "grow up" to mature when I went to college.

    II. Body:

        A. I learned to get along with all types of people by living in a dormitory.

        B. I discovered the importance of budgeting my money the first time some bills arrived.

        C. I realized I didn't "know it all" when I entered my first college class.

(3) Concluding paragraph.

The concluding paragraph for our example essay should recap our purpose and intended message for the examples and illustrations we provided in the essay. For example, we can conclude the previous outline like this:

    III. Conclusion: Among the many important experiences a college education offers, the opportunity to mature was the most valuable to me.

Sample 2

Violence in the Morning

In recent years, television networks have come under increasing attack for the violent programs that fill their schedules. As we discussed in class, psychologists and communications experts, such as Dr. George Gerbner at the University of Pennsylvania, have formulated scales to measure the death and destruction that comes into American homes daily. Sociologists have discussed the possible effects of this situation on the viewing public. One area that is currently receiving attention is children's television. As even a brief glance at weekly cartoon shows reveals, children are being exposed to a steady diet of violence that surpasses that of the prime-time shows their parents so eagerly watch.

Children's cartoons have traditionally contained much violence, and this situation is something we have learned to accept as normal. Consider how much a part of our landscape the following situations are. The coyote chases the roadrunner and finds himself standing in midair over a deep chasm. For a fraction of a second he looks pathetically at the audience; then he plunges to the ground. Elmer Fudd puts his shotgun into a tree where Buggs Bunny is hiding. Buggs bends the barrel so that, when Elmer pulls the trigger, the gun discharges into his face. A dog chases Woody Woodpecker into a saw mill and, unable to stop, slides into the whirling blade of a circular saw. As the scene ends, the two halves of the dog fall to the ground with a clatter.

Where these so-called traditional cartoons depict violence as an isolated occurrence, newer cartoons portray it as a normal condition of life. Teenage Mutant Ninja Turtles is a good example of this. Every Saturday these characters battle a series of villains that seem intent upon destroying the world. Every week the plot stays essentially the same; only the participants in the combat seem to change. And every week the message to young viewers remains the same: Only by violent action can the problems of the world be confronted and solved. Neither the turtles nor their human friends ever attempt to negotiate with their enemies or to find a peaceful solution to their seemingly endless combat. It is only when the turtles use their considerable physical skills to defeat their adversaries that the status quo is restored. Oddly enough, no one is ever killed or seriously injured during all this fighting. It would seem that in an effort to avoid criticism, the producers of this show have decided to present combat as a game in which violence has no lasting effect on those involved. Ironically, these combative turtles—Michelangelo, Donatello, Raphael, and Leonardo—are named after four Renaissance artists whose work represents the highest achievement of the human spirit.

Even more shocking is the violence in G. I. Joe, a thirty-minute action cartoon that presents a daily battle between the individuals in a commando unit (the forces of good) and COBRA (the forces of evil). In this series violence and evil are ever present, threatening to overwhelm goodness and right. Each day COBRA, an organization that appears to operate freely all over the world, destroys defense installations, blows up power plants, attacks cities, or somehow challenges the ingenuity of G. I. Joe. The two sides have apparently fought to a stalemate. COBRA's desire to rule the world is at the heart of the conflict. How COBRA started or how it is able to operate as freely as it does is never fully explained. In one episode, COBRA scientists discover a "computer virus" that can destroy any computer in which it is placed. COBRA plans to insert this virus into all the police computers in the world to wipe out their records. The G. I. Joe commandos fight a pitched battle on the streets of Las Vegas and eventually find and destroy the virus in the computers of a resort hotel. As is the case with Teenage Mutant Ninja Turtles, human beings are never killed or seriously injured, but the young viewers of the show must know, even though it is not shown, that many people are killed when lasers explode and buildings fall.

Violence on children's television is the rule rather than the exception. Few shows, other than those on cable or public television, attempt to go beyond the simplistic formulas that cartoons follow. As a result, children are being shown that violence is superior to reason and that conflict and threats of violent death are normal conditions for existence. In addition, because human beings never get killed in these cartoons, children are encouraged to see war and fighting as harmless. Perhaps the recently convened government commission to study violence on children's television will help end this situation, but until it does parents will continue to shudder each time their children sit down in front of television for a morning of fun.

(By Arden Jensen, Ph. D., Professor of English, from http://webpages.leeu.edu)

Task 4.11

Answer the questions according to the essay.
1. What is the thesis in the essay?
2. What are the examples the author use to support his opinion?

Sample 3

The Effects of Advertising

How many times have you visited the grocery store and come back with a lot of things that you later realize you do not need but you just bought because they looked good at the time? This is the power of advertisements. Marketers use various techniques in order to make promotions for products so that they look really appealing and attractive to the customers. These people use various cues that target the various emotions and values of the consumers and the people are pulled into buying the products. Some marketing techniques are so successful that they attract even those people who really do not need the product in the first place! This means that advertising makes us buy things that we really do not need.

Many critics of the media and literature have criticized advertising. Many philosophers have also gone ahead and said that advertising corrupts the society and the culture and that it should not be allowed. I have seen many magazine articles and read many books that criticize advertising as being bad. Many people think that it is manipulative and therefore morally reprehensible. Others think that it is very expensive and therefore a waste of the important resources. Many believe that advertising diverts our attention from important problems of society such as poverty, class divisions and inequality. And worst of all, it wastes consumers' money because it is responsible for making them buy things that they really do not want.

I remember that once I was watching television with my sister and we both saw an advertisement for some new lamp that they have made that boasted perfect lighting for the eyes and were giving out promises that it can improve your grade. We were both laughing at the ad because we both thought that it was a very stupid idea. In addition, none of us needed a new lamp because we have plenty of them in our house. But to my amazement, I saw my sister walk in the house a few days later, carrying the lamp in her hands! I asked her why she had bought it because we clearly did not need it and she told me that it was because the advertisement convinced her that it would be a good buy. She told me that it looked good in the ad and that she had to buy it to see the great light that they were talking about. Later we found out that it was just another ordinary lamp with a fancy name and design.

There have been times when I go to the grocery store to buy something that I have needed, and have come back with so much more that I later realize was totally unnecessary. Why do I do this? It is because I see the posters, the banners, and the flyers that are advertising those products and I am lured into buying them. This means that the marketers do this on purpose: they include such cues and materials into the advertisements that attract the customers and sometimes those customers who really do not want the product in the first place.

Other times when I have experienced this phenomenon is when I have seen kids ask their parents for things that they really do not need. This is all because the advertising of these products have been done in such a way to target and attract all kinds of customers.

I am definitely of the opinion that advertising can make people buy unnecessary things that they do not really need. I have seen this happen to people I know and I have read about this in various places. I have experienced it first hand and that is when I was convinced. Many critics may argue that advertising helps us by spreading awareness. I agree with this, but it also waste the money of the consumer by attracting them into buying things that they really do not need.

(from http://www.tailoredessays.com/samples/effects-of-advertising.htm)

Task 4.12

Find the thesis in the essay and make an outline of the essay.

Sample 4

Fairy Tales and Modern Stories

The shortcomings of the realistic stories with which many parents have replaced fairy tales is suggested by a comparison of two such stories— "The Little Engine That Could" and "The Swiss Family Robinson"— with the fairy tale of Rapunzel. The Little Engine That Could encourages the child to believe that if he tries hard and does not give up, he will finally succeed. A young adult has recalled how much impressed she was at the age of seven when her mother read her this story. She became convinced that one's attitude indeed affects one's achievements that if she would now approach a task with the conviction that she could conquer it, she would succeed.

A few days later, this child encountered in first grade a challenging situation: she was trying to make a house out of paper, gluing various sheets together. But her house continually collapsed. Frustrated, she began to seriously doubt whether her idea of building such a paper house could be realized. But then the story of "The Little Engine That Could" came to her mind; twenty years later, she recalled how at that moment she began to sing to herself the magic formula "I think I can, I think I can, I think I can...." So she continued to work on her paper house, and it continued to collapse. The project ended in complete defeat, with this little girl convinced that she had failed where anybody else could have succeeded, as the Little Engine had. Since "The Little Engine That Could" was a story set in the present, using such common props as engines that pulled trains, this girl had tried to apply its lesson directly in her daily life, without any fantasy elaboration, and had experienced a defeat that still rankled twenty years later.

Very different was the impact of "The Swiss Family Robinson" on another little girl. The story tells how a shipwrecked family manages to live an adventurous, idyllic, constructive, and pleasurable life—a life very different from this child's own existence. Her father had to be away from home a great deal, and her mother was mentally ill and spent protracted periods in institutions. So the girl was shuttled from her home to that of an aunt, then to that of a grandmother, and back home again, as the need arose. During these years, the girl read over and over again the story of this happy family who lived on a desert island, where no member could be away from the rest of the family.

Many years later, she recalled what a warm, cozy feeling she had when, propped up by a few large pillows, she forgot all about her present predicament as she read this story. As soon as she had finished it, she started to read it over again. The happy hours she spent with the Family Robinson in that fantasy land permitted her not to be defeated by the difficulties that reality presented to her. She was able to counteract the impact of harsh reality by imaginary gratifications. But since the story was not a fairy tale, it merely gave her a temporary escape from her problems; it did not hold out any promise to her that her life would take a turn for the better.

Consider the effect that "Rapunzel" had on a third girl. This girl's mother had died in a car accident. The girl's father, deeply upset by what had happened to his wife (he had been driving the car), withdrew entirely into himself and handed the care of his daughter over to a nursemaid, who was little interested in the girl and gave her complete freedom to do as she liked. When the girl was seven, her father remarried, and, as she recalled it, it was around that time that Rapunzel became so important to her. Her stepmother was clearly the witch of the story, and she was the girl locked away in the tower. The girl recalled that she felt akin to Rapunzel because the witch had "forcibly" taken possession of her, as her stepmother had forcibly worked her way into the girl's life. The girl felt imprisoned in her new home, in contrast to her life of freedom with the nursemaid. She felt as victimized as Rapunzel, who, in her tower, had so little control over her life. Rapunzel's long hair was the key to the story. The girl wanted her hair to grow long, but her stepmother cut it short; long hair in itself became the symbol of freedom and happiness to her. The story convinced her that a prince (her father) would come someday and rescue her, and this conviction sustained her. If life became too difficult, all she needed was to imagine herself as Rapunzel, her hair grown long, and the prince loving and rescuing her.

"Rapunzel" suggests why fairy tales can offer more to the child than even such a very nice children's story as "The Swiss Family Robinson". In "The Swiss Family Robinson", there is no witch against whom the child can discharge her anger in fantasy and on whom she can blame the father's lack of interest. The Swiss Family Robinson offers escape fantasies, and it did help the girl who read it over and over to forget temporarily how difficult life was for her. But it offered no specific hope for the future.

"Rapunzel", on the other hand, offered the girl a chance to see the witch of the story as so evil that by comparison even the "witch" stepmother at home was not really so bad. "Rapunzel" also promised the girl that her rescue would be effected by her own body, when her hair grew long. Most important of all, it promised that the "prince" was only temporarily blinded that he would regain his sight and rescue his princess. This fantasy continued to sustain the girl, though to a less intense degree, until she fell in love and married, and then she no longer needed it. We can understand why at first glance the stepmother, if she had known the meaning of "Rapunzel" to her stepdaughter, would have felt that fairy tales are bad for children. What she would not have known was that unless the stepdaughter had been able to find that fantasy satisfaction through "Rapunzel", she would have tried to break up her father's marriage and that without the hope for the future which the story gave her she might have gone badly astray in life.

It seems quite understandable that when children are asked to name their favorite fairy tales, hardly any modern tales are among their choices. Many of the new tales have sad endings, which fail to provide the escape and consolation that the fearsome events in the fairy tale require if the child is to be strengthened for meeting the vagaries of his life. Without such encouraging conclusions, the child, after listening to the story, feels that there is indeed no hope for extricating himself from his despairs. In the traditional fairy tale, the hero is rewarded and the evil person meets his well-deserved fate, thus satisfying the child's deep need for justice to prevail. How else can a child hope that justice will be done to him, who so often feels unfairly treated? And how else can he convince himself that he must act correctly, when he is so sorely tempted to give in to the asocial prodding of his desires?

(Bruno Bettelheim)

Task 4.13

Read the essay carefully and answer the following questions.

1. What is the main purpose in this article?
2. Explain how this article is an example of an illustration essay. What are some characteristics that distinguish it as illustrating examples of some argument or purpose?
3. In addition to providing examples of fairy tales and modern stories, what is the author's main argument or conclusion about the two types of stories?
4. Did the fairy tale about Rapunzel help one girl cope with the harsh realities of her family life?
5. Explain why the author favors fairy tales for providing hope for children.

Common Transitions in an Illustration Essay:

For example	An illustration of this is
For instance	This is illustrated by
To illustrate	This is exemplified by
An example of this is	This is evidenced by
As an illustration	

Task 4.14

Write an illustration essay on one of the following topics.

1. Failure Is a Better Teacher Than Success.
2. First Impressions Are Often The Best/Worst Means of Judging People.
3. Participation in (a Particular Sport, Club, Hobby, Event) Teaches Valuable

Lessons.
4. Job Hunting Today Is a Difficult Process.
5. One Important Event Can Change The Course Of a Life.
6. Travel Can Be The Best Medicine.

Task 4.15

Choose your own topic and write an illustration essay in single (extended) example type or multiple examples type.

Use the following revision form to check for the basics in your illustration essay draft.

Overall

1. Does the essay provide ideas, examples and/or illustrations and have an analytical purpose?
   (Yes/No)
2. Does the essay include specific examples in the body paragraph and provide an analytical setup, and a concluding paragraph?
   (Yes/No)
3. Are the paragraphs broken up well and about the right length?
   (Yes/No)

Introduction

4. Is the title interesting and in the correct format?
   (Yes/No)
5. Is there a general introduction that gives background information for the essay's purpose?
   (Yes/No)
6. Is there a clear thesis statement that explains the significance/message of the examples/illustrations being provided an expository purpose?
   (Yes/No)

Body

7. Do the body paragraphs have support and develop the examples well and flow smoothly?
   (Yes/No)
8. Are transitions used between and, when needed, within the paragraphs?
   (Yes/No)
9. Do the body paragraphs have descriptive details and analysis to enhance the examples?
   (Yes/No)

Conclusion

10. Does the concluding paragraph sum up the process and re-emphasize the purpose set up in the introductory paragraph and thesis, without adding new ideas?
    (Yes/No)

Editing

11. Circle the following errors you think you see in this draft: spelling errors, fragments, run-ons/comma splices, errors in comma and semicolon/colon use, pronoun disagreement, reference fault errors, and errors in parallelism, apostrophe use, verb use/tense, and passive voice construction.
12. Other types of grammar or sentence-level errors:

Comments

4.5 A Comparison and Contrast Essay

> **Thinking over the Questions before Writing**
>
> ➤ What two objects, people, or concepts am I going to compare and/or contrast?
> ➤ Are they in the same general category?
> ➤ Am I going to focus on similarities, differences, or both? Are the two subjects mostly alike, mostly different, or some of each?
> ➤ How will I set up my comparisons/contrasts, and how will I arrange my paragraphs? In subject-by-subject (block) arrangement or point-by-point (alternating) arrangement?
> ➤ What examples and details should I include for support?
> ➤ What do I want my readers to learn or understand after reading this comparison and/or contrast essay?
> ➤ How will I conclude my essay?

Comparison points out how two things are the same or similar.

For example: *A Ford costs $20,000. A Toyota costs $20,000.* We can compare the two cars as follow:

1. The Ford is **as** expensive **as** the Toyota.
2. The Ford is **the same** price **as** the Toyota.
3. The Ford costs **as many** dollars **as** the Toyota.
4. The Ford costs **as much** money **as** the Toyota.
5. The Ford costs **as much as** the Toyota.
6. The Ford and the Toyota are **both** $20,000.
7. **Both** the Ford and the Toyota are $20,000.
8. **Neither** the Ford nor the Toyota are as expensive as a Porsche.

Another example: *The Ford has four doors, power steering, and a top speed of 140kph. The Toyota has four doors, power steering and a top speed of 135kph.* We can compare the cars as follow:

1. The Ford and the Toyota are **similar** cars.

2. The Ford is **similar to** the Toyota.
3. The Ford and the Toyota are **alike**.
4. The Ford is **like** the Toyota.
5. The Ford and the Toyota are **almost the same**.

Contrast shows how two, or more, things are different.

For example: *The Toshiba computer costs* $3,500. *The NEC computer costs* $4,000.

1. The Toshiba is **not as** expensive **as** the NEC.
2. The Toshiba **is cheaper than** the NEC.
3. The NEC is **more** expensive **than** the Toshiba.
4. The Toshiba is **less** expensive **than** the NEC.
5. The Toshiba does **not** cost as **many** dollars **as** the NEC.
6. The Toshiba does **not** cost as **much** money **as** the NEC.

A *Comparison* or *Contrast* essay is an essay in which we either compare something or contrast something. A comparison essay is an essay in which we emphasize the similarities, and contrast essay is an essay in which we emphasize the differences. We use comparison and contrast thinking when deciding which university to attend, which car to buy, or whether to drive a car or take a bus or an airplane to a vacation site.

There are two ways to arrange a comparison and contrast essay. One is called **subject-by-subject** or **block arrangement** of ideas, in which we discuss the various aspects of one thing before moving on to the other; the other is called **point-by-point** or **alternating arrangement** of ideas, where we discuss both things under each of the various aspects compared or contrasted.

Suppose we are interested in showing the differences between vacationing in the mountains and vacationing at the beach. We will then write a contrast composition. One way to arrange our material is to use the *block* arrangement which is to write about vacationing in the mountains in one paragraph and vacationing at the beach in the next. If we mention a particular point in the mountains paragraph, we must mention the same point in the beach paragraph, and *in the same order*. Study the following outline, which shows this kind of organization. The introductory paragraph is followed by the *mountains* paragraph, the *beach* paragraph, then the conclusion; the fully developed essay is just four paragraphs.

> **Subject-by-Subject or Block Arrangement**
> **I.** Introduction in which you state your purpose which is to discuss the differences between vacationing in the mountains or at the beach
> **II.** Mountain
>   A. Climate
>   B. Types of Activities
>   C. Location
> **III.** Beach
>   A. Climate
>   B. Types of Activities
>   C. Location
> **IV.** Conclusion

A second way to organize this material is to discuss a particular point about vacationing in the mountains and then immediately to discuss the same point about vacationing at the beach. This is called *point-by-point* or *alternating* arrangement. An outline of this organization follows.

> **Point-by-Point or Alternating Arrangement**
> **I.** Introduction in which you state your purpose which is to discuss differences between vacationing in the mountains or at the beach.
> **II.** First difference between mountains and beaches is climate.
>   A. Mountains
>   B. Beach
> **III.** Second difference between mountains and beaches are types of activities.
>   A. Mountains
>   B. Beach
> **IV.** Third difference between mountains and beaches is the location.
>   A. Mountains
>   B. Beach
> **V.** Conclusion

Sample 1

Vacationing at the Beach or in the Mountains

People are always looking forward to their vacation period. There are many options where to choose. I think that the two most common places people choose for taking a vacation are the beaches and the mountains. Both places offer a variety of fun activities. The beach offers activities that the mountain cannot offer and vice versa. The mountain and the beach are totally different in the aspects of climate, types of activities and locations.

As the mountain goes, climate is always important in order to enjoy vacations. If a person dislikes cold weather, he or she might have a hard time in the mountains. The cold climate in the mountains is the first barrier to enjoying them, but the climate and the temperature of these zones also determine the types of activities they offer. Snow boarding, mountain climbing, mountain biking, hiking, and skiing are some activities people can enjoy when going to the mountains. There are many regions that have mountains where people can go and have a great vacation. Canada is a country located in North America and contains many mountain vacation sites where people can go and have fun.

When it comes to the beach, warm climate is one of the most important features that the beach has. Sun and fun are two words that describe the beach. The temperature in those places is always hot. The sea and the warm climate determine the activities that are available at the beach. People can swim, play volleyball, play soccer, and ride water bikes. In most coastal sites, there are discos and restaurants where people can dance or party throughout the night. Mexico offers many amazing coastal sites to visit. Acapulco and Cancun are two of the most beautiful and famous beaches in the word.

It doesn't matter what place a person decides to choose. The fun is 100% guaranteed. People often choose one of these two options to spend their vacations. Depending on what the person likes is what he or she will choose. I like the beach better than the mountains, but sometimes it is better to take a risk and try a different place to enjoy.

Task 4.16

Answer the questions according to the essay

1. Is it a comparison essay, a contrast essay, or both? Can you give your reason?
2. Please rewrite the essay by using *point-by-point arrangement*.

Sample 2 is based on the following supportive evidence. Please read the information in the table carefully, and then pay attention to the arrangement of the essay.

Restaurant	Prices ($)		Services	Facilities
Linda's Restaurant	Salads	$3.50	opens from 7 a.m. to 9 p.m.	clean bathrooms
	Sandwiches	$4.00	drive-in service	12 tables / 48 chairs
	Soup	$3.00	carry-out	20 parking spaces
	Drinks	$1.50	home delivery	playground for kids
	Desserts	$2.00	three cashiers in rush hours	air conditioner
José's Restaurant	Salads	$4.50	opens from 7 a.m. to 7 p.m. drive-in service NO home delivery 2 cashiers in rush hours	clean bathrooms
	Sandwiches	$4.50		8 tables/32 chairs
	Soup	$3.50		10 parking spaces
	Drinks	$2.00		NO playground for kids
	Desserts	$3.00		ceiling fans only

Sample 2

Two Restaurants

Have you eaten at Linda's Restaurant lately? If you haven't, you have missed all the great improvements that she has added to her beautiful and inviting restaurant. I used to be a regular customer at José's Restaurant down the corner. But after discovering all of the new secrets at Linda's, I said: No way José! The more affordable prices, the great service, and the improved facilities are some of the reasons why I prefer Linda's restaurant over José's.

First of all, you feel more relaxed eating at Linda's because of the reasonable prices. For example, salads cost $3.50 and sandwiches are at a low $4.00. On the other hand, both of these items cost $4.50 at José's Restaurant. At Linda's, you can eat soup for just $3.00, but you have to pay $3.50 at José's for the same soup. Last but not least, drinks and desserts cost $1.50 and $2.00 at Linda's, whereas at José's they go up to $2.00 and $3.00 respectively.

In addition to the lower prices, Linda's Restaurant offers a better service. For instance, it opens from 7 a.m. to 9 p.m. giving its customers two extra hours that they cannot have at José's. Although both restaurants have a convenient drive-in service, Linda has added a home delivery service to satisfy her customers at their homes. During rush hours, Linda has three cashiers working to speed up the line but José has only two, which usually slows down the line and makes the customers become impatient.

Finally, the improved facilities at Linda's Restaurant make the place more comfortable than José's. To begin with, when you get there, you have 20 parking spaces available at Linda's, different from the only 10 limited spaces at José's. Once inside the restaurant, there is a lot more space and room because Linda has expanded the place to accommodate 12 tables with 48 chairs, while José has kept his 8 tables and 32 chairs. Linda also bought a brand new central air conditioner that provides absolute coolness to her restaurant. On the contrary, José still has his traditional ceiling fans, which sometimes become an annoyance to the customers. To top it off, Linda constructed a colorful playground for kids, which has become her customers' favorite attraction. Now, they can eat and relax while their children play. At José's Restaurant, the kids look out the window trying to see the colorful playground at the other side of the street.

In conclusion, Linda's Restaurant has considerable advantages over José's. Little by little, all of José's customers are going to run away and jump into Linda's air conditioned facilities the way I did. If José doesn't do anything to improve his restaurant in the near future, he is going to be out of business!

Read sample 3 carefully and see where the essay uses the subject-by-subject method and where it uses the point-by-point method?

Sample 3

Learning to Write is Like Learning to Play a Musical Instrument

Even if you've never tried to learn a musical instrument, you can probably relate to the way learning to write can be compared to learning a musical instrument. They both require a set of skills and both, when they're performed well, can be considered an art with power to greatly move audiences.

In the first place, learning any musical instrument can be a grueling process, but once you learn to play competently, you're rewarded by the beautiful sound of music at your fingertips. Once you gain control over the notes you're trying to reach, and the tones those notes create, you can consciously set a mood, create an atmosphere. You can make people dance for joy or make them weep. But you don't gain that control overnight. Learning an instrument requires a big time investment, a lot of patient practice. Your fingers have go over and over the same positions as you learn scales and practice exercises that increase dexterity. The sounds you produce may be ugly at first: discordant, disjointed, off rhythm. But through continued practice you'll begin to play more smoothly, with greater feeling, and with fewer mistakes. Pretty soon, you'll feel like you've arrived. You can play.

Similarly, writing well is an art in the sense that it has an "aesthetic" experience to offer us—when we're finished we may have created something truly beautiful. Reading a good piece of writing, we can experience its truth and beauty. It has the power to affect us intellectually, emotionally. But learning to write well is a skill we can acquire only through time and patience. In the beginning, "process" is as important as "product". While we're learning drafting, revising, and editing skills, our first attempts may be fumbling or unfocused, incoherent, and full of error, but if we keep practicing the fundamentals, before long we get the hang of it. Concepts like structure, unity, coherence, development, style, and syntax aid rather than intimidate us. They provide the solid foundation upon which we express new ideas.

Writing and making music aren't always similar. In a few key ways, these skills are more different than they are the same. First, whereas music and writing both have the power to evoke strong feeling, writing is probably better at making audiences think. Second, whereas music is often created collaboratively, writing is often created solo. Even when writing projects are collaborative, individual writers often work separately on unique tasks and then assemble the group's work into a whole. They rarely do the work of writing face to face with other group members, though they may seek advice and feedback from group members. Finally, the biggest difference between writing and making music is that, unless a person is a professional musician, we don't use music skills on a daily basis in the variety of environments that we use writing.

Given that learning to write and learning to play music can be so similar, it makes sense to evaluate a writer's skills at the end of a course rather than at the beginning. It isn't what students know when they start that counts, or even what you know along the way; it's what a student can do by the end that really matters.

Sample 4

American Space, Chinese Place

Americans have a sense of space, not of place. Go to an American home in exurbia, and almost the first thing you do is drift toward the picture window. How curious that the first compliment you pay your host inside his house is to say how lovely it is outside his house! He is pleased that you should admire his vistas. The distant horizon is not merely a line separating earth from sky, it is a symbol of the future. The American is not rooted in his place, however lovely: his eyes are drawn by the expanding space to a point on the horizon, which is his future. By contrast, consider the traditional Chinese home. Blank walls enclose it.

Step behind the spirit wall and you are in a courtyard with perhaps a miniature garden around the corner. Once inside the private compound you are wrapped in an ambiance of calm beauty, an ordered world of buildings, pavement, rock, and decorative vegetation. But you have no distant view: nowhere does space open out before you. Raw nature in such a home is experienced only as weather, and the only open space is the sky above. The Chinese is rooted in his place. When he has to leave, it is not for the promised land on the terrestrial horizon, but for another world altogether along the vertical, religious axis of his imagination.

The Chinese tie to place is deeply felt. Wanderlust is an alien sentiment. The Taoist classic Tao Te Ching captures the ideal of rootedness in place with these words: Though there may be another country in the neighborhood so close that they are within sight of each other and the crowing of cocks and barking of dogs in one place can be heard in the other, yet there is no traffic between them; and throughout their lives the two peoples have nothing to do with each other. In theory if not in practice, farmers have ranked high in Chinese society. The reason is not only that they are engaged in the root industry of producing food but that, unlike pecuniary merchants, they are tied to the land and do not abandon their country when it is in danger.

Nostalgia is a recurrent theme in Chinese poetry. An American reader of translated Chinese poems will be taken aback even put off by the frequency as well as the sentimentality of the lament for home. To understand the strength of this sentiment, we need to know that the Chinese desire for stability and rootedness in place is prompted by the constant threat of war, exile, and the natural disasters of flood and drought. Forcible removal makes the Chinese keenly aware of their loss. By contrast, Americans move, for the most part, voluntarily. Their nostalgia for home town is really longing for childhood to which they cannot return: in the meantime the future beckons and the future is out there, in open space. When we criticize American rootlessness we tend to forget that it is a result of ideals we admire, namely, social mobility and optimism about the future. When we admire Chinese rootedness, we forget that the word place means both location in space and position in society: to be tied to place is also to be bound to one's station in life, with little hope of betterment. Space symbolizes hope; place, achievement and stability.

(Yi – Fu Tuan, *Space and Place: The Perspective of Experience*)

Task 4.17

1. List two characteristics of this article that distinguish it as a contrast article.
2. Who do you think the main intended audience is for this article, Americans or Chinese? Why?
3. Provide one reason suggested in the article for the different perspectives of the Chinese and Americans toward their homes.

Comparison/Contrast Transitions

Transitions showing **similarity**:	Transitions indicating **difference**:
also	although
and	but
along with	compared with
as well as	conversely
as if	differ
as	different from
besides	even though
both	furthermore
comparatively	however
even when	in contrast to
in comparison	in contrast
in the same way	instead
in the same manner	less than
in addition	more than
just as	nevertheless
like	notwithstanding
likewise	on the other hand
moreover	on the contrary
most important	otherwise
same	rather than
similar to	regardless
similar	still
similarly	though
the same as	to the contrary
too	unless
	unlike
	whereas
	while
	yet

Task 4.18

Write a comparison and/or contrast essay on one of the topics:
1. A Memory of a Person or Place and a More Recent Encounter
2. A Hero Today and Yesterday
3. Two Places You've Lived or Visited or Two Schools You've Attended
4. Two Instructors or Coaches Whose Teaching Styles Are Effective But Different
5. Your Attitude Toward a Social Custom or Political Belief and Your Parents' (or grandparents') Attitude Toward That Belief or Custom

Task 4.19

Choose your own topic and write a comparison and/or contrast essay by using subject-by-subject arrangement and/or point-by-point arrangement.

Use the following revision form to check for the basics in your comparison and/or contrast essay draft.

Overall

1. Does the essay clearly develop comparison and/or contrast analysis with a clear purpose/analytical conclusion
   (Yes/No)
2. Does the essay use a clear order (subject by subject or point by point or an effective combination of the two) in the body paragraphs with an analytical conclusion drawn from the comparison or contrast?
   (Yes/No)
3. Are the paragraphs broken up well and about the right length?
   (Yes/No)

Introduction

4. Is the title interesting and in the correct format?
   (Yes/No)
5. Is there a general introduction that gives the purpose for the comparison and contrast analysis? Is the process and organization clear?
   (Yes/No)
6. Is there a clear thesis statement that explains the purpose of the comparisons and/or contrasts and the overall purpose?
   (Yes/No)

Body

7. Do the body paragraphs develop the ideas and analysis well and flow smoothly?
   (Yes/No)
8. Are transitions used between and, when needed, within the paragraphs?
   (Yes/No)
9. Do the body paragraphs include support and descriptive details for development?
   (Yes/No)

Conclusion

10. Does the concluding paragraph sum up the process and re-emphasize the purpose set up in the introductory paragraph and thesis, without adding new ideas?
    (Yes/No)
11. Does the writer demonstrate the significance of the similarities and differences (both or just one of the two)?
    (Yes/No)

Editing

12. Circle the following errors you think you see in this draft: spelling errors, fragments, run-ons/comma splices, errors in comma and semicolon/colon use, pronoun disagreement, reference fault errors, and errors in parallelism, apostrophe use, verb use/tense, and passive voice construction.
13. Other types of grammar or sentence-level errors:
   _____
   _____
   _____

Comments

_____
_____
_____

4.6 A Cause and Effect Essay

Thinking over the Questions before Writing

▶ What process or event is the subject of my cause-and-effect analysis?
▶ What are the benefits of doing a cause-and-effect analysis of my chosen topic?
▶ Why did this process or event happen what was the original cause(s)?
▶ What is the result(s) (effect/s) of this process or event?
▶ What do I want my readers to learn from reading about the cause(s) and/or effect(s) of this event or process?
▶ How will I conclude this essay?

Many phenomena, events, situations and trends can be better understood by describing their causes and effects. The cause and effect essay explains what happens and why it happens. Logic is the most important factor in a cause-effect essay. Usually we have three common patterns:

(1) One cause producing one effect:

e.g. **Cause**: I am out of gas.
  Effect: My car won't start.

(2) Many causes contributing to a single effect:

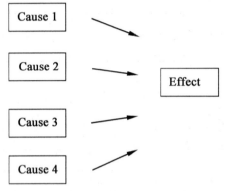

e.g. **Causes**: I liked business in high school.
    Salaries in the field are high.
    I have an aunt who is an accountant.
    I am good with numbers.
  Effect: I will choose to major in accounting

(3) Many effects resulting from a single cause:

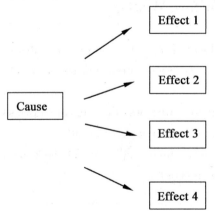

e. g. **Cause**: reducing work hours
Effects: less income
employer is irritated
more time to study
more time for family and friends

(4) Cause-Effect-Chain

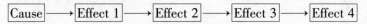

e. g. Thinking about friend... forgot to buy gas... car wouldn't start... missed math exam... failed math course.

Among these patterns of cause-effect-essay, pattern 2 and pattern 3 are used more commonly. Read sample 1 and sample 2 carefully, and try to sum up the characteristics of cause essay and effect essay.

Sample 1

Why are Cities Becoming Overcrowded?

The fact that the world's cities are getting more and more crowded is well-known. Cities such as Tokyo, Sao Paolo, Bombay and Shanghai are now considered "mega-cities", because of their enormous size and huge populations. There are two main reasons why these and other cities are becoming so crowded; one economic, the other socio-cultural.

First, the primary cause of cities becoming so crowded is economic. As a country develops, its cities become the engines of development, thus jobs are available in these areas. Frankfurt, Istanbul, Bombay and Sao Paolo are all the economic centers of their countries. For example, Tokyo was the motor for Japan's rapid economic development in the 1960's and 70's; as a result, its population increased rapidly. People moved to Tokyo because they could find employment and establish economic security for themselves and their families there.

Second, another factor in the huge increase in urban populations is the socio-cultural factor. Thousands of people migrate to the cities not only for jobs but also for educational and personal reasons. The better universities are always located in big cities and this attracts thousands of students every year, and these students stay on and work in the city after they graduate. Moreover, young people will move to the city as the villages and rural areas are more custom and tradition oriented. Therefore, young people believe this is an obstacle to their personal freedom.

In conclusion, economic and cultural factors are the major causes of huge urban population. People will always move to the areas which provide opportunity and to the places which can give them the freedom they desire.

Sample 2

What effects has the computer had on our lives?

The twenty-first century is already turning out to be the century of the computer. The computer revolution that started after the Second World War is now developing exponentially and computers are beginning to influence and take over nearly every aspect of our lives. Computers are clearly changing and affecting society in many ways. The two main areas in which computers have brought about a profound change in our lives are in the economic field and in the field of communications.

The computer has led to immense changes in economic and business life. First, businesses now have to be computerised or they risk failure. Every big corporation bases its operations on computing, regardless of which sector they are in. For example, Coca-Cola, the BBC and Levi's market and sell different products and services, yet they all share one basic property—without computers their operations would collapse. Second, computing is an economic dynamo. Japan, China, India and many other countries have large IT sectors which drive their economies upwards. Furthermore, the developed world is moving from an industrial-based economy to a computer and IT-based one.

It is not just in business that computers have affected us so profoundly; communication has been revolutionised totally. Firstly, whereas before, people wrote letters, which would often take weeks to reach their destinations, or speak on the phone, which was terribly expensive, now they e-mail. For instance, instead of waiting weeks for a letter now, we can read it instantly, seconds after it's been written. Secondly, many people use computers to communicate with people all around the world using chat rooms and chat programs, this was impossible before the computer became widespread. As a result, now people who live thousands of kilometres away from each other can communicate as much as they want and whenever they want using e-mail and/or chat rooms.

In conclusion, computers have had a profound effect on our lives in many ways and it is in business and communication that they have had the greatest influence. In the future, if the computer continues evolving at such speed, our business practices and methods of communication will undergo even more radical changes.

Task 4.20

Underline transition words in sample 1 and sample 2, and make distinction between cause-essay and effect-essay.

4.6.1 Introductory Paragraph

We should begin our cause and effect essay with a general introduction to the topic, and end our introductory paragraph with a thesis statement that sets up the purpose for our essay.

4.6.2 Body Paragraphs

The body paragraphs and topic sentences set up the order and the examples we shall develop for our cause-and-effect analysis. We could arrange the causes and/or effects in separate paragraphs from least to most important (or vice versa) or arrange them in time order. We should use transitional words and phrases to lead our readers from one cause or effect to the next. Be sure to use plenty of specific examples and details to illustrate the particular causes or effects in our body paragraphs. The topic sentence in body paragraphs are also important, for they will indicate which causes or effects we will be explaining in each paragraph.

4.6.3 Concluding Paragraph

Our essay will need a concluding paragraph that briefly restates the cause-and-effect analysis and the purpose for studying the causal relationship. Re-emphasize what we want our readers to realize about the cause-and-effect connections after they've read our essay.

Sample 3 is a cause-and-effect essay about fast food—how it becomes so popular and what its effects have been. Pay attention to the structure of the essay.

Sample 3

Fast Food

In the past people in the United Arab Emirates used to eat healthy, freshly prepared food with their families in the home. Today however, many people, particularly young people, prefer to eat fast food such as hamburgers, fried chicken, shawarma, or pizza. There are many reasons why this change has occurred, but this essay will also outline the serious effects of this move towards fast food on individuals and society.

There are many reasons for the popularity of fast food. One of the main reasons is the change in lifestyle. Many people in the UAE are working long hours, shifts, or extended school days. They don't have time to find ingredients or prepare good food. Women are now starting to work in the Emirates, and this can result in less time being available for preparing family meals. Another cause is the huge number of young, affluent people in the United Arab Emirates. The rapid development of the country has meant that young people, who comprise over 75% of the population, have money to spend. A third reason is advertising. The UAE is a modern, free-market country, with all forms of media such as the Internet and satellite television, and people like to try new products and different kinds of fast food.

However, this change in diet can have some serious effects. One effect is on health. Many individuals in the UAE are becoming obese. These people will be less productive and have conditions such as heart disease and diabetes. Another result of fast food culture is the loss of the family tradition of eating together. Children and adults rarely eat together now, and thus get less opportunity to talk. A further effect is on the economy. Although fast food is not very expensive, it is more expensive than cooking properly for yourself. Many of the fast-food companies are franchisees of foreign corporations, so profits leave the country.

In conclusion, fast food, although it is convenient and a tasty addition to a diet, can have serious health and social effects. People should learn to choose fast food carefully and remember the pleasure of eating good food in good company.

Let's look at the structure of sample 3:

Introduction

    General introduction: People used to eat;
                              What people eat now
    Thesis: This change has had many effects

Body

    Causes: 1. Lifestyle: Many people working long hours, no time Women working
                 2. More money: Young people have money to spend
                               More eating outside the home
                 3. Modern Life: Advertising
                               Less time with family
                               New things, desire for change
    Effects: 1. Health: Obesity
                           Heart Disease
                           Diabetes
                           Less energy
                 2. Families: Family not eating together
                               Family not talking over a meal
                 3. Economic effects: Waste of money
                                     Multinational companies own fast food chains
                                     New things, desire for change

Conclusion

    Both sides: Fast food is tasty but...
                      ...fast food also has a downside
    Future: We need to look after our health in future

In sample 4, the author discusses both causes and effects of obesity, pay attention the signal words in the essay.

Sample 4

Obesity

Obesity has become a major problem in the UAE. Over 60% of Emirati nationals are overweight. **This is a difficult problem with many serious effects on the individual and country.**

Obesity can be divided into three main causes—diet, lifestyle and education. **One of the chief causes is diet.** Young Emiratis eat more and more high-carbohydrate, high-fat burgers and pizza in fast-food restaurants. However, some traditional foods are also very oily, and **because of increasing affluence** are eaten more often than in the past. Lifestyle is a second main cause of obesity. **As a result of cheap foreign labour**, many Emiratis now have sedentary jobs, and do not exercise regularly. **However, one of the main causes** is lack of education and awareness. The society's attitude to food often **leads to** overconsumption. Parents do not teach good eating habits to children, and many people lack knowledge about good nutrition or a balanced diet.

Obesity affects the individual and the country. **The biggest effect** is on the individual. First of all, being overweight **has health risks.** Obesity **can lead to** heart disease, diabetes, and other conditions. The quality of life suffers, as it is difficult to enjoy exercise or move. **Another result is lack of** self-esteem. This can **lead to** depression, eating disorders and crash diets. The country is also **affected.** It becomes very expensive for the government to provide advanced medical care such as heart transplants. Unhealthy citizens are also less productive, and their children learn poor eating habits.

Obesity or even being overweight **has serious effects** on the individual and the society. Both need to take action to examine the causes of this problem and find solutions.

Task 4.21

Please list the causes and effects of obesity according to the essay.

Sample 5

The Dangers of Too Much TV

Television is a great invention, and it is a great element of most homes, as long as it is watched in moderation. Unfortunately, these days, too many children are watching too much TV every day. Studies show that students watch an average of two to four hours of TV a day. There are several negative effects of watching too much TV.

The first negative effect for children who watch too much TV is lack of exercise due to sitting passively in front of the tube all day. Unfortunately, many children do not spend as much time outside playing with their friends as they did in the past. With the constant availability of kid's programming, such as cartoons played 24 hours a day, more children choose to stay on the couch watching shows than going outside and playing with their friends. It used to be that cartoons were only available at certain times, so the fact that they are on 24/7 may have added to the increase in TV watching.

A direct result of increased TV watching has been the increase in childhood obesity in America. Many children are more inactive due to increased TV watching, and, in addition, they tend to snack more when indoors watching TV all day. Both of these reasons lead to increased weight in a child.

Another negative effect of too much TV is a decrease in reading and imaginative play by children. When children spend hours watching TV, then they spend a lot less time reading or engaging in imaginative play. For instance, many children these days rarely play board games or work on puzzles. These interactive types of play are much more intellectually stimulating than passive TV viewing.

Overall, the increase in TV viewing by children over the last couple of decades has led to negative consequences for many of them. Their health and intelligence are put in jeopardy when they watch too much TV. Hopefully, parents will take these negative effects seriously and take action to decrease the amount of time their kids spend in front of the tube and strongly encourage them to participate in physical activities, imaginative play, and reading.

Task 4.22

Find the thesis, topic sentences, and transition words in this essay.

Sample 6

Some Lessons from the Assembly Line

Last June, as I stood behind the bright orange guard door of the machine, listening to the crackling hiss of the automatic welders, I thought about how different my life had been just a few weeks earlier. Then, I was writing an essay about French literature to complete my last exam of the spring semester at college. Now I stood in an automotive plant in southwest Michigan, making subassemblies for a car manufacturer.

I have worked as a temp in the factories surrounding my hometown every summer since I graduated from high school, but making the transition between school and full-time blue-collar work during the break never gets any easier. For a student like me who considers any class before noon to be uncivilized, getting to a factory by 6 O'clock each morning, where rows of hulking, spark-showering machines have replaced the lush campus and cavernous lecture halls of college life, is torture. There my time is spent stamping, cutting, welding, moving or assembling parts, the rigid work schedules and quotas of the plant making days spent studying and watching "Sports Center" seem like a million years ago.

I chose to do this work, rather than bus tables or fold sweatshirts at the Gap, for the overtime pay and because living at home is infinitely cheaper than living on campus for the summer. My friends who take easier, part-time jobs never seem to understand why I'm so relieved to be back at school in the fall or that my summer vacation has been anything but a vacation.

There are few things as cocksure as a college student who has never been out in the real world, and people my age always seem to overestimate the value of their time and knowledge. After a particularly exhausting string of 12-hour days at a plastics factory, I remember being shocked at how small my check seemed. I couldn't believe how little I was taking home after all the hours I spent on the sweltering production floor. And all the classes in the world could not have prepared me for my battles with the machine I ran in the plant, which would jam whenever I absent-mindedly put in a part backward or upside down. As frustrating as the work can be, the most stressful thing about blue-collar life is knowing your job could disappear overnight. Issues like downsizing and overseas relocation had always seemed distant to me until my co-workers at one factory told me that the unit I was working in would be shut down within six months and moved to Mexico, where people would work for 60 cents an hour.

Factory life has shown me what my future might have been like had I never gone to college in the first place. For me, and probably many of my fellow students, higher education always seemed like a foregone conclusion: I never questioned if I was going to college, just where. No other options ever occurred to me. After working 12-hour shifts in a factory, the other options have become brutally clear. When I'm back at the university, skipping classes and turning in lazy rewrites seems like a cop-out after seeing what I would be doing without school. All the advice and public-service announcements about the value of an education that used to sound trite now ring true.

These lessons I am learning, however valuable, are always tinged with a sense of guilt. Many people pass their lives in the places I briefly work, spending 30 years where I spend only two months at a time. When fall comes around, I get to go back to a sunny and beautiful campus, while work in the factories continues. At times I feel almost voyeuristic, like a tourist dropping in where other people make their livelihoods. My lessons about education are learned at the expense of those who weren't fortunate enough to receive one. "This job pays well, but it's hell on the body," said one co-worker. "Study hard and keep reading," she added, nodding at the copy of Jack Kerouac's *On the Road* I had wedged into the space next to my machine so I could read discreetly when the line went down.

My experience will stay with me long after I head back to school and spend my wages on books and beer. The things that factory work has taught me—how lucky I am to get an education, how to work hard, how easy it is to lose that work once you have it—are by no means earth-shattering. Everyone has to come to grips with them at some point. How and when I learned these lessons, however, has inspired me to make the most of my college years before I enter the real world for good. Until then, the summer months I spend in the factories will be long, tiring and every bit as educational as a French-lit class.

(Andrew Braaksma)

Task 4.23

Answer the questions according to the essay.

1. What cause-effect relationship is presented in this essay? Does this essay focus primarily on causes or effects?
2. What are some of the important lessons Braaksma has learned? Learning these lessons at this point in his life inspired Braaksma in what new way?
3. What strategy does Braaksma use to begin his essay, and why? How is this strategy continued throughout the essay?
4. In paragraph 2, what descriptive details and verbs are particularly effective in characterizing the work that Braaksma did at the factories?
5. What does the use of dialogue in paragraph 6 add to this essay?
6. Evaluate Braaksma's conclusion. Why does he refer to his French-lit class?

Cause and Effect Transition Words

because	because of	due to
since	on account of	for that reason
therefore	thanks to	consequently
accordingly	thus	hence
as a result	the result of	the effect of
result in	lead to	have an effect on
the reason for	for this reason	the cause of
so that	such that	seeing that
so as to	now that	for fear that

Task 4.24

Write a cause and effect essay on one of the following topics:

1. Effects of Pollution
2. Internet Influence on Kids
3. Effects of Laughter
4. Reasons for the changes which have occurred in your neighborhood or home

town over time

5. Effect(s) of a parent, teacher, coach or friend on you

Task 4.25

Choose your own topic and write a cause and effect essay. Pay attention to the logic of the cause(s) and effect(s).

Use the following revision form to check for the basics in your cause and effect essay draft.

Overall

1. Does the essay clearly develop cause-and-effect analysis with a clear purpose?
   (Yes/No)
2. Does the essay use a clear order in the body paragraphs?
   (Yes/No)
3. Are the paragraphs broken up well and about the right length?
   (Yes/No)

Introduction

4. Is the title interesting and in the correct format?
   (Yes/No)
5. Is there a general introduction that gives the purpose for the cause-and-effect analysis? Is the process clear?
   (Yes/No)
6. Is there a clear thesis statement that explains the results of the cause(s) and effect(s) and the overall purpose?
   (Yes/No)

Body

7. Do the body paragraphs develop the ideas and analysis well and flow smoothly?
(Yes/No)
8. Are transitions used between and, when needed, within the paragraphs?
(Yes/No)
9. Do the body paragraphs include support and descriptive details for development?
(Yes/No)
10. Does the essay demonstrate the relationship of the cause(s) and the effect(s) and the importance of their interrelatedness?

Conclusion

11. Does the concluding paragraph sum up the essay with an analytical frame that re-emphasizes the introductory paragraph and thesis, without adding new ideas?
(Yes/No)

Editing

12. Circle the following errors you think you see in this draft: spelling errors, fragments, run-ons/comma splices, errors in comma and semicolon/colon use, pronoun disagreement, reference fault errors, and errors in parallelism, apostrophe use, verb use/tense, and passive voice construction.
13. Other types of grammar or sentence-level errors:
_____
_____

Comments

_____
_____
_____

4.7 A Classification Essay

Thinking over the Questions before Writing

➤ What basis or principles will I use to classify the topic?
➤ How can I subdivide my categories or classifications?
➤ What do I want to explain or prove as a result of this classification and division?
➤ Have I unfairly or inaccurately classified my subjects or oversimplified complex divisions?
➤ What do I want my readers to learn or understand after reading this essay?

When we do the laundry, we usually begin by separating the clothing into piles, putting all the whites in one pile and all the colors in another. Or we might classify the laundry not according to color, but according to fabric-putting all cottons in one pile, polyesters in another, and so on. Classifying is the process of taking many things and separating them into categories. We generally classify to better manage or understand many things. Librarians classify books into groups (novels, travel, health, etc.) to make them easier to find. A scientist sheds light on the world by classifying all living things into two main groups: animals and plants.

Dividing, in contrast, is taking one thing and breaking it down into parts. We often divide, or analyze, to better understand, teach, or evaluate something. For instance, a tinkerer might take apart a clock to see how it works; a science text might divide a tree into its parts to explain their functions. A music reviewer may analyze the elements of a band's performance—for example, the skill of the various players, rapport with the audience, selections, and so on.

In short, *if we are classifying, we are sorting numbers of things into categories. If we are dividing, we are breaking one thing into parts.* It all depends on our purpose—we might classify flowers into various types or divide a single flower into its parts.

When we write a classification or division essay, the most important thing is to be certain that our categories are logical and do not overlap. To divide group of students into "boys, girls, and athletes," for instance, would be inaccurate because "athletes" obviously includes individuals from the first two groups. Be certain that our parts account for all elements of the object. To divide the federal government of United States into the judicial and legislative branches would be incomplete because the executive branch is omitted. Finally, when classifying, make certain that every item fits into a category and that there are no items left over. Decide on what basis of division we will classify or divide our subject and then be consistent throughout our essay.

Read the following samples carefully and see what categories the writer chooses.

Sample 1

Three Kinds of Dogs

A city walker will notice that most dogs fall into one of three categories. First there are the big dogs, which are generally harmless and often downright friendly. They walk along peacefully with their masters, their tongues hanging out and big goofy grins on their faces. Apparently they know they're too big to have anything to worry about, so why not be nice? Second are the spunky medium-sized dogs. When they see a stranger approaching, they go on alert, They prick up their ears, they raise their hackles, and they may growl a little deep in their throats. "I could tear you up," they seem to be saying, "but I won't if you behave yourself." Unless the walker leaps for their master's throat, these dogs usually won't do anything more than threaten, The third category is made up of the shivering neurotic little yappers whose shrill barks could shatter glass and whose needle-like little teeth are eager to sink into a friendly outstretched hand, Walkers always wonder about these dogs—don't they know that people who really wanted to could squash them under their feet like bugs? Such dogs are only one of the potential hazards that the city walker encounters.

Sample 2

The Chronicle of Levis

How often does anyone ever stop to think about the life of a plain, ordinary pair of Levis? Mine seem to go through various phases in which they are completely different: from the new to the not so new and finally to the very old.

In their first stage, my Levis are brand new. I am very conscious of my new Levis when I wear them because they are usually very stiff and feel somewhat tight. They are also very crisp, and I can almost smell the newness of the unfaded, dark blue color. Somehow I feel very dressed up, like a soldier in his military blues, when I wear brand new Levis.

In their second stage, my Levis are beginning to loosen up and are starting to conform more to my body. The original dark, denim blue is a little lighter now. Although they no longer leave the wash water blue, they are still nice and bright. I have seen pictures of President Carter wearing his stage-two Levis; he must enjoy them as much as I do.

In their final days, my Levis have gotten almost white from lots of wear and repeated washings. Like a baby's cheek, they are soft to the touch, and they have become as comfortable as the proverbial old shoe. Even though they are very worn and have a few small holes, I like them best at this stage.

My Levis and I go through a lot together, and each stage serves a purpose. When I am a senior citizen, I will probably still be wearing them.

Sample 3

Florida's Trapped Tourists

Florida is the nation's virtual melting pot for many reasons. One of the biggest reasons is that the state is awash in tourist attractions. The Sunshine State's variety of attractions often makes it easy for those who live there to identify and classify the tourists: South Florida's natural attractions hint of adventure;

Orlando's theme parks lure families and newlyweds; West Palm Beach promises a snobby, luxurious life-style; and Key West offers hedonistic escapades.

One classification of Florida tourists is the tropical adventurer, easily distinguishable by an ever-present camera or video recorder. Although even Floridians occasionally take pictures, cameras provide one clue that someone is a visitor to the state. For example, a man wearing a pith helmet, a fifty-pocket photo vest, Banana Republic shorts, and L. L. Bean super-duty sandals while taking pictures of children looking miserably cute in the glaring sun could be a Floridian; however, if the guy in the pseudo-adventurer garb is telling the children to move closer together so he can include a palm tree, airboat, stuffed alligator, or bikini-clad bimbo, he is a tourist. This man falls into the tropical adventurer category because he is not trying to capture a special moment in his children's lives, but endeavoring to record a particular object that proves to friends and family that he has indeed led his brood upon a Sunshine State safari. It is always the background that this type is focused on, the proof of tropical adventure.

Another type of easily identified tourists includes those drawn like lemmings to the magical, mystical, or confined-animal theme parks. These people may include families or hand-holding, smooching newlyweds. They are all under the impression that a park such as Rodent World is the perfect fun or romantic getaway. These tourists obviously find it fun and romantic to stand in long lines among rude teenagers and whiny toddlers who are constantly being chastised by grumpy, overweight, under-dressed, sweaty parents — all suffering from the heat and habitual humidity or the punctual afternoon thunderstorms. When the storms do strike, a bizarre scenario unfolds: The individual tourists are transformed into a giant pulsating entity composed of a zillion bright yellow plastic ponchos bearing a portrait of "the Rodent". Battalions of these tourists, all clad in these fourteen-dollar-bright-yellow slickers are a true testament of the Rodent's mass-marketing magic. If it isn't raining, this variety of tourist is distinguishable by goofy-looking hats and T-shirts bearing the likenesses of various princesses, ducks, mice, dogs, chipmunks, or various other cutesified critters.

The Palm Beach set also stands out as a distinct variation of tourists. Often, these are successful businessmen (or their sons) and their wives, all of whom showcase deep tans from leisurely or sporting activities. They often wear expensive, name-brand resort clothes, or nautical-motif attire. The women can be identified by "name-dropping" shopping bags, enormous sunglasses, strange hats, and expensive sandals on perfectly pedicured feet. The men are usually found on the golf course or in the country club lounge, where they brag of luxury cars, sailboats, stock market prowess, or deep-sea fishing conquests. Because some of these people spend many months in the state, they have even convinced themselves that they are true "Floridians", not tourists.

Daytona Beach also adds to Florida's melting-pot of tourism, but Daytona visitors arrive by season: In February and July, it's auto-racing fans; in March and April, it's college students on spring break; and in the fall, it's Speed Week bikers. However, if a member of one group tends to stray into another group's season, it's still easy to sort out who's who. Auto racing fans wear shirts with giant numbers that barely cover giant bellies; the college kids don't wear shirts at all; and the bikers are the totally nude, tattooed dudes (and dudettes) spraying one another down in the car washes.

The final group of tourists is far more difficult to spot because it is easy to blend into the locale: Key West. There are few places, for example, where a large man can slip into a small, tight-fitting, zebra-striped dress; plant a cheap, blond wig on his head; toss on a pair of spiked heels; and fit right in with the crowd.

Although the Key West carnival atmosphere can make tourists more difficult to spot, they are not completely invisible. Pale skin, fiery red skin, or peeling skin are clues. So are new Hawaiian shirts, designer swim suits, and the stench of Coppertone. So too are the stunned looks at restaurants when visitors learn that the glass of water they requested costs more than the rum-laden planter's punch. By happy hour, however, all differences tend to dissolve in Margaritaville as everything becomes a tropical blur, and all are totally uncaring of who is native and who is tourist.

Of course, all of this is not to say that Floridians begrudge tourists their "traps" because the "natives" often visit them, too. In fact, many Floridians visit theme parks, the Palm Beaches, Daytona, or Key West because they enjoy watching tourists. The tourists who flock to Florida attractions become Florida attractions themselves.

(Jamie Harris)

Task 4.26

When writing a classification essay, we should stick to the single principle of classification. In each of the groups, cross out the one item that has not been classified on the same basis as the other three.

1. Water
   a. Cold
   b. Lake
   c. Hot
   d. Lukewarm
2. Eyes
   a. Blue
   b. Nearsighted
   c. Brown
   d. Hazel
3. Household pests
   a. Mice
   b. Ants
   c. Roaches
   d. Flies
4. Vacation
   a. Summer
   b. Holiday
   c. Seashore
   d. Weekend
5. Mattresses
   a. Double
   b. Twin
   c. Queen
   d. Firm
6. Books
   a. Novels
   b. Biographies
   c. Boring
   d. Short stories
7. Wallets
   a. Leather
   b. Plastic
   c. Stolen
   d. Fabric
8. Zoo animals
   a. Flamingo
   b. Peacock
   c. Polar bear
   d. Ostrich
9. Newspaper
   a. Wrapping garbage
   b. Editorials
   c. Making paper planes
   d. Covering floor while painting
10. Exercise
    a. Running
    b. Swimming
    c. Gymnastics
    d. Fatigue
11. Students
    a. First-year
    b. Transfer
    c. Junior
    d. Sophomore
12. Leftovers
    a. Cold chicken
    b. Feed to dog
    c. Reheat
    d. Use in a stew

Sample 4

What Is Really in a Hot Dog?

Now that baseball season is wrapping up, and you've likely eaten your share of ballpark dogs (9 percent of all hot dogs purchased are bought at baseball stadiums, after all), it's the perfect time to delve into what's really in one of America's favorite foods: the hot dog. It's the subject of many urban legends, the object of many grade-schoolers' double dares: do hot dogs contain pig snouts and chicken feathers, or are they really made from high-quality meat?

The debate certainly hasn't put a damper on Americans' enthusiasm for the food. The U.S. population consumes about 20 billion hot dogs a year, according to the National Hot Dog and Sausage Council. That works out to about 70 hot dogs per person, per year. And, an estimated 95 percent of U.S. homes serve hot dogs at one meal or another. Wondering how many hot dogs are sold each year? In 2005, retail stores sold 764 million packages of hot dogs (not including Wal-Mart), which adds up to more than $1.5 billion in retail sales.

What's in a Hot Dog?

On to the million-dollar question: what are hot dogs made of ? According to the National Hot Dog and Sausage Council: All hot dogs are cured and cooked sausages that consist of mainly pork, beef, chicken and turkey or a combination of meat and poultry. Meats used in hot dogs come from the muscle of the animal and looks much like what you buy in the grocer's case. Other ingredients include water, curing agents and spices, such as garlic, salt, sugar, ground mustard, nutmeg, coriander and white pepper. However, there are a couple of caveats. "Variety meats", which include things like liver, kidneys and hearts, may be used in processed meats like hot dogs, but the U.S. Department of Agriculture requires that they be disclosed in the ingredient label as "with variety meats" or "with meat by-products". Further, watch out for statements like "made with mechanically separated meats (MSM)." Mechanically separated meat is "a paste-like and batter-like meat product produced by forcing bones, with attached edible meat, under high pressure through a sieve or similar device to separate the bone from the edible meat tissue," according to the U.S. Food Safety and Inspection Service (FSIS).

Although the FSIS maintains that MSM are safe to eat, mechanically separated beef is no longer allowed in hot dogs or other processed meats (as of 2004) because of fears of mad cow disease. Hot dogs can contain no more than 20 percent mechanically separated pork, and any amount of mechanically separated chicken or turkey. So if you're looking for the purest franks, pick those that are labeled "all beef" "all pork" or "all chicken, turkey, etc." Franks labeled in this way must be made with meat from a single species and do not include by-products. (But check the label anyway, just to be sure. Turkey and chicken franks, for instance, can include turkey or chicken meat and turkey or chicken skin and fat in proportion to a turkey or chicken carcass.)

Are Hot Dogs Unhealthy?

Eating lots of processed meats like hot dogs has been linked to an increased risk of cancer. Part of that risk is probably due to the additives used in the meats, namely sodium nitrite and MSG. Sodium nitrite (or sodium nitrate) is used as a preservative, coloring and flavoring in hot dogs (and other processed meats), and studies have found it can lead to the formation of cancer-causing chemicals called nitrosamines. MSG, a flavor enhancer used in hot dogs and many other processed foods, has been labeled as an "excitotoxin", which, according to Dr. Russell Blaylock, an author and neurosurgeon, are "a group of excitatory amino acids that can cause sensitive neurons to die".

If you love hot dogs and are looking for a healthier alternative, opt for nitrate free, organic varieties (available in health food stores and increasingly in regular supermarkets) that contain all meat, no byproducts and no artificial flavors, colors or preservatives.

(from *SixWise. com*)

Task 4.27

Answer the following questions according to the essay.

1. How does this article illustrate division rather than classification?
2. What is the main purpose of this article? What kinds of readers might be especially interested in this topic?
3. Why the author include the figures on hot dog consumption and sales?
4. What is gained by quoting directly from such organizations as the U. S. Department of Agriculture and the U. S. Food Safety and Inspection Service?
5. What warnings about hot dog variety are presented through use of description, definition, and examples? Were any of the details surprising to you?
6. Did this article successfully persuade you to follow the advice given in its conclusion? Why or why not?

Sample 5

Race in America

Because of intermarriage, most Americans have multiple ethnic and racial identities. Some persons of mixed lineage prefer to assume culturally nondescript identities. For example, they have become white people, black people, Indians, Latinos, Asians, or just plain Americans in order to somehow deflect from themselves any connection with their ancestors. The task of tracing their families has become too taxing or too insignificant. Even so, the effects of ethnicity and race are pervasive: disparate patterns of community relationships and economic opportunities haunt us. At some time in their history, all ethnic groups in the United States have been the underclass. Also, at different times, all ethnic groups have been both the oppressed and the oppressors.

Ethnicity is the most distinguishing characteristic of Americans, where we are sorted primarily on the basis of our cultural identities or nationalities. An ethnic group is a culturally distinct population whose members share a collective identity and a common heritage. Historically, the overwhelming majority of ethnic groups emerged in the United States as a result of one of several responses to the following processes: ① migration, ② consolidation of group forces in the face of an impending threat from an aggressor, ③ annexation or changes in political boundary lines, or ④ schisms within a church. Hence, ethnic minority presupposes people different from the mainstream or dominant cultured persons.

But it is the erroneous belief that people who come to America can be placed in categories based on their unique gene pools that has resulted in the most blatant instances of discrimination. Races, however defined, do not correspond to genetic reality because inbreeding world populations share a common gene pool. A much more practical dictum, and one that has often been ignored throughout American history, is that all people belong to the same species. Unfortunately, too few individuals believe that the only race of any significance is the human race.

A Brief History

At the time of the American Revolution, the American population was largely composed of English Protestants who had absorbed a substantial number of German and Scotch-Irish settlers and a smaller number of French, Dutch,

Swedes, Poles, Swiss, Irish, and other immigrants. The colonies had a modest number of Catholics, and a smaller number of Jews. Excluding Quakers and Swedes, the colonists treated Native Americans with contempt and hostility, and engaged in wars against them that bordered on genocide. They drove natives from the coastal plains in order to make way for a massive white movement to the West. Although Africans, most of whom were slaves, comprised one-fifth of the American population during the Revolution, they, similar to Indians, were not perceived by most white colonists as being worthy of assimilation.

The white peoples of the new nation had long since crossed Caucasian lines to create a conglomerate but culturally homogeneous society. People of different ethnic groups English, Irish, German, Huguenot, Dutch, Swedish mingled and intermarried. English settlers and peoples from western and northern Europe had begun a process of ethnic assimilation that caused some writers to incorrectly describe the nation as melted into one ethnic group: American. In reality, non-Caucasian Americans were not included in the Eurocentric cultural pot.

During the 150 years immediately following the Revolution, large numbers of immigrants came to the United States from eastern European countries. They were the so-called new immigrants. During the latter part of that period, slaves were emancipated, numerous Indian tribes were conquered and forced to relocate to reservations, portions of Mexico's land were taken, and Asians began emigrating to the United States. The English language and English-oriented cultural patterns grew even more dominant. Despite a proliferation of cultural diversity within the growing ethnic enclaves, Anglo-conformity ideology spawned racist notions about Nordic and Aryan racial superiority. This ideology gave rise to nativist political agendas and exclusionist immigration policies favoring western and northern European immigrants.

Non-English-speaking western Europeans and northern Europeans were also discriminated against. The slowness of some of those immigrants, particularly Germans, to learn English, their tendency to live in enclaves, and their establishment of ethnic-language newspapers were friction points. Such ethnic-oriented lifestyles prompted many Americanized people to chide: If they don't like it here, they can go back to where they came from. But that solution was too simplistic. Immigrants from all countries and cultures, even those who were deemed socially and religiously undesirable, were needed to help build a nation to work the farms, dig the ore, build railroads and canals, settle the prairies, and otherwise provide human resources.

Beginning in the 1890s, immigrants from eastern and southern Europe were numerically dominant. That set the stage for racist statements about inferior, darker people threatening the purity of blond, blue-eyed Nordics or Aryans through miscegenation. Intermixture was perceived as a deadly plague. Although the immigrants from eastern and southern Europe were not suitable marriage partners, their critics stated, they could be properly assimilated and amalgamated. This kind of ethnocentrism prevented large numbers of other immigrants and indigenous peoples of color from becoming fully functioning citizens. And the legacy for the children of people denied equal opportunities was second-class citizenship. We can easily document the negative effects of second-class citizenship: abhorrent inequalities, unwarranted exclusions, and atmospheres of rejection.

Immigrants who lived in remote, isolated areas were able to maintain some semblance of being ethnic nations within America. But the growth of cities brought about the decline of farming populations and ethnic colonies. A short time was required for the white immigrants who settled in cities to discard their native languages and cultures. But it is erroneous to think of any ethnic group as melting away without leaving a trace of its cultural heritage. All ethnic groups have infused portions of their cultures into the tapestry of American history.

Early twentieth-century eastern European immigrants were a very disparate mixture of peoples. They came from nations that were trying to become states Poland, Czechoslovakia, Lithuania, and Yugoslavia; from states trying to become nations Italy, Turkey, and Greece; and from areas outside the Western concept of either state or nation. All of them included people such as Jews who did not easily fit into any of those categories. Through social and educational movements, laws, and superordinate goals such as winning wars and establishing economic world superiority, eastern Europeans and other white ethnic groups were able to enter mainstream America.

The cultures and colors of Third World ethnic groups were in stark contrast to European immigrants. Those differences became obstacles to assimilation and, more importantly, to people of color achieving equal opportunities. Nonwhite groups in the United States occupied specific low status niches in the workplace, which in turn resulted in similarities among their members in such things as occupations, standard of living, level of education, place of residence, access to political power, and quality of health care. Likenesses within those groups facilitated the formation of stereotypes and prejudices that inhibited the full citizenship of nonwhite minorities.

Immigrants who held highly esteemed occupations lawyers, artists, engineers, scientists, and physicians became Americanized much faster than those who held less esteemed positions unskilled laborers, farm workers, coal miners, and stock clerks. But even in those instances there were pro-European biases and stereotypes. For example, French chefs, Italian opera singers, Polish teachers, German conductors, and Russian scientists were more highly recruited than Africans, Hispanics, and Asians who had the same skills. Racial and quasi-racial groups including American Indians, Mexican Americans, Asian Americans, African Americans, and Puerto Ricans were not nearly so readily absorbed as various Caucasian ethnic groups. And that is generally the situation today. Despite numerous and impressive gains during the past century, a disproportionate number of peoples of color are still treated like pariahs.

What Does the Future Hold?

If U.S. Census Bureau population projections are correct, our nation is undergoing mind-boggling demographic changes: Hispanics will triple in numbers, from 31.4 million in 1999 to 98.2 million in 2050; blacks will increase 70 percent, from 34.9 million to 59.2 million; Asians and Pacific Islanders will triple, from 10.9 million to 37.6 million; Native Americans and Alaska Natives will increase from approximately 2.2 million to 2.6 million. During the same period, the non-Hispanic white population will increase from 196.1 million to 213 million. Also, the foreign-born population, most of them coming from Asia and Latin America, will increase from 26 million to 53.8 million. The non-Hispanic white population will decrease from 72 percent of the total population in 1999 to 52 percent in 2050, and the nation's workforce will be composed of over 50 percent racial and ethnic minorities and immigrants. Who then will be the pariahs?

Without equal opportunities, the melting pot will continue to be an unreachable mirage, a dream of equality deferred, for too many people of color. This does not in any way detract from the significance of the things minorities have achieved. Ethnic-group histories and lists of cultural contributions support the contention that each group is an integral part of a whole nation. Although all American ethnic minority groups have experienced continuous socioeconomic gains, the so-called playing field that includes white participants is not yet level. Simply stated, the rising tide of economic prosperity has not yet lifted the masses of people of color. Whatever our life circumstances, the citizens of the United States are bound together not as separate ethnic groups but as members of different ethnic groups united in spirit and behavior and locked into a common destiny.

There is little doubt that our nation is at a crossroads in its race relations. Where we go from here is up to all of us. We can try segregation again, continuance of the status quo, silence in the face of prejudice and discriminatory practices, or activism. The choice is ours.

Segregation of ethnic minorities is not a redeeming choice for the United States. It did not work during earlier times, and it will not work now. There have never been separate but equal majority-group and minority-group communities in the United States. And the pretense of such a condition would once again be a particularly pernicious injustice to all citizens. Racial segregation diminishes both the perpetrators and their victims. Preserving the status quo in education, employment, health care, and housing, which so often is little more than codified racial discrimination, is not justice for minorities either.

Inaction by people who witness oppressive acts is equally unacceptable. Even though they may be shocked and frustrated by the problems, standing in wide-eyed horror is not an adequate posture to assume. While they may be legally absolved of any wrongdoing, these silent people must come to terms with what others believe to be their moral culpability. Of course, silence may be prudent. Usually, there is a high price to be paid by those who would challenge racism in community institutions. Friends, jobs, promotions, and prestige may be lost. Furthermore, few victories come easily, and most of the victors are unsung heroes.

Individuals who choose to challenge purveyors of bigotry and unequal opportunities must also take care that in their actions to redress racial injustices, they do not emulate the oppressors whom they deplore. That might makes right, that blood washes out injustices these too are false strategies for achieving justice. It does not matter much to a slave what the color of his master is, a wise black janitor once said. We, the descendants of migrants, immigrants, and slaves, can build a better nation a place where all people have safe housing, get a top-quality education, do meaningful work for adequate wages, are treated fairly in criminal-justice systems, have their medical needs met, and in the end die a timely death unhurried by bigots. This is the kind of history that should be made.

(From *a special issue on race in America in the spring* 2000 *issue of National Forum* by George Henderson)

Task 4.28

Answer the questions according to the essay.
1. What techniques, organization patterns, and details distinguish this as a *classification* essay?
2. In your own words, what is the author's view of people who identify themselves by race?
3. Can you provide two examples of injustices that have happened in American society as a result of racial differences as mentioned by the author?

Transition words for classification or division essays

classify	divide
classification	division
kinds	types
aspects	classes
parts	categories
factors	regions
sources	attributes
characteristics	qualities
kinds of	basic kinds
minor	primary
secondary	opposite
opposing	differences
similar	similarities
dissimilar	dissimilarities

according to   with respect to

fall into... categories

can be divided into... kinds/types/classes/parts

Task 4.29

Below are four topics to develop into a classification paragraph. Each one is classified into three categories. Choose one topic to develop into a paragraph.

Topic 1
Supermarket Shoppers
1. Slow, careful shoppers
2. Average shoppers
3. Hurried shoppers

Topic 2
Eaters
1. Very conservative eaters
2. Typical eaters
3. Adventurous eaters

Topic 3
Types of Housekeepers
1. Never clean
2. Clean on a regular basis
3. Clean constantly

Topic 4
Attitudes toward Money
1. Tight-fisted
2. Reasonable
3. Extravagant

Task 4.29

Write a classification or division essay on one of the following topics:

1. Attitudes Toward Life
2. Presents
3. Mothers (or Fathers)
4. Commercials
5. Neighbors

Use the following revision form to check for the basics in your classification/division essay draft.

Overall

1. Does the essay categorize two or more subjects with specific characteristics?
   (Yes/No)
2. Does the essay use specific categories consistently and clearly?
   (Yes/No)
3. Are the paragraphs broken up well and about the right length?
   (Yes/No)

Introduction

4. Is the title interesting and in the correct format?
   (Yes/No)
5. Is there a general introduction that sets up the thesis and categories?
   (Yes/No)
6. Is there a clear thesis statement that explains the purpose of the classifications being made?
   (Yes/No)

Body

7. Do the ideas in the body paragraphs develop the categories and flow smoothly?
   (Yes/No)
8. Are transitions used between and, when needed, within the paragraphs?
   (Yes/No)
9. Do the body paragraphs include support (descriptive details and examples)?
   (Yes/No)

Conclusion

10. Does the concluding paragraph sum up the categories with analysis and re-emphasize the purpose developed in the introductory paragraph and thesis, without adding new ideas?
(Yes/No)

Editing

11. Circle the following errors you think you see in this draft: spelling errors, fragments, run-ons/comma splices, errors in comma and semicolon/colon use, pronoun disagreement, reference fault errors, and errors in parallelism, apostrophe use, verb use/tense, and passive voice construction.
12. Other types of grammar or sentence-level errors:
   _____
   _____
   _____

Comments

_____
_____
_____

4.8 An Argumentative Essay

Thinking over Questions before Writing

➤ What is my stand on this issue?
➤ Is there a plan of action I can propose to solve a problem?
➤ Who would disagree with my stand or solution, and why? (What are the counterarguments?)
➤ What examples and evidence can I provide to support my arguments and claims?
➤ How will I organize my arguments and evidence?
➤ How will I conclude my essay?

Some argumentative essays declare the best solution to a problem; others argue a certain way of looking at an issue; still others may urge adoption of a specific proposal or plan of action. Whatever our exact purpose, our argumentative essay should be composed of a clear thesis and body paragraphs that offer enough sensible reasons and persuasive evidence to convince our readers to agree with us.

4.8.1 Purpose of Argumentative Essays

An argument follows when two groups disagree about something. People can have different opinions and can offer reasons in support of their arguments. However, sometimes it might be difficult to convince the other group because the argument could be based on a matter of preference, or religious faith. Therefore, **arguments of preference, belief or faith are NOT the type of arguments.** The kind of argument that can be argued logically is one based on an opinion that can be supported by **evidence** such as facts.

An argumentative essay is also one that attempts/tries to **change the reader's mind, to convince the reader to agree with the point of view of the writer.** For that reason, the argumentative essay attempts to be **highly**

persuasive and logical. For example, a thesis such as "My first experiences with Americans were shocking" has a central idea 'shocking' but it is *not* really strongly persuasive, and it is certainly not argumentative.

When we write an argumentative essay, assume that the reader disagrees with us. But remember that our reader *is no less* intelligent than us. So, write **objectively**, **LOGICALLY and RESPECTFULLY.** Try to understand our opponent's point of view. If we do not, we are not likely to convince the reader.

4.8.2　Errors on Logic When Constructing Arguments

Argument essays are apt to fall prey to logical fallacies—that is, errors in reasoning. The tone and fair-minded logic of our essay's arguments are essential to persuading our readers of our point and maintaining our credibility. We need to assess our intended audience carefully in order to choose the most effective tone, approach, and evidence to provide in support of our claims and arguments. Moreover, we need to make sure we haven't oversimplified the subject, our arguments, or our oppositions arguments. we must appear logical or our readers will reject our point of view. Here is a short list of some of the most common *logical fallacies*. Check your rough drafts carefully to avoid these problems.

4.8.3　Common Logical Fallacies Include

(1) Hasty generalization: The writer bases the argument on insufficient or unrepresentative evidence.

  e. g. I believe all poodles are vicious dogs because my two poodles both bit me.

  I'm certain the students lack of motivation is related to changes in modern music.

(2) Non sequitur ("it doesn't follow"): The writer's conclusion is not necessarily a logical result of the facts.

  e. g. Professor Smith is a famous chemist, so he will be a brilliant chemistry teacher.

  We know why it rained today: because I washed my car.

(3) Begging the question: The writer presents as truth what is not yet proven by the argument.

  e. g. Good parenting would have prevented all of these social problems. All of our society's major problems are a direct result of bad parenting.

(4) Red herring: The writer introduces an irrelevant point to divert the readers' attention from the main issue.

  e. g. I hear that many soldiers suffer from depression after returning home from Iraq. Has anyone looked into why these soldiers signed up for the military in the first place?

  I know I forgot to deposit the check into the bank yesterday. But, nothing I do pleases you.

(5) Post hoc, ergo porpter hoc ("after this, therefore because of this"): The writer assume that because one event follows another in time, the first event caused the second.

Most of our superstitions are *post hoc* fallacies; we now realize that bad luck after walking under a ladder is a matter of coincidence, not cause and effect.

  e. g. I decided to wear my striped shirt the day I aced my chemistry exam, so if I wear it again today, I should do great in my English test.

(6) Argument *ad hominem* ("to the man"): The writer attacks the opponent's character rather than the opponent's argument.

  e. g. Dr. Bloom can't be a competent marriage counselor because she's been divorced.

  He is so stupid that his argument couldn't possibly be true.

(7) Faulty use of authority: The writer relies on "authorities" who are not convincing sources.

Although someone may be well known in a particular field, he or she may not be qualified to testify in a different area.

  e. g. To find out whether or not sludge-mining really is endangering the Tuskogee salamander's breeding grounds, we interviewed the supervisors of the sludge-mines, who declared there is no problem.

(8) Argument *ad populum* ("to the people"): The writer evades the issues by appealing to readers' emotional reactions to certain subjects.

Instead of arguing the facts of an issue, a writer might play on the readers' negative response to such words as "socialism" "terrorist" or "radical", and their positive response to words like "God" "country" "liberty" or "patriotic".

 e. g. If you are a true American, you will vote against the referendum on flag burning.

 The majority of people like soda. Therefore, soda is good.

(9) Circular thinking: The argument goes in an endless circle, with each step of the argument relying on a previous one, which in turn relies on the first argument yet to be proven.

 e. g. I am a good worker because Frank says so. How can we trust Frank? Simple: I will vouch for him.

 God exists because the Bible says so. The Bible is inspired. Therefore, we know that God exists.

(10) Bandwagon appeal: The writer tries to validate a point by intimating that "everyone else believes in this".

Such a tactic evades discussion of the issue itself. Advertising often uses this technique.

 e. g. Everyone who demands real taste smokes Phooey cigarettes.

 Popular/beautiful/"cool"/rich people use/buy/wear "X"; if you use "X", you too will be popular/beautiful/etc.

(11) False dilemma fallacy: This fallacy is also known as the either/or fallacy. The writer presents only two sides to a complex issue that may have many sides.

 e. g. You're either with us or against us.

 If you don't support our request for more library funding, then you are anti student success.

(12) Faulty analogy: The writer uses an extended comparison as proof of a point.

 e. g. Education is like cake; a small amount tastes sweet, but eat too much and your teeth will rot out. Likewise, more than two years of education is bad for a student.

(13) Equivocation: Using the same term in an argument in different places but the word has different meanings.

 e. g. Plato says the end of a thing is its perfection; I say that death is the end of life; hence, death is the perfection of life.

Here the word *end* means "goal" in Plato's usage, but it means "last event" or "termination" in the author's second usage. Clearly, the speaker is twisting Plato's meaning of the word to draw a very different conclusion.

4.8.4 Thesis Statement in Argumentative Essays

The argumentative thesis takes **a side of an issue**; frequently it proposes an approach of action which is often expressed with the modal ***should***.

In the argument concerning the **nuclear power plant**, the thesis for a paper on this topic might be:

Governments **should ban further construction** of nuclear power plants.

Someone else might argue:

The U.S **should continue building** nuclear power plants.

4.8.5 Organizing the Argumentative Essay

When **planning the argumentative essay**, we should be aware that the essay contains the following characteristics.

(1) The argumentative essay should **introduce and explain the issue or case.** The reader needs to understand what the issue is going to being argue.

(2) The essay should **offer reasons and support** for those reasons. In other words, the essay should prove its point.

(3) The essay should **refute opposing arguments.** (refute: to prove wrong by argument or to show that something is invalid/untrue/illogical)

(4) The conclusion of the essay should **impress the audience.**

Sample 1 is an argumentative essay **giving opinions.** Look at the organization pattern of this kind of essay:

I. Introduction: State your opinion clearly without using too many personal opinion words.

II. Body: Give the first point supporting your opinion.

Give the second point supporting your opinion.

Give the last point supporting your opinion.

III. Conclusion: Restate your opinion, using different words.

Sample 1

The Right to Die

A difficult problem that is facing society is euthanasia, another word for mercy killing. Thousands of young people are mortally ill because of incurable disease. They are all kept alive in artificial ways. They have no chance to recover completely, but most of the legal systems do not allow doctors to end their lives. However, fatally ill patients should be allowed to die for several reasons.

The first reason is that medical costs are very high. The cost of a hospital room can be as much as a hundred dollars per day and even more. The costs of medicines and medical tests are also high. The family of the patient is responsible for these expenses. Consequently, they would be a terrible financial burden for them for a long time.

The second reason is that the family suffers. The nurses can only give the terminally ill patient minimum care. The family must spend time to care for the special needs of their loved one. They should talk, touch, and hold the patient even though he or she may be in a coma. For example, Karen Quinlan's parents visited her every day even though she was unable to speak or to see. Also, it is very difficult to watch a loved one in a coma because his or her condition does not improve.

The third and most important reason is that the patients have no chance of recovery. They can never lead normal lives and must be kept alive by life-support machines. They may need a machine to breathe and a feeding tube to take in food. They are more dead than alive and will never get better. For example, in 1975, Karen Quinlan became unconscious after the she swallowed some drugs and drank alcohol. She was kept alive by machines. Her parents knew that her body and brain would never be normal. Therefore, they asked the court to allow their daughter to die. The judge agreed, and Karen's breathing machine was turned off. She was able to breathe on her own, but she died nine years later in June of 1985.

In conclusion, because terminally ill patients have no chance to live normal lives, they should be allowed to die with dignity. Therefore, the family should have the right to ask to turn off the life-support machines or to stop further medical treatment.

Task 4.31

Underline transition words in the essay.

Task 4.32

Read the essay carefully and answer the questions.
1. What is euthanasia?
2. What would be a terrible financial burden for the family?
3. How does the family suffer?
4. Which sentence expresses the writer's opinion about the right to die?
5. Do you agree with the writer's argument? Why or Why not?

  The following two samples are about the question whether dangerous sports, such as boxing or motor-racing, should be banned. Compare the different points the authors hold.

Sample 2

Dangerous Sports: No

  Millions of people play sport every day, and, inevitably, some suffer injury or pain. Most players and spectators accept this risk. However, some people would like to see dangerous sports such as boxing banned. In my opinion, dangerous sports should be banned for a number of reasons.

  The first reason is that some sports are nothing but an excuse for violence. Boxing is a perfect example. The last thing an increasingly violent world needs is more violence on our television. The sight of two men (or even women) bleeding, with faces ripped open, trying to obliterate each other is barbaric. Other sports, such as American football or rugby, are also barely-concealed violence.

  Some people argue that the players can choose to participate. However this is not always the case. Many boxers, for example, come from disadvantaged backgrounds. They are lured by money or by social or peer pressure and then cannot escape. Even in richer social groups, schools force unwilling students to play aggressive team sports, claiming that playing will improve the students' character (or the school's reputation), but in fact increasing the risk of injury.

Even where people can choose, they sometimes need to be protected against themselves. Most people approve of governments' efforts to reduce smoking. In the same way, governments need to act if there are unacceptably high levels of injuries in sports such as football, diving, mountaineering, or motor-racing.

I accept that all sports involve challenge and risk. However violence and aggression should not be permitted in the name of sport. Governments and individuals must act to limit brutality and violence, so that children and adults can enjoy and benefit from sport.

Sample 3

Save our Sports!

Today, many sports are becoming increasingly regulated. Boxing, rugby, soccer, and other games are being targeted by sports bodies and medical organizations in an effort to improve safety standards and to reduce injuries. However, for some people, this is not enough, and they would rather see some dangerous sports banned completely. In this essay, I will examine some arguments against banning dangerous sports.

Sports, competition, and games seem to be natural to humans. Young children learn their own limits and strengths through play with others, but they also learn valuable social lessons about what acceptable behavior and the rights of others. Sport therefore is not just a physical phenomenon, but a mental and social one.

Challenging sport provides a healthy, largely safe, physical outlet for aggression. There is very little evidence to show that people who take part in dangerous sports become violent as a result. In fact it is more likely that apart from the many friendships created in playing, sport acts as a safety valve for a society by reducing stress. Moreover, sport teaches and requires discipline, training, and respect for the rules—valuable lessons in any society.

Almost all sports involve some risk. Young rugby players are paralysed every year in scrums. Scuba-diving accidents can lead to brain damage or death. Even golf or jogging can lead to pain or injury. Without some elements of risk or challenge, sport becomes meaningless. A marathon runner trying to improve his time, basketball players fiercely battling an opposing team, or a sky-diving team defying gravity—all are trying to push themselves to their maximum. There is therefore no sport without danger.

There is also the issue of freedom. Without a wide range of sports, many people would feel trapped or limited. People should be free to participate in activities with others as long as it does not affect the safety of non-participants.

There also should be limits to the power of governments to ban sports. If one sport is banned because of alleged danger, then what sport would be next? Boxing is the most common target of opponents of dangerous sports. But if boxing is banned, would motor racing follow, then rugby, wrestling, or weightlifting? Furthermore, many sports would go underground, leading to increased injury and illegal gambling.

Nobody denies that regulation is needed. Medical bodies have introduced safety rules in boxing, in soccer, and these safety regulations have been welcomed by players. But the role of government should be reduced.

In conclusion, our society would be healthier if more people took part in sports of all kinds. We should continue to try to prevent accidents and injuries. However, we should also ensure that sports are challenging, exciting, and, above all, fun.

Sample 4 and sample 5 are argumentative essays expressing Pros and Cons. There are three possible organization patterns. Which pattern do they belong to?

Pattern 1:

I. Introduction: Thesis statement

II. Body: Pros

        Con(s) + Refutation(s)

III. Conclusion

Pattern 2:

I. Introduction: Thesis statement

II. Body: Con(s) + Refutation(s)

        Pros

III. Conclusion

Pattern 3:

I. Introduction: Thesis statement

II. Body: Con idea 1 ⟶ Refutation

　　　　　Con idea 2 ⟶ Refutation
　　　　　Con idea 3 ⟶ Refutation
　Ⅲ. Conclusion
Pattern 4:
　Ⅰ. Introduction: Thesis statement
　Ⅱ. Body: Pros
　　　　　Cons
　Ⅲ. Conclusion: Giving a well-balanced consideration

Sample 4

Which is Better—Raising Children to Be Competitive or Cooperative?

　There are two schools of thought on how to bring up children so that they can take their place in society. These choices are competition and co-operation. In my opinion, encouraging children to be co-operative is better than making them competitive but there are two sides to the argument.

　One reason why I believe cooperation is better is that society needs people who are willing and able to work with others. This is because teamwork is very important in many jobs today. Another issue is that adults who are able to collaborate are able to listen and give advice to others. This will make society stronger as everyone moves forward. Last, I would also argue that teaching children to co-operate will turn them into responsible adults who are willing to share their knowledge and skills with their family, friends, and colleagues.

　However, there are also arguments in favour of encouraging competition among children. One is that society needs leaders to drive us onwards. Entrepreneurs are people who rise to the top by being competitive and they create jobs for other people. Another point is that in areas like sports, even though teamwork is important, athletes still need to be competitive in order to succeed. Finally, people often have to compete in the real world and there is a danger of being left behind if they haven't learned how to make the best of themselves.

　Both competition and cooperation have strong merits. Children who have been taught to work together will probably become more valuable members of society but the ability to compete should not be overlooked.

Sample 5

Health and Healing at Your Fingertips

Throw out the bottles and boxes of drugs in your house. A new theory suggests that medicine could be bad for your health, which should at least come as good news to people who cannot afford to buy expensive medicine. However, it is a blow to the medicine industry, and an even bigger blow to our confidence in the progress of science. This new theory argues that healing is at our fingertips: we can be healthy by doing Reiki on a regular basis.

Supporters of medical treatment argue that medicine should be trusted since it is effective and scientifically proven. They say that there is no need for spiritual methods such as Reiki, Yoga, Tai Chi. These waste our time, something which is quite precious in our material world. There is medicine that can kill our pain, X-rays that show us our fractured bones or MRI that scans our brain for tumors. We must admit that these methods are very effective in the examples that they provide. However, there are some "every day complaints" such as back pains, headaches, insomnia, which are treated currently with medicine. When you have a headache, you take an Aspirin, or Vermidon, when you cannot sleep, you take Xanax without thinking of the side effects of these. When you use these pills for a long period, you become addicted to them; you cannot sleep without them. We pay huge amounts of money and become addicted instead of getting better. How about a safer and more economical way of healing? When doing Reiki to yourself, you do not need anything except your energy so it is very economical. As for its history, it was discovered in Japan in the early 1900s and its popularity has spread particularly throughout America and Western Europe. In quantum physics, energy is recognized as the fundamental substance of which the universe is composed. Reiki depends on the energy within our bodies. It is a simple and effective way of restoring the energy flow. There are no side effects and it is scientifically explained.

Opponents of alternative healing methods also claim that serious illnesses such as HIV/AIDS and cancer cannot be treated without drugs. They think so because these patients spend the rest of their lives in the hospital taking medicine. How can Reiki make these people healthy again? It is very unfortunate that these patients have to live in the hospital losing their hair because of chemotherapy, losing weight because of the side effects of the medicine they take. Actually, it is common knowledge that except for when the cancer is diagnosed at an early stage, drugs also cannot treat AIDS or cancer. Most of the medicine these patients use are to ease their pain and their sufferings because of the medical treatment they undergo. Instead of drugs which are expensive and have many side effects, you can use your energy to overcome the hardships of life, find an emotional balance, leave the stress of everyday life and let go of the everyday worries. Most of the chronic conditions such as eczema or migraine are known to have causes such as poor diet and stress. Deep rooted anger or other strong emotions can contribute to viral infections as well. Since balancing our emotions and controlling our thoughts are very important for our well-being, we should definitely start learning Reiki and avoid illnesses before it is too late.

Some people may still maintain that in our material world, everything depends on time. It is even "lacking time" that causes much of the stress that leads to the illnesses we mentioned. How would it be possible to find time to do Reiki to ourselves and the people around us when we cannot even find time to go to the theater? This is one good thing about Reiki; it does not require more than 15 minutes of our time. There is no need for changing clothes or special equipment. It is a wonderfully simple healing art, an effective method of relaxation and stress-relief. Most important of all, it is less time consuming than medicine if we think of all the time we spend taking medicine for some complaints and taking some more for the side effects as well.

Having said these, resistance to Reiki would be quite illogical. Reiki is natural and drug-free. What is more, it is easy to learn by anyone, regardless of age and experience. It can be used anywhere, anytime. It also enhances physical, mental, emotional and spiritual well-being and the benefits last a lifetime. It is definitely high time to get away from the drug boxes we store in our drug cabinet!

(by Oya Ozagac, September 2004 Copyright @ 2005 Bogazici University SFL)

Sample 6 is an argumentative essay of the advantages and disadvantages. You can start your essay by making a *general statement* and then *divide the advantages and disadvantages into two separate paragraphs.*

Sample 6

Importance of Tourists and Tourism

This question can be looked at from several points of view. Firstly, tourism should be considered in relation to a country's economy. Secondly, it can be seen in terms of its effect on the countryside and environment. Thirdly, the influence of the tourist industry on culture must be taken into account.

The economy of a country often benefits as a result of tourism; foreign visitors come and spend their money, and this creates jobs for those who run hotels and restaurants. However, there are also certain drawbacks. Whereas the people directly involved in the industry may benefit, others may find that they are worse off. This is because the cost of living goes up and goods become more expensive since tourists are prepared to pay more for them.

As far as the effect on the environment is concerned, tourism is often a bad thing. While it is true to say that development results in better roads being built improvements for poorer areas, it is sometimes also very harmful. In some countries, huge hotels and skyscrapers have ruined areas of unspoilt beauty.

The cultural influence of tourism is difficult to measure. In some countries foreign influence can destroy the local way of life. On the other hand, countries which do not encourage tourism may miss the benefits that foreign technology and investment can bring.

In conclusion, it can be seen that tourism has both advantages an disadvantages; if it is controlled properly, it can be good for a country, but there will always be a danger that it may do a great deal of harm.

Sample 7

Can You Be Educated from a Distance?

By almost any measure, there is a boom in Internet-based instruction. In just a few years, thirty-four percent of American colleges and universities have begun offering some form of what's called distance learning (DL), and among the larger schools, it s closer to ninety percent. If you doubt the popularity of the trend, you probably haven't heard of the University of Phoenix. It grants degrees entirely on the basis of online instruction. It enrolls 90,000 students, a statistic used to support its claim to be the largest private university in the country.

While the kinds of instruction offered in these programs will differ, DL usually signifies a course in which the instructors post syllabi, reading assignments, and schedules on websites, and students send in their written assignments by e-mail. Other forms of communication often come into play, such as threaded messaging, which allows for posting questions and comments that are publicly viewable, as a bulletin board would, as well as chat rooms for real-time interchanges. Generally speaking, face-to-face communication with an instructor is minimized or eliminated altogether.

The attraction for students might at first seem obvious. Primarily, there's the convenience promised by courses on the Net: you can do the work, as they say, in your pajamas. But figures indicate that the reduced effort results in a reduced commitment to the course. While the attrition rate for all freshmen at American universities is around twenty percent, the rate for online students is thirty-five percent. Students themselves seem to understand the weaknesses inherent in the setup. In a survey conducted for Cornell, the DL division of Cornell University, less than a third of the respondents expected the quality of the online course to be as good as the classroom course.

Clearly, from the schools perspective, there's a lot of money to be saved. Although some of the more ambitious programs require new investments in servers and networks to support collaborative software, most DL courses can run on existing or minimally upgraded systems. The more students who enroll in a course but don't come to campus, the more the school saves on keeping the lights on in the classrooms, paying custodians, and maintaining parking lots. And, while there's evidence that instructors must work harder to run a DL course for a variety of reasons, they won't be paid any more, and might well be paid less.

But as a rule, those who champion distance learning don't base their arguments on convenience or cost savings. More often, they claim DL signals an advance in the effectiveness of education. Consider the vigorous case made by Fairleigh Dickinson University (FDU), in Madison, New Jersey, where students regardless of their expectations or desires are now required to take one DL course per year. By setting this requirement, FDU claims that it recognizes the Internet as a premier learning tool of the current technological age. Skill in using online resources prepares our students, more than others, for life-long learning—for their jobs, their careers, and their personal growth.

Moreover, Internet-based courses will connect FDU students to a global virtual faculty, a group of world-class scholars, experts, artists, politicians, and business leaders around the world.

Sounds pretty good. But do the claims make much sense? First, it should be noted that students today and in the future might well use the Internet with at least as much facility as the faculty. It's not at all clear that they need to be taught such skills. More to the point, how much time and effort do you suppose world-class scholars (much less politicians and business leaders) will expend for the benefit of students they never meet or even see? Probably a lot less than they're devoting to the books, journal articles, and position papers that are already available to anyone with access to a library.

Another justification comes from those who see distance learning as the next step in society's progress toward meritocracy. A recent article in Forbes magazine cites Professor Roger Schank of Northwestern University, who predicts that soon students will be able to shop around, taking a course from any institution that offers a good one. ... Quality education will be available to all. Students will learn what they want to learn rather than what some faculty committee decided was the best practical compromise. In sum, says Professor Schank, who is also chairman of a distance-learning enterprise called CognitiveArts, Education will be measured by what you know rather than by whose name appears on your diploma.

Statements like these assume education consists in acquiring information (what you know). Accept that and it's hard to disagree with the conclusions. After all, what does it matter how, or through what medium, you get the information? But few truly educated people hold such a mechanistic view. Indeed, traditionally, education was aimed at cultivating intellectual and moral values, and the information you picked up was decidedly secondary. It was commonplace for those giving commencement speeches to note that, based on etymology, education is a drawing out, not a putting in. That is, a true education educes, or draws out, from within a person qualities of intellect and character that would otherwise have remained hidden or dormant.

Exactly how this kind of educing happens is hard to pin down. Only in part does it come from watching professors in the classroom present material and respond to student questions, the elements of education that can be translated to the Net with reasonable fidelity. Other educational experiences include things like watching how professors joke with each other (or not) in the hallways, seeing what kinds of pictures are framed in a professor's office, or going out for coffee after class with people in your dorm. Such experiences, and countless others, are sometimes labeled (and dismissed) as social life on campus. But they also contribute invaluably to education. Through them, you learn a style, in the noblest sense of that term, a way of regarding the information you acquire and the society you find yourself in. This is what the philosopher Alfred North Whitehead meant when he called style the ultimate acquisition of a cultivated mind. And it's the mysterious ways of cultivating that style that the poet Robert Frost had in mind when he said that all that a college education requires is that you hang around until you catch on.

Hang around campus, that is, not lurk on the Net.

(James Barszcz)

Task 4.33

Answer the following questions according to the essay.
1. What is the main purpose in this article?
2. Is the drop out (attrition) rate for distance learning (online) students is higher than traditional students?
3. What counterarguments does the author provide to his arguments against distance learning?
4. Can you give an example of one of the author's refutations to one of the counterarguments?
5. What does the author mean, in the last paragraph of the article, when he talks of the importance of learning a style in college?

Transition words for argumentative essays

First	First of all	To begin with
Second	Secondly	In addition
Next	Then	Lastly
Finally	Most of all	For example
For instance	In order to	In addition
Another	Besides	Together with
Along with	Let's not forget	Let's remember
As I just mentioned	For this reason	In fact
Surprisingly	Again	Remember
Please consider/reconsider	In conclusion	This is important because

Task 4.34

Write an argumentative essay on one of the following topics
1. Drivers' Use of Cell Phones while Vehicles Are in Motion Should Be Prohibited
2. Both Parents Should Assume Equal Responsibility in Raising a Child
3. Romantic Love Is a Poor Basis for Marriage
4. College Students Should Have Complete Freedom to Choose Their Own Courses
5. Students Should Not Be Required to Take Physical Education Courses
6. People Have Become Overly Dependent on Technology

Task 4.35

Choose one of the subjects listed below for an argument essay, and narrow that subject to a manageable topic. Then, take a stand on that issue (for or against or proposing a change). Be sure to include the opposition's view and counterarguments, and address them thoroughly.

    traffic problems
    mandatory foreign language classes

obesity in children
overpopulation
beauty contests
chemical fertilizers
pesticide use
genetic engineering
globalization
global warming
nuclear energy
city housing
loss of farmland

Use the following revision form to check for the basics in your argumentative essay draft.

Overall

1. Is the chosen problem from school, your job, or where you live, and is it clear?
   (Yes/No)
2. Is there a clear purpose and argument for change—a plan for a solution?
   (Yes/No)
3. Is the plan for change reasonable—not too extreme? Is it specific?
   (Yes/No)

Introduction

4. Is the title interesting and in the correct format?
   (Yes/No)
5. Is there a good attention grabber and general explanation of the problem?
   (Yes/No)
6. Is the thesis statement a brief and specific summary of the plan for change— a solution? Are the words "should", "must", or "needs to" used to help clarify the proposed plan of action?
   (Yes/No)

Body

7. Do the body paragraphs have clear topic sentences?
   (Yes/No)
8. Does the body of the essay develop, explain, and elaborate the problem with ideas, examples, analysis, and support?
   (Yes/No)
9. Does the body explain in detail exactly how the plan for change will resolve the problem and make a positive change?
   (Yes/No)
10. Does the solution include all details for who, how, and why the solution will work?
    (Yes/No)
11. Does each body paragraph have a good concluding sentence?
    (Yes/No)
12. Are transitions used well both within and between paragraphs?
    (Yes/No)

Conclusion

13. Does the concluding paragraph sum up well without adding new ideas?
    (Yes/No)

Editing

14. Circle the following errors you think you see in this draft: spelling errors, fragments, run-ons/comma splices, errors in comma and semicolon/colon use, pronoun disagreement, reference fault errors, and errors in parallelism, apostrophe use, verb use/tense, and passive voice construction.
15. Other types of grammar or sentence-level errors: _____

Comments

Part II Practical Writing Skills

Chapter 5 Writing for Job Application

An application for employment, job application, or application form (often simply called an application) is a form or collection of forms that an individual seeking employment, called an applicant, must fill out as part of the process of informing an employer of the applicant's availability and desire to be employed, and persuading the employer to offer the applicant employment.

From the employer's perspective, the application serves a number of purposes. These vary depending on the nature of the job and the preferences of the person responsible for hiring, as "each organization should have an application form that reflects its own environment". At a minimum, an application usually requires the applicant to provide information sufficient to demonstrate that he or she is legally permitted to be employed. The typical application also requires the applicant to provide information regarding relevant skills, education, and previous employment. The application itself is a minor test of the applicant's literacy, penmanship, and communication skills-a careless job applicant might disqualify themselves with a poorly filled-out application.

The application may also require the applicant to disclose any criminal record, and to provide information sufficient to enable the employer to conduct an appropriate background check. For a business that employs workers on a part-time basis, the application may inquire as to the applicant's specific times and days of availability, and preferences in this regard. It is important to note, however, that an employer may be prohibited from asking applicants about characteristics that are not relevant to the job, such as their political view or sexual orientation.

For many businesses, applications for employment can be filled out online, and do not have to be submitted in person. However, it is still recommended that applicants bring a printed copy of their application to an interview.

Before knowing exactly about what business writing is, we may as well ask what writing is. People communicate in verbal and nonverbal methods. The verbal way means involving the use of words, either written or spoken, while the nonverbal one refers to the use of facial expressions, gestures, generally regarded as body language. Writing happens to be one of the two ways of verbal communication, the other being speaking. In comparison with speaking, or other verbal ways, writing lacks immediate and face-to-face responses. However, it has clear advantages, too. It usually allows people more time to think logically. And it is easier to record human activities with a pen before the invention of multimedia. So it is at least equal to, if not better than, speaking in its communication power.

The type of writing is always an issue in question. In the development of writing studies, a variety of modifiers have been added to the word "writing", which it leads to a long list of different and overlapping subordinate concepts, for example, expository writing, academic writing, technical writing, etc., and business writing here is familiar course on college programs. Why it is so may be the difference in standards of classification. In other words, people look at writing from different point of view. Another effort is made to distinguish "writing for general purposes" from "writing for specific purposes". The former usually discusses basic writing skills from the choice of words and sentence patterns, through the development paragraphs, to the completion of four discourses, that is to say, narrative, description, exposition and argumentation. The latter is a large family in which business writing is one solid member. Other members include writing for scientific purposes such as a lab report by a scientific after an experiment, or writing for academic purposes such as a graduate thesis by a student.

In short, business writing is writing for business purposes. In the long history of human beings, writing has been serving different purposes in business. As purposes differ, so do the written documents for achieving the purposes. Therefore people often hear businessmen taking about e-mails, memos, minutes, letters, reports, proposals, etc. Among those, letters, memos, e-mails and reports are generally considered as the most basic types of business documents based on their frequency and characteristics in business practices.

When it comes to business writing, people often use different terms, some of which are similar in meaning, such as content and message, format and layout, etc., causing unnecessary inconvenient and even confusion. Based on definition found in some dictionaries, common synonyms are listed as follows:

(1) Content and message.

The word "content" is the topic or matter treated in a written work; the word "message" is a communication in writing, in speech, or by signals. Both refer to what is written in the body of the document.

(2) Form, format, layout and style.

The word "form" is an orderly method of arrangement. The word "format" is a general plan of organization. The word "layout" is the plan or design or arrangement of something laid out. The word "style" is a distinctive quality, form, or type of something. Among these, "style" is the most confusing, as it has many uses. Only when used as in the "full block style" of letters is it close in meaning to "format" or "layout" focusing on the visual arrangement of the document.

(3) Genre, type, category.

A "genre" is a kind, sort, or a category of artistic, musical, or literary composition characterized by a particular style, form, or content; a "type" is one having qualities of a higher category; a "category" is a division within a system of classification.

(4) Tone, attitude.

These two words may often replace each other. The "tone" in writing refers to the writer's attitude toward the reader and the subject of the message. The overall tone of a written message affects the reader just as one's tone of voice affects the listener in everyday communication.

As the definitions suggest, these terms do overlap to some extent, which may partially explain why they are sometimes used interchangeably within each group in business writing. For their simplicity and high frequency of appearance, "content", "format", and "type" are preferred in the rest of this book, though others are also used sometimes.

5.1 Application Letter

A cover (or covering) letter is short and introductory document in the standard business letter format. Generally attached to other documents, a cover letter serves as a brief introduction or provides additional information. In other words, it is a letter that "covers" or introduces something else. For example, a writer may attach a cover letter to the manuscript being sent to a publisher. In the job-application context, a cover letter refers to the self-introducing letter prepared by a job applicant and is sent with the person's CV or resume to a prospective employer.

There are many types of job-related letters serving different purposes at different stages in the whole process of job searching. For example, a letter of inquiry asks questions about possible job opportunities. A thank-you letter shows the interest a candidate has in a position after a job interview. An acceptance letter states that the candidate is accepting the job offered. A declination (or refusal) letter informs the employer that the candidate is no longer interested in the position of offered. A job-application cover letter differs from all these above because it is written, together with the resume, to attract the interest of the employer and finally get the job interview.

5.1.1 How to Write an Application Cover Letter

Application letter plays a vital role in applying for a job in every company. Thought the resume is the last resort for further evaluation, application letter serves as the springboard for the Personnel Officer or the HR head in charge of evaluating applicants' data to be stimulated to go within the resume. This application letter should be well organized, because if it's not, your resume will no longer be seen and surely it will go to the trash bin because the company is not keeping any document without value or if the officers are courteous enough, they will send it back to you.

Application is not an ordinary letter. It should be written with careful attention on the details and the format as well. This letter is to be read by people within the company who's eying for the best applicant to be hired. Thus, organization and of the presented data should be taken into extra-ordinary consideration. You have to watch your subject and verb agreement and the modifiers used.

Application is considered a business letter. Therefore, it is advisable that you follow the "block" type of letter. The date, the name and position of the person addressed for the letter should all be written on the left side of typewriting pad or bond paper (8.5" x 11"). Do not put "Subject" because this is only used in making reports.

You can start your letter with "Sir/Madam:", but if you know the gender of the Officer you may remove the other one. The punctuation colon indicates that the letter is a formal letter. On your first paragraph, you state who you are, your educational attainment, the name of the school where you graduated and the date of your graduation.

On the second paragraph, you should state where you got the information that their company is in need of additional employee and that you qualified for the position. You can use also this information as the introduction of your letter. You can interchange both the information about yourself and this one. But both should not be placed on the third or fourth paragraph.

On the third paragraph, you should state that your knowledge and skills is suited for the duties and responsibilities of the position. As much as possible, elaborate some of your experiences during college days or on your work experience of if you have that you are really fitted for the job and that you are willing to be called up for an interviewed for further evaluation.

A complete job application consists of a cover letter and a resume. The cover letter is meant to highlight your individuality or personality, and to make you stand out from among hundreds of other applicants. When there are more job seekers around than job vacancies, human resource personnel tend to be more selective when short listing candidates for interview. Hence, you should use the cover letter as a tool to win the heart of a prospective employer. Market yourself to create a positive first impression in the cover letter, so that the person will read your resume, shortlist you for an interview, and offer you a job. A poorly written cover letter is likely to get instant rejection from the employer given the current job market.

As there is no standard format for cover letter, you are encouraged to write a particular cover letter, one at a time, to apply for the position of your interest. Cover letter should not be generic, i. e. you should not use the same cover letter for all the companies you wish to approach. This is because details like where and when you learnt about the vacancy, why you are interested to apply, what you have to offer to the company etc. are different for each of these companies.

Generally, a well written cover letter should provide answers to what the employers want to know:

Are you the kind of person they are looking for?
Do you have the relevant education, work experience and skills?
Can you handle the work demands, based on the job description?

Have you shown a commitment to this particular field of interest?
How well can you communicate with others?
Are you a team player?
Have you any leadership qualities?
Guidelines for writing a cover letter:
Organize your thoughts carefully
Express yourself clearly and reasonably
Use strong action words to describe your achievements
Use active rather than passive voice
Avoid jargon
Avoid long sentences
Avoid bad grammar and spelling mistakes
Limit the length to one page only
Proof read before you send via e-mail

5.1.2 Layout of a Cover Letter

(1) Opening

Include your name and address, the date, employer's designation and address, salutation and subject.

(2) Introduction

Nominate the job for which you are applying for. Indicate the source and date of the job information. Mention briefly your qualifications. Indicate your interest, career objective or goal.

(3) Sales pitch

Highlight the extent to which you match the requirements of the job. State your relevant experience gained from industrial attachments, projects, vacation or part-time jobs. Give a brief summary of your educational achievements, experience, qualities, capabilities and skills. Outline any further points in your favor related to the job and mention the attached resume. Mention your interest in the organization and your reason for applying for that particular position.

(4) Request for further action

Write that you look forward to a call or letter. State your availability for interview. Thank the person for his or her time and consideration.

(5) The complimentary close

Remember to sign personally and include your name. State your enclosures such as your attached resume, academic results or references.

5.1.3 Tips for Writing Winning Application Letters

To write the letter to a specific person—the person you think is the one who would hire you, you will be specific about the job you are seeking—hirers are not your employment counselor, do your research—demonstrate that you know something about the company. In the letter, you may tell the reader what you can do for the company. Meanwhile, you try to individualize your letter, which is short and to the point, and also to make it easy on the eyes and close it with an invitation for the reader to act—"Please give me a call at..."

5.1.4 Useful Expressions

(1) Opening

Conventional opening stating the purpose of the letter, where and when you saw the vacancy advertised etc.

I am writing to apply for the vacancy/post of... advertised in... on...

With reference to your advertisement in... on..., I should like to apply for the post/position of...

I would like to apply for admission to your Graduate School/University/Institute to pursue a Doctoral/Master's/Bachelor's Degree in...

I am interested in your research program/MA course/diplomas course in... and wish to enter this program starting from...

I wish to obtain admission to your Ph. D./graduate/undergraduate program in.... My intended date of entry is...

(2) Body

What you have to offer (key skills, personal qualities, relevant experience, achievements...) Use the job description and person specification to fit yourself to the job-give evidence.

1) About education:

I am now a (senior/third-year student/sophomore/freshman) in... Department of... University.

I went to... (name of school) in... (date) and studied there for...

(length of years)

I was trained at... (place) in... (subject) from... to... (date)

I major/specialize in...

I expect to graduate in...

I graduated from... (name of school) in... (date) with excellent grade in... (subjects).

I obtained/ received the... degree in... (date).

2) About work experience:

After completing my studies, I joined... (name of the work unit) and worked as a... (post) On finishing my training, I took up the position of... with... (name of the work unit), and I have been at that post ever since.

For the last... years, I have been working as a ...(post)

I was promoted to the post of... in... (date)

3) About sentence to conclude education and experience:

I am confident that my education and experience are extremely appropriate for the position.

I am confident that I am fully qualified for the job.

I am sure that I have excellent qualifications for the post.

4) About scores of standard tests taken:

I took the TOFEL in... (date) and achieved a score of..., which I hope will meet your requirements.

I have taken the TOFEL and GRE. My scores on the two tests were... and... respectively.

5) About foreign language proficiency:

I speak English well and can also write in English. I believe that such foreign language proficiency will be taken into favorable consideration.

Since you are an import-export company, you will no doubt be pleased to know that I speak English very well.

I passed the national College English Test (Band 4) in... (date) (Photocopies of Certificate enclosed).

6) About awards:

I was awarded the prize of... in... for my outstanding performance in ...

I won/received the prize/award of... in...

7) About financial status or aids:

I have sufficient financial resources to provide for my own education as well as other living expenditures.

If possible, I wish to obtain a teaching assistantship so that I may support myself and obtain more practical experience while pursuing graduate study.

I should be grateful if you can send me application forms for any scholarships you may offer to overseas students.

8) About reasons for application:

One of the main reasons I am applying is...

The reason I would like to work with you is to...

This explains why I am now seeking another post.

My work with the ··· has always been interesting and rewarding, and I personally would not have chosen to move. However...

(3) Closing—How you will follow-up

1) Requesting an interview:

If these meet your requirements, please grant me an interview.

I would very much appreciate the chance to talk to you.

2) Referring to enclosures:

I enclose three references and a full curriculum vitae as requested.

Please refer to my enclosed resume for details.

I have enclosed my CV for your reference. Please let me know if further information is needed.

3) Urging attention:

I feel that my application deserves your serious consideration.

I hope that you will give my application the serious consideration which I feel it deserves.

4) Requesting an early reply:

I look forward to hearing from you at your earliest convenience.

Please let me know the result of my application in due course.

5) Offering further contacts:

I can be contacted at the address above or on telephone...

I would be available in (every afternoon...). Please contact me if necessary.

Sample of a cover latter

101 Yangming Street
Harbin, 150000
Tel: 04518558855
E-mail: sidenyliu@163.com
September 9, 2007
Mr. Dave Clayton
HR Manager
ABC, Inc.
140 Chaoyang Street
Harbin, 150000

Dear Mr. Clayton:

  I came to know about a managerial job opening in the marketing team at your company from Robert Woods of United Services. With my work experience and MBA in marketing, I feel that I am an ideal candidate for the position.

  I have been following the progress of ABC, Inc. since last two years from newspapers and trade journals. I am keenly interested in the online-offline model developed by your company to sell products on the Internet and in retail outlets. Before I started my MBA, I worked extensively in marketing and retailing products on e-commerce websites. Currently, I am sharpening my skills in the traditional marketing areas with my MBA studies. I plan to graduate in December 2008 with an emphasis in marketing. I find a great synergy between your company and my background and experience. I am sure, that as a marketing manager in your company, I will be able to take the department to new heights.

  I am eager to talk to you and learn more about the managerial position. I want to discuss with you, the new ideas which I have for ABC, Inc. Please review my resume. I will contact you after a week to know about the possibility of arranging a meeting with you.

  Your time and consideration is greatly appreciated.

Yours sincerely,
Sidney Liu
Enclosure: Resume

Task 5.1 Writing Practice

1. Write a cover letter according to the following situation.

You are a junior student of the Foreign Languages Department. One day, you read an ad on the website that the Campus office at your university is looking for a student assistant in the coming winter. Good computer skills and English proficiency are required. You think you are the right person for the post because you have successful office experience in your department from April 2010 till now. Write a formal application letter to Mr. Wang in the Campus Office expressing your interest in the positions. Use your own personal information where necessary.

2. Translate the following sentences.

(1) I would like to apply for the post of accountant advertised in today's Morning post.

(2) Since my present position offers little prospect for advancement, I would prefer to be employed in an expanding company as yours.

(3) I would like to accept the post, and look forward to joining your firm on March 21.

(4) It is with great pleasure to receive your appointment letter of June 6 and the enclosed introduction of your company.

(5) Letters of recommendation from employers and professors, as well as my resume, are enclosed as requested.

(6) My master's degree in Business Administration and my varied management experience make me well qualified for this position.

5.2 Resume (Curriculum Vitae)

In English dictionaries' the word "resume" is usually defined as a summary of your educational and work experiences. The special spelling comes from the past participle of the French word "résumer" meaning "to summarize". In North America English, it is also sometimes spelled as "résumé" or "resume". In Commonwealth English, it is often used the same way as a curriculum vitae or CV for short which is a Latin term meaning "the course of one's life".

5.2.1 The keys to Resume

A resume is a written self-introduction to your future employers. It is meant to lead to an interview—the opportunity for a one-on-one talk between you and your employers. As the first impression you may leave with your future employer, a resume can be a great help for you to get a job offer if written very well. Like selling a product, you write your resume to "sell" yourself to your "customer", i. e. your future employer who may have special needs for a certain position. In order to convince your "customer" of your values in helping with their business or solving their problems, you can never be too careful in writing your resume.

The key to a successful resume is preparation, which involves at least the following aspects:

(1) In preparing your resume, the more you know about the position for which you are appling, the better. A good understanding of your employer's needs may help your better present your values.

(2) As in any type of marketing material, it is important to present the information so that it captures your customer's interest quickly. Your goal is to encourage the reader to stay with your document as long as possible. Your chance for a more detailed reading increases when you give the reader that information which he or she most wants to secure, early in the document.

(3) The layout of your resume is extremely important. Your resume needs to maintain a "clean" and professional appearance. It should allow the reader to access the information quickly. Neat margins, adequate "white space" between groupings, and indenting to highlight text, aid the ease of reference and retention of the material. Use "bolding" and italics sparingly. Overuse of these features actually diminishes their effectiveness of promoting the material they are intended to highlight.

(4) Your contact information is the most important information in the entire document. Make certain your name, address, phone number, and email address are clearly visible and at the top of your document. If you are including additional pages, be certain that your name is on these secondary pages in case your sheets become separated.

(5) The standards for resume length have changed. It used to be typical

for resumes to be on-page in length, and no longer. But for candidates with years of experience, having held multiple positions, or with outstanding achievements, this one-page constraint often results in a document that is unreadable with very small fonts. Actually, you may use as much space as you need to concisely, accurately, and effectively tell your reader about your skills, history, achievements and accomplishments, so long as these relate to the position you are applying for. Just remember, if a two-page resume can be clear enough to successfully lead to an interview, why do you want to turn to the third page? Leave something for the interview.

A Curriculum Vitae (CV) is like a resume in many ways, but is more specifically focused on academic achievements, especially when you are applying for positions in the fields of medicine and education. A CV summarizes educational and academic history, and may include details about teaching experience, publications, and academic honors and awards. Use a CV rather than a resume for teaching or research opportunities, applying for fellowships or for future academic training. Some research positions in industry may also prefer a CV rather than a resume. CVs are frequently longer than resumes, since the emphasis is on completeness rather than brevity. While there is no single correct format or style for writing a CV, the following types of information are generally included, and typically organized in this way:

- Name and Address
- Education
- Dissertation
- Fellowships & Awards
- Prepared to Teach or Areas of Research/Interest or Areas of Specialization
- Teaching Experience
- Research Experience
- Publications & Presentations
- Works in Progress
- Related Professional Experience
- Languages
- Other
- References
- Dissertation Abstract

Putting together a resume is very serious business. Often it is the first impression you will make on a prospective employer. Hopefully, after looking over your resume, the employer will grant you the opportunity to make a second impression.

If we look at the job search as a marketing campaign, as was discussed in the article, Personal Marketing Strategy, we can then look at the resume as a print advertisement or a marketing brochure. If you take a look through a magazine you will see many ads. Try to find one that tells you to buy a product because the company needs to increase its profits. You will be hard pressed to find such a beast. The ads you see tell you what the manufacturer's product can do for you—make your smile bright, your hair shiny, or simply make your life better. When putting together your resume, evaluate the needs of the employer and then determine how you can fill those needs. If you have access to a computer (which you do if you are reading this article) and a quality printer, you can design a targeted resume for every job for which you apply. If you have to mass produce your resume, you will have to do a little guesswork to come up with one that will impress everyone.

5.2.2 Choosing a Resume Format

Next you must determine what type of resume format to use. There are three basic types: chronological, functional, and a combination of the two. The following sections will explain what each of these types is and when to choose one type over another.

5.2.3 Chronological Resume

The chronological resume is probably the one with which most people are familiar. On it, work experience is listed in reverse chronological order (most recent job first). The period of time during which you were employed is listed first, followed by the name of the employer and then the employer's location. A description for each job is also included. Following work history is a section on education. If you are trying to show career growth, a chronological resume may be the way to go. If your most recent job is store manager, while the one before that is department manager, and the one before that is sales clerk, you can show a history of promotion. However, if your work history has been spotty or if it has been stagnant you shouldn't use a chronological resume. If you are changing careers, a chronological resume is not for you either.

5.2.4 Functional Resume

A functional resume categorizes skills by function, emphasizing your abilities. This is useful if you are changing careers and want to show how you can transfer your skills. As stated previously, it is important to show prospective employers what you can offer them. A functional resume does just that. A functional job objective is given first, followed by several paragraphs, each discussing a different job function. Examples of functions are: Supervision and Management, Accounting, and Writing and Editing. Begin with the one you want to emphasize most. If you are customizing your resume for different employers, you can change your functional job objective as well as the order in which you list the functions. However, if you don't list your previous jobs, the person reviewing your resume may be suspicious.

5.2.5 Combination Resume

A combination resume is exactly what it sounds like—it combines a functional resume with a chronological one. An objective is listed at the top, after your name and address, of course. Following that are paragraphs describing job functions. A section titled "Employment Experience" comes next. That is where the chronological part of the resume comes in. List employers and dates in this section. Do not offer further descriptions here as you have already described your abilities in the functional part of this resume. This is a useful format if you are changing careers but have a solid employment history. I also find it useful if your job duties on a single job were very diverse and you want to stress your various abilities. If you spent a long time at one job but moved up through the company, you might want to use a combination resume.

All job seekers ultimately ask one basic question—"Why do I need a good resume?" The answer is simple. You need a good resume to market yourself, have a written record of your skills and accomplishments and to sow the seeds of interest in the minds of recruiters and potential employers. In short, if you want a rewarding, fulfilling career, you need a good resume.

A Good Resume Evolves From Your Credentials and Not From Writing Skills

How very true! But of late, this fact seems to have moved to the background. Yes, with good resume writing skills you can really project your skills. However, realize that you have to have good, marketable skills and credentials—and no one, not even a resume writer, knows them better than you do. So, if you are writing your own resume, how do really make yours stand out from the crowd?

There are 3 principles of writing a good resume that holds true for nearly everyone, yet not everyone follows them (though everyone should). Here it is called "radical steps", because landing a job (a good job) sometimes requires new, radical techniques.

Radical Step 1: You Can't Have A Single Resume for Multiple Job Targets

You must have noticed that within a single field, there are many skills required even though the core needs of employers remain the same. Let's simplify this. Let's say that an accountant's job description remains same across industry segments at the core. Still, there are varying degrees of "desirable/preferable" qualifications across different sectors. More often than not, this plays a major role in selecting a suitable candidate.

So here is a suggestion: keep your standard resume the same while making room for accommodating different requirements. Your resume should never be so inflexible that you can't apply minor changes when need be.

Radical Step 2: Your Resume Must Make Sense To The Reader

This may seem apparent, but it is not always followed, sometimes inadvertently. The fact is that an awkward resume can be fatal to your job search (or a resume that appears awkward to an employer). Of course, neatness is of the utmost importance, but common mistakes such as writing personal goals in the "objectives" section and overstating your qualifications (especially when you are applying for junior to middle positions) can leave an awkward impression in the mind of the reader. In order to have your resume make sense to the reader, you must make sure that you format your resume using an uncluttered, logical layout that highlights the following:

(1) Core competencies.

(2) Work experience in reverse chronology.

(3) One core accomplishment that stands out and why.

(4) Educational qualifications.

It goes without saying that you should proofread your resume when finished. Then have someone else do so. Two of the unforgivable sins of resume writing are spelling mistakes and typos.

Radical Step 3: Make Clear Your Value To An Organization

Make no mistake; when you write your resume, you are absolutely marketing and selling yourself. As with marketing any product, you need to impress upon the reader the value of the product (that's you) and why they should buy it (hire you). The sad fact is that too many resumes just don't do this. Writing a generic description of your duties and job titles isn't going to cut it. You have to make clear what the organization will get out of hiring you. For example, if the position is for a marketing manager, you can highlight your sales abilities by including relevant, specific facts (think numbers, percentages and sales targets).

The crucial key to remember when writing (or editing) your resume—hence the 3 steps above—is to tailor it to the job that you are searching for. You can't hit the bull's eye without targeting it.

Writing a resume in English can be very different than in your native tongue. The following how to outlines a standard resume format.

Here's How:

(1) First, take notes on your work experience—both paid and unpaid, full time and part time. Write down your responsibilities, job title and company information. Include everything!

(2) Take notes on your education. Include degree or certificates, major or course emphasis, school names and courses relevant to career objectives.

(3) Take notes on other accomplishments. Include membership in organizations, military service and any other special accomplishments.

(4) From the notes, choose which skills are *transferable* (skills that are similar) to the job you are applying for—these are the most important points for your resume.

(5) Begin resume by writing your full name, address, telephone number, fax and email at the top of the resume.

(6) Write an objective. The objective is a short sentence describing what type of work you hope to obtain.

(7) Begin work experience with your most recent job. Include the compa-

ny specifics and your responsibilities—*focus on the skills you have identified as transferable.*

(8) Continue to list all of your work experience job by job progressing backwards in time. Remember to focus on skills that are transferable.

(9) Summarize your education, including important facts (degree type, specific courses studied) that are applicable to the job you are applying for.

(10) Include other relevant information such as languages spoken, computer programming knowledge etc. under the heading: Additional Skills.

(11) Finish with the phrase: REFERENCES Available upon request.

(12) Your entire resume should ideally not be any longer than one page. If you have had a number of years of experience specific to the job you are applying for, two pages are also acceptable.

(13) Spacing: ADDRESS (center of page in bold) OBJECTIVE double space EXPERIENCE double space EDUCATION double space ADDITIONAL SKILLS double space REFERENCES. Left align everything except name/address.

Writing a resume is often required in University application or job application. You can find many tips and samples on line, but most of them just give you a very general introduction. Maybe you need some special help when writing something Chinese which you don't know its English equivalent. Here you can find something useful.

Here are a few pointers on how to arrange these items on your resume:

List general organization memberships and activities where you had no real leadership experience. For the more important items, e.g. a leadership role in a campus organization, include one or two sentences describing your responsibilities.

Use active-voice verbs in describing experience. Avoid using the personal pronoun "I". The information can be listed either in the order "time, title, responsibility" or "title, time, responsibility".

Samples:

1. Listing (put the most recent first and work backward)

Sept 2007 to present: Deputy Head of campus life section of the student union

Sept 2005 to present: Member of the foreign film society

Sept 2005 to 2006: Member of the chess club

2. Leadership responsibility

President of the environmental organization BREATHE, Sept 2005 to Present:

Responsibilities included meeting with corporate partners, raising funds and leading teams of volunteers at clean-up sites

3. Project responsibility

Project manager of the "University Star" competition, March 2007:

The project selected students to appear in university promotional material, such as posters and pamphlets. Responsibilities included project oversight, writing selection criteria for student models, conducting interviews and consulting with university officials.

When you apply for a job, you will use your summarizing and writing skills to prepare an effective resume and application letter. You will use your resume to introduce yourself to potential employers. The resume is a brief (usually one-page) record or summary of your experience (that is, your personal background) and your qualifications for a job. Written before your application letter, the resume provides background information to support your letter. In turn the application letter will emphasize specific parts of your resume and will discuss how your background is suited to that job. The resume gets you the interview, not the job. As for employers, when you give them a resume, they look for an obvious and persuasive answer to this question. What can you do for us? They expect a resume: to look good (conservative and tasteful, on high-quality paper), to read easily (headings, typeface, spacing, and punctuation that provide clear signals), and to provide information the employer needs to make an interviewing decision.

The common formats of resumes or CV are as follows:

(1) Traditional.

> Name:
> Sex:
> Date of Birth:
> Address for correspondence:
> Telephone:
> E-mail:
> Education:
> Experience:
> Honors/Hobby:
> References:

(2) Modern.

```
                           Name:
                          Address
                      Telephone/E-mail
    Objective: (position sought)
    Summary of qualifications:
    Education:
    Experience:
    Personal data: (sex, health, nationality...)
    References:
```

(3) Functional.

```
                           Name:
                          Address
                      Telephone/E-mail
    Objective: (position sought)
    Training:
    Skills: (computer skills, communication skills)
    Experience:
    Education:
    References:
```

Resume for job application

```
                     Curriculum Vitae
    Name: Wang Gang
    Sex: male
    Address for correspondence:
    Dept. of Computer Control Engineering
    Beijing Institute of Aircraft Design
    Beijing 100028
    Telephone: 86-10-88227712
    Education: 1992 to 1995: Dept. of Electronics
               Wuhan University
          Major: Electronic communication technology
```

Experience: 1995 to present
                Engineer (full-time)
                Dept. of Computer Control Engineering
                Beijing Institute of Aircraft Design
                Evening class instructor (part-time)
Hobby: languages, travel, tennis
Qualifications: CET-4 and CET-6 Certificates
                TOEFL score: 624

Resume for school or scholarship admission

                          Zhang Fang

Sex: Female
Date of Birth: April 20, 1981
Address for correspondence: 110 Nanshan Rd.
                            Zhongshan District
                            Dalian 116002
                            Liaoning Province
                            PR China
Telephone: 86-411-6668946
E-mail: Zhangfang@sina.com.cn
Hobby: classical music, reading, mountain climbing and swimming
EDUCATION
    2000 to present: graduate student
                Dept. of Computer Science and Engineering
                Dalian University of Technology
                Dalian, Liaoning Province
                PR China
                Field of study: software design
                Degree to be awarded: MS in June 2002
    1996 to 2000: undergraduate student
                Dept. of Computer Science
                Tsinghua University
                Major: computer science

> Degree awarded: Bachelor of Science
> EXPERIENCE
> 2000 to present: member of Prof. Li Lie's research group
> 1998: Third prize winner of The 3rd Computer Program Design Contest
> Reference: available on request

Despite some variation in format, a resume should be clear to read and present an attractive image. It is important to highlight the features which will interest the reader. The following are the tips on writing resume:

(1) Avoid highly colored modifiers, opinion words or intensifiers.

e. g. provided persistent leadership, led the lab intelligently..., my extremely valuable contribution

(2) Avoid vague expressions. It's better to use concrete, specific nouns and action verbs.

e. g. Extensive experience with computers—used Quicken, Lotus 1-2-3,...

(3) Use paralleled structures.

e. g. created a new database, familiar with different softwares, being manager of...

—created a new database, used different softwares, managed the office of...

(4) Avoid repetition.

e. g. provided accurate data, provided valuable assistance to top management, provided useful training to...

—provided accurate data, assisted top management, trained...

(5) Try to use Power Words.

accelerated accomplished achieved adapted administered analyzed approved conceived conducted completed controlled coordinated created delegated demonstrated designed developed directed earned effected eliminated established evaluated expanded expedited facilitated found generated guided implemented improved increased influenced initiated inspected instructed interpreted launched led lectured maintained managed mastered motivated operated ordered originated organized participated performed pinpointed planned prepared produced programmed proposed proved provided proficient(in) purchased recommended reduced   reinforced reorganized revamped   reviewed revised scheduled simplified   set up   solved   supervised supported surpassed   taught   trained translated used utilized won wrote chair a committee, coordinate a program, develop a method,   conduct research,   create a database, direct a center, establish clientele,   initiate a partnership, install a new system, keep records, manage an office,   research the market,   test a new software, provide analysis, run a lab, train new employees, operate a machine, implement a policy, investigate a problem, organize a conference , considered an enthusiastic worker, analytical and critical thinking skills

Sample 1

Sanjay Dixit

282 HSR Layout, Koramangala, Bangalore 560012, India

Email: sanjay_dix@ userhome. com

Phone: 91-80-1234-5678

EDUCATION

B. Tech. Computer Science and Engineering, Indian Institute of Technology, Chennai (2001 **to** 2005)

Thesis Title: Efficient Algorithm for Terrain Simplification for Fast Rendering

Advisor: Janaki Rajagopalan

Summary: Improves the state of the art in occlusion plane detection given terrain data. My implementation showed a user controlled drive-through of a complex scene with real-time rendering of 3 million polygons using a 16 node Beowulf cluster. A paper was published in Graphics Interface '04.

St. Xavier's School, New Delhi (Graduated 2000)

Ranked 1st in school in 12th C. B. S. E. Board Examination.

PROJECT WORK (B. Tech)

(1) Built an optimizing compiler for mC + +, a C + + subset with support for dynamic object migration over the network between compatible typespaces.

(2) Built a user-level distributed file system based on NFS with write-through caching, fault tolerance and consistency guarantees.

WORK EXPERIENCE

(1) **Research Assistant, TIFR, Mumbai (Aug to Dec** 2004): Imple-

mented a library of image processing functions for edge detection and de-skewing on scanned images. Adapted an off-the-shelf OCR package to operate on scanned mail images with 99% address recognition accuracy at the city/pin-code level and 85% at the street level.

(2) **Project Trainee, Kreativ Networks, Bangalore**: (Jan 2005 to present): Joined a 7 person startup implementing campus-wide video-on-demand system for corporate training. Implemented the streaming video component with buffering for jitter reduction. Also, bit-rate reduction in the event of congestion to meet frame-rate guarantees. Extensive performance testing was conducted.

COMPUTER SKILLS

(1) **Software**: SQL Server, Apache, CVS, Mathematica, Latex. Also, audio/video formats and codecs.
Languages: C/C++, STL, Python, Javascript/C#
(2) **Platforms**: Linux, FreeBSD, Windows 98, NT 4.0, 2000.

PUBLICATIONS

Occlusion Culling using Hyperplane Projection and Frequency Domain Splicing. Pavan Pleasant, Amit Ganguly, and Janaki Rajagopalan. Graphics Interface '01(2004) pp. 323-333.

AWARDS

· Best B. Tech thesis – 2004. Dept of Computer Science. IIT Chennai
Silver Medalist at the International Mathematical Olympiad (IMO), 2003. Seoul, S. Korea.
· Ranked 18th in IIT Joint Entrance Examination – 2001.

REFERENCES

· Prof. R. K. Ravindranath, Dept. of Computer Science, IIT Chennai
Prof. Janaki Rajagopalan, Dept. of Computer Science, IIT Chennai

- Dr. B. Sanghal, TIFR, Mumbai

Sample 2

CURRICULUM VITAE
CHETHAN. M. V   Email: chethan2005_pesce @ yahoo. co. in
#1255, 5ᵗʰ **main**, 2ⁿᵈ **cross, Ph** : (0821) 2561192
Vivekanandanagar, Mysore
Karnataka   570 023

OBJECTIVE
Seeking full time career with an organization, which will permit me to use and contribute my abilities in software development and also to enhance my knowledge and contribute towards its growth by committed and high quality work. My Motto in life is Problems are opportunities and never accept defeat in life.

EDUCATION
Bachelors Degree in **COMPUTER SCIENCE AND ENGINEERING**
People Education Society College of Engineering, MANDYA.
Visveswaraiah Technological University.

Percentage Marks in Individual Semesters:

Semester (2001 to 2005)	Percentage of marks
First semester	61.9%
Second semester	57%
Third semester	57.8%
Fourth semester	61.9%
Fifth semester	62.5%
Sixth semester	70.3%
Seventh semester	77.3%

Aggregate % marks for 7 semesters: 64.1%

TECHNICAL SKILLS

Programming language	C++, C, Java
Relational Database	Oracle
Operating System	Windows 95/98/2000, Linux

PRE – DEGREE QUALIFICATIONS

Institution	Board	Examination passed	Year of passing	Percentage of marks
Sree cauvery composite junior College, Mysore	Karnataka Secondary Education Examination Board	SSLC	1999	85%
Marimallappa Pre-University College, Mysore	Karnataka State Pre-University Board	PUC	2001	65%

PROFILE SUMMARY:

He is very exciting and full of energy, who can make atmosphere around him very vibrant. He is very determined and hardworking, who is much focused to achieve what he intends to. He is very friendly, open-minded and levelheaded person. He likes to work in a team. He can get along with the People nicely. He loves his family & friends, they are his motivation. He wants to be recognized.

PROJECT DETAILS

(1) Implementation of cryptography over networking.

Cryptography is the art of manipulating information into an intermediate form and hence secures it from getting it into wrong hands. In our application we have implemented network security using the famous and efficient ciphers BLOWFISH. An attractive user interface being given using GTK Glade tool. The application allows the user to either pass or receive messages across the network and these messages are made secure through the BLOWFISH cipher.

Operating System: Linux   Red Hat version 7.0

Language: C

Team Size: 4

(2) Placement cell automation.

The main aim of this database project is to fulfill need of having an efficient application to the placement cell Management, pertaining toward its needs. we have done this for our college placement cell.

Front End: Visual Basic 6.0

Back End: Oracle 8

Platform: Windows 98

Team size: 2

(3) Design and development of VRRP.

Virtual Router Redundancy Protocol is designed to eliminate the single point of failure inherent in the static default routed Environment. It specifies an election protocol that dynamically assigns responsibility for a virtual router to one of the VRRP Routers on a LAN.

Operating System: Linux
Language: C
Team Size: 4

PERSONAL DETAILS

Date of birth	10/12/1983
Permanent address	#1255, 5th main, 2nd cross, Vivekanandanagar, Mysore Karnataka-570023
Nationality	Indian
Gender	male
Languages known	English, Hindi, and Kannada

SKILLS AND STRENGH

Excellent grasping capability and understanding the concepts clearly.
Ability to adjust to the situation.
Sense of Responsibility and a very hard worker.
A Self motivated team player, with excellent confidence & commitment.

OTHER ACTIVITEIES

I was an N.C.C. cadet in High School level. I am interested in playing cricket. I listen to music. I love traveling. I am deeply attracted by the ideas and thoughts of Swami Vivekananda.

DECLARARTION

I hereby declare that the information furnished above is true to the best of my knowledge.

PLACE: Mysore (CHETHAN. M. V)

Sample 3

Sample Engineering Resume

This sample engineering resume will give you a quick start on building an effective and optimized resume for your job application. Visitors can feel free to customize and edit our sample engineering resume as per their requirement for job application. We hope that our sample engineering resume will go a long way in portraying your abilities and skillsets efficiently.

Richard Anderson

    1234, West 67 Street,

    Carlisle, MA 01741,

    (123)-456 7890.

OBJECTIVE:

To gain employment with a company where my leadership experience and knowledge, especially in the area of thermodynamics, can be used effectively.

EDUCATION:

University Of Colorado at Boulder

B.S. Mechanical Engineering, expected May 2003

Cumulative GPA: 3.2

    · Relevant Projects: Designed, built, and tested an evaporative cooler, Spring 2002

    · Relevant Courses: Advanced Thermodynamics, Intro to Combustion, Failure of Engineering Materials

UNITED STATES AIR FORCE ACADEMY, Summer 1998 to Summer 2000

Mechanical Engineering, Cumulative GPA: 3.5

Academically ranked 12th out of 1,000 cadets at time of honorable discharge

EXPERIENCE :

BYRD CONSTRUCTION, Longmont, CO

Carpenter/General Laborer, Summer 2002

    · Learned valuable skills which can be applied to improving the actual implementation of design in the field

OFFICE OF FINANCIAL AID, CU-BOULDER, Boulder, CO (worked 15 hours per week)

    Advisor/Customer Service Representative, Spring 2001 to Spring 2002

    · Gained valuable experience assisting customers with their confidential financial aid accounts

LEADERSHIP :

UNITED STATES AIR FORCE, USAF ACADEMY, Colorado Springs, CO

Cadet, active duty military, Jun 1998 to Juy 2000
- Cumulative Overall Performance Average (OPA): 3.25
- Chief Clerk, Fall 1999—charged with leading 3rd Class Cadets in my squadron in performing their duties to standard
- Secret Clearance gained from Combat Survival Training
- Basic Cadet Training, Recognition, Combat Survival Training (CST), Parachuting, Gliding

COMMUNITY SERVICE :

CU-VOLUNTEER DAY, Nov 2001
- Painted the walls of an elementary school to improve its aesthetic appeal

BIG BROTHERS/BIG SISTERS—FALCON CLUB, 1998 to 2000
- Served as Big Brother for a young teen who lived with his single mother
- Participated in various events with the club

Task 5.2 Writing Practice

1. Write a letter of application to a university overseas for pursuing Ph. D program there and supply your resume.
2. Write a letter and a resume applying for a post in a Sino-American joint venture.

Chapter 6　Writing for Routine Job

6.1　Notices

As signs put in a public place that announce something or warn people about something, the writing of notices varies in forms from one to another. They may be written on blackboard or bulletin board. They may be written as memos delivered to the desk of officials. They can also be written as letters to notify people of something in detail.

It may be an announcement of a meeting, a party, a film or video show, a contest, a match, etc. Such a notice includes at least three parts:

(1) Date—day of the week—time

(2) Place

(3) Activity

(4) Audience

For lectures or talks, the notices should also include:

(5) Background information about the speakers, and for tours

For notice or written announcement drafting, writers should pay attention to what has happened or what will happen and as well as to when and where something has happened or will happen. Besides, to whom the information is given should be included. As far as language is concerned, it should be concise, simple, accurate and somewhat formal.

Notices are mainly classified into three categories:

(1) Notifications and warnings—about certain events in formal terms, with precise structure and concise words.

(2) Brief notices—about meetings and activities (such as speeches, games and parties) including the time, place and contents of the meetings or activities.

(3) Detailed notices—on activities with background information about a certain person, organizations and arrangement of activities.

What should be included in a notice are heading (to attract the reader's attention using the word Notice or NOTICE), body (to inform the public of certain events or activities. The body includes the purpose for issuing the notice; detailed information about the event; and the rounding off remarks.), signature: to inform the readers who the organizer is. It is usually put at the end of the body, and date (to inform the readers when the notice is made. The date appears below the signature, centered or in the bottom left-hand corner. Some notices, especially notifications and warnings may omit the last part. Sometimes even the heading is omitted).

Generally, notices should be presented in a brief and straightforward way so as to be understood easily by the public. On the notices, the time (the specific day, month, date and even the hour) and the place for the meetings or activities should be clearly and exactly stated so that there will be no misunderstanding of them. A few words about the meetings or activities should also be included in order that the readers of the notices can decide whether participation is compulsory or optional, or whether it is worth the time or not. As for the presentation of the time, usually the day of the week is put at the very beginning, followed by the month, date and hour.

For notice or written announcement drafting, writers should pay attention to what has happened or what will happen and as well as to when and where something has happened or will happen. Besides, to whom the information is given should be included. As far as language is concerned, it should be concise, simple, accurate and somewhat formal.

Useful expressions

There will be a... (meeting) at... (time) in/at... (place)
I am pleased to tell you that...
I am writing to inform you that...
Please informed that...
I'd like to tell you that...
All the staff members are expected at the meeting.
You are invited to attend...
The session is organized by... sponsored by...
I/ we have pleasure in informing you that...

Each participant will be given 5 minutes for speech.
All the students in our class have been arranged to visit. . .
Passengers are requested to note that. . .
It is hereby announce that. . .
This is to notify that. . .
Your attention, please.
I was careless and lost. . .
Will the finder kindly send it to. . . or ring me up to fetch it back?
Whoever knows her whereabouts or has got any information which may lead to her location is requested to phone me. . .
A green leather bag was left at the. . .
The club announces with regrets that owing to the rain, the trip to. . . scheduled for tomorrow is to be cancelled.
If interested, please contact me.
Passengers are requested to note that the new timetable comes into effect from. . .
All are welcome to be present at the contest to cheer the. . .
Owing to. . . our company finds it necessary to remove to. . .
Please to be advised that the name of…will be changed to
Meals and accommodation will be provided at moderate charges. . .
Recruit other highly qualified teachers on a part time or full time basis. . .

Sample 1

English Teaching & Research Group
NOTICE

There will be an English lecture on the differences between American English and British English by a famous English professor, Mr. Alexander, the author of *Follow Me and New Concept English* which are well known to us all. It will be given in the Lecture Hall from 7:00 to 9:00 on Saturday evening, September 23. Those who are interested in it are warmly welcome. And you may also invite your friends of other schools to attend it. Be sure not to be late. After the lecture, you may have a picture taken with Mr. Alexander.

September 2, 2012

Sample 2

MEETING NOTICE

Date: Saturday, May 21, 2008
Time: 9:00A. M to 3:00 P. M.
Location: College Hall
Sessions include:
    * The Scientific Research of the Students
    * Education Reform in the Teaching of English
    * Teaching Practice of the Students
All teachers are required to be present at the session.
Students are welcome.

College Office

May 19, 2008

Sample 3

NOTICE
All are Warmly Welcome
Under the auspices
Of the College Literature Association
a report will be given
on Dream of Red Mansion
by famous speaker Wang Zhu
in the College Hall
On Wednesday, April 18, 2012 at 1:30 P. M.
College Literature Association
April 8, 2012

Sample 4

NOTICE

It is hereby announced that upon the decision of the Board of Directors Mr. Wang Liming is appointed secretary of the marketing.

The Director's Office

February 15, 2011

Sample 5

NOTICE GIVING A HOLIDAY

May 22, 2012

As the Dragon Boat Festival is approaching, our school is scheduled to be closed from May 28th to May 30th, and classes will be resumed as usual on May 31th.

College Office

Sample 6

NOTICE

In order to improve the speaking ability of students, the Students' Union has decided to organize an English speaking Contest.

The English speaking Contest is going to be held in the school's auditorium in the fifth floor at 4:00 p.m. on June 9th. All the students who are in the second year are welcome to this activity. Those who want to take part in the contest are requested to sign up for it at the Student's Union office before May 25th. If you are one of the first five students, you will receive a beautiful present from the Student's Union.

The Student's Union

May 20, 2010

Sample 7

Notice of Removal

Dear Sir or Madam,

Due to the development of new business, our company will move to Room 2022 Zhongxin Building No. 17 Zhongshan Road from December 10, 2011. Our new telephone and fax numbers are 025-83321145 and 025-83326542 respectively.

We are very sorry for the inconvenience brought to you. We would also like to take this chance to thank you for your continued support over the years and hope that we can keep on working together in the future.

Yours faithfully,
Clare Tao
General Secretary

Sample 8

A Jacket Lost

In the playground, May 12, a Jacket, green in colour and with a zipper in the collar lost, finder please return it to the owner, Krutch. Room 203, Dormitory 9.

Sample 9

Female Clerk wanted

Interesting and rewarding position in the Huatian Hotel. Age 20 to 22, at least 2-year working experience. Salary according to experience will be between RMB ￥500 and RMB ￥800 per month. Transport can be provided from Town Center Plus other benefits including shopping discount. Please contact Miss Wen at 8108888.

Sample 10

Found

A pair of glass was found in the reading room on the morning of April 10th. Will the owner please ring 6254318?

Sample 11

NOTICE OF ENGAGEMENT

Mr. and Mrs. Holand Walshman have the honour to announce the engagement of their daughter, Miss Lucy, to Mr. Samual Russell on Saturday, August 11, 2011.

Sample 12

FOUND

1. A bunch of keys, in the dining hall on the evening of February 14.
2. A sweater, white in color, on the football field, on the moring of March 11.
3. A red leather wallet, in the bathroom, on the evening of May 8.

Please apply at the Lost Property Office, Room 102, on the 3rd floor of the office building. Open from 8:00 to 11.30 A. M. and 1.30 to 4.30 P. M.

Lost Property Office

May 28, 2011

Sample 13

ENGLISH EVENING
by
Students of Grade 1, English Department
7 p. m. Saturday, June 2, at Main Hall

Sample 14

PROGRAMME

1. Opening Speech by the Chairman
2. Group Singing

"Workers, Unit for the Battle!"

"We Shall not be moved."

3. Recitation of a Poem
4. Story-Telling : An English Fork-Tale
5. A Sketch : The Devoted Friend
6. A Play: The Art Scholarship
7. Closing Speech by Dean of the English Department

Sample 15

BASKETBALL

Financial Dept. Vs Human Resources Dept.

Time: 5:00 p.m., April 20

Place: Company Gymnasium

Please apply at the Labor Union for tickets. Admission freet.

Labbor Union

April 18, 2006

Task 6.1 Writing Practice

(1) As the secretary of your department, write a meeting notice to inform all of the teachers in your department to have a meeting this Wed. afternoon at two o'clock in Classroom 232 to discuss the preparation for the final exams.

(2) As the monitor of your class, write a notice about the English corner. Make up the time and place by yourself.

(3) Write a lecture notice of your own. You can make up the lecturer, the topic, the time, and the place.

(4) Analyze the Structure of a Notice

Directions: Read the following notice carefully. Then try to find the six parts of a notice.

Subscribe Now

Subscription fees for the 2009 to all newspapers and periodicals are to be handed to the Teacher's Reading Room before noon on Friday, October 15. Late payment will not be accepted.

Department Office

September 25th, 2008

---

1) The title:

2) The activity:

3) The place for the activity:

4) The time and date for the activity:

5) The name of the person/unit announcing the notice:

6) The date of announcing:

6.2 Notes

Notes are brief letters which are usually written to ask for favors, to send an invitation, to express thanks, sympathy, congratulations, and apologies or to ask after one's health. In this part, we will concentrate on notes in the following ten situations: asking for leave; sending an invitation; accepting an invitation; declining an invitation; canceling an appointment; showing sympathy or condolence; asking after one's health; regretting not seeing someone; a note of returning something borrowed and a note of accompanying a present.

As far as the layout is concerned, a regular note should have five necessary semantic elements. They are the heading, the salutation, the body, the closing form and signature.

6.2.1 Heading

The heading of a note suggests when the note is written. Just like the heading of a Christmas card, we only write the date on the top right corner and we need not write the writer's address. The date is often put between the month and the year such as "March 1, 2012". We often use the abbreviation forms for some of the months such as: Jan., Feb., Aug., Sept., Oct., Nov., Dec.. But we have to write the following months in full: March; April; May; June; July. Sometimes, especially for friendly informal note, we just write down the day or the time when we write the note such as: "Sunday morning", "Monday noon" or "7:00 a.m." when we are leaving a note to a very familiar person. Also in informal notes, the heading is often omitted.

6.2.2 Salutation

The function of the salutation is to show to whom the note is written. The form of salutation varies according to the different relationship between the writer and the reader. If you are writing to a person you do not know very well, you should use the more formal salutation "Dear Mr. (Mrs., Miss, Ms., Professor) the family name of the receiver", e. g. , Dear Mr. Black; Dear Mrs. Clinton; Dear Professor Liu. Always put a comma after the name. If you are writing to your friends, use their first names together with "dear", e. g. Dear Tom. Never begin a note with the salutation "Dear Friend" or "Dear Teacher". When writing to your relatives, you may begin with: Dear mother, Dear Aunt Alice, but never " Dear Cousin" or " Dear cousin Fred".

6.2.3 The body

The body is the most important part of a note for it tells the reader why the writer writes this note. The necessary semantic elements varies according to the different writing purposes.

(1) If you are writing a note to ask for a leave of absence, the necessary semantic elements should include the writing purpose (asking for leave), the specific demands, and the reason why you ask for a leave and your expectation and thanks to the writer.

(2) If you are writing a note to send an invitation, the necessary semantic elements will include the writing purpose (sending an invitation); the detailed information about the activity which you ask the reader to attend (what activity, when and where); your expectations from the reader.

(3) If you are writing a note to accept an invitation, the necessary semantic elements are usually as follows: showing thanks; writing purpose (accepting the invitation); offering some help.

(4) If you are writing a note to decline an invitation, the necessary semantic elements in the body are as follows: showing thanks for being invited; writing purpose (your regret not being able to attend it); your reasons for declining the invitation; your good wishes sometimes.

(5) If you are writing a note to cancel an appointment which you have made with the reader, the following are usually the necessary semantic elements in the body: your writing purpose (canceling an appointment); your reasons for canceling the appointment; suggesting another appointment.

(6) Suppose you are writing a note to show your condolence, the necessary semantic elements in the body are as follows: writing purpose (showing your condolence); recalling the good deeds the dead has performed; comforting the reader; offering your help.

(7) If you are writing a note accompanying a gift, the regular necessary semantic elements in the body will be as follows: writing purpose (mentioning what you are sending for a gift); your reason to send the gift; your expectation of the gift.

(8) Suppose you are writing a note of regretting not seeing someone, in the body, you need to include the necessary elements showing your regret at not seeing someone and your reason for leaving this note.

(9) If you are writing a note of returning something borrowed, the following two semantic elements are usually necessary in the body: showing thanks to the reader; mentioning that your have returned what you have borrowed from the reader.

6.2.4 The closing form

A closing form serves no real purpose, but it is an expected courtesy in a respectful communication. Among friends or family members, we may end a note with the closing form of "Yours," "Love," or nothing of the kind, but not "Yours". A comma must be used after the closing form.

Yet in a formal business note, we often use the closing forms of "Yours sincerely," "Yours truly," "Sincerely,". Again, a comma is used after the closing.

6.2.5 Signature

How you sign your name depends on how well you know the person you are writing to or how formal the note is meant to be. If you are writing a note to a person you do not know very well, or if this is a formal or business note, you use your full name. If you are writing a note to your friend or family members, you may use only your first name, or even a nickname. Your signature must be readable and it must come under the closing of a note.

Since notes are defined as brief letters usually to promote personal relationship in a society, the language used in notes is generally informal. Simple declarative sentences with active voice are preferred in note writing. The following are the common and useful expressions which are often used in notes to express the different writing purposes in the above situations.

6.2.6 Useful sentences

(1) Asking for a leave.

May I have a two-day's leave of absence from...?

I am writing to ask you for a leave of absence from...?

I'd like to have the a three-day's leave of absence from work from...

I'd like to ask you for a day's leave from...

I'd like to request a half-day's leave of absence this afternoon.

I wonder if you could allow me to have a two-day's leave of absence from work from...

I'd appreciate it very much if you could give me a three-day's leave of absence from work from...

(2) Sending an invitation.

We are going to have a birthday party for Mr. Liu next Sunday. Come and join us.

Will you please come and attend my 18th birthday party next Wednesday afternoon?

Would you like to attend our evening party this coming Saturday?

I'm writing to invite you to attend my teacher's 50th birthday party this coming Saturday.

We'd like to invite you to attend our seminar on functional linguistics this Monday evening.

(3) Accepting an invitation.

Thanks a lot, John and I will be happy to come to your house for a BBQ this Saturday.

Thank you very much for inviting us. We are very pleased to accept the invitation to the gathering next weekend in your house.

It's so kind of you to invite me to attend... I will certainly be glad to join you.

I will be happy to be invited to attend... I will definitely make it to the party then.

(4) Declining an invitation.

Thanks a lot. I am sorry I won't be able to come for the BBQ.

I would love to accept your invitation. I am afraid that I won't be able to join you.

We are so sorry that we won't be able to make it to your gathering.

I regret to say that I won't be able to make it to your forum this coming weekend.

How I wish I could accept your invitation! Unfortunately, I'll have to decline it.

(5) Canceling an appointment.

I am sorry but I won't able to keep the appointment with you...

I am sorry but I have to cancel the appointment with your because...

I would like to express my apology for not being able to keep the appointment with you because...

(6) Showing sympathy or condolence.

I am sorry to hear the news that...

I was so sad to hear that...

I was shocked and sad to learn the news that.

(7) Showing regret for not seeing someone.

I was sorry to have missed you in your office...

How I regretted that I failed to meet you in my hometown.

(8) Asking about one's health.

I am sorry to hear that you are down with headache these days. How are you feeling now?

I am sorry to hear that you are suffering from a bad cold these days. How are you feeling now?

I am sorry to hear that you are suffering from headache these days. Are you feeling better now?

Sample 1

Note

Dear Aunt Susan,   June 1

I was shocked and saddened to learn of Uncle Smith's death on Monday. He was a wonderful man and one of my favorite people. We will all miss him so much. How are you and little Mike holding up? Is there anything I can do for you? If there is anything at all that I can do to help, please don't hesitate to give me a call. I am at your disposal.

Yours,
Amy

Sample 2

Note

Dear Mr. John,

I was so sorry to have missed you at the office this afternoon. I was in that section of the city and I thought I would take a chance and see if you were free for a cup of tea. I should have known better with your busy schedule. I will telephone you later this week and we can discuss those sales figures.

Yours sincerely,
Mary Smith

Task 6.2 Writing Practice

Practice writing notes based on the following situations:

(1) Situation 1

Your uncle John died in a car crash at the age of 40, leaving his wife Susan and a little son Tommy. Write them a note of condolence and also offer your help.

(2) Situation 2

You go to visit your former teacher Mr. Liu, but he is out. Write him a note of regret and request another meeting. You should also suggest the exact time for the meeting.

(3) Situation 3

Your classmate Mary is suffering from headache these days and is staying at home. Write her a note to ask after her health and give her some suggestions on how to recover soon.

(4) Situation 4

You borrowed a bike from your classmate Xiao Wang to go shopping this morning. Now you have come back and put the bike somewhere near the teaching building. Write him a note of returning the bike you borrowed.

(5) Situation 5

Your cousin Susan has been enrolled by Heilongjiang University. You are going to send her an English dictionary as a present. Write her a note accompanying the present.

6.3 Memo

Memos or memorandums are business messages, which transmit information between colleagues or department within a business organization. As they go between co-workers and colleagues, they play an important role in keeping the different parts of a company in touch. Memos are simple because they do not have the formality of the letterhead, inside name and address, etc. And they are efficient because they convey the writers' ideas quickly and directly to the readers.

Memos, as a common means of internal communication, differ greatly from letters which usually go outside the company. Memos are generally less formal in style and tone than letters. Of course, memos can be formal in case the messages are highly serious, or they are sent, for example, to the president or the managing director. Besides, memos are short, usually two pages at most. Longer messages are handled, instead, in the form of a report.

6.3.1 Parts of a memo

The format for memos varies from company to company. However, all memos, regardless of format, include the following five guide words:

Memorandum or Memo, or Interoffice Memorandum

Date: (*the date on which the memo is written and sent*)

To: (*the name of the person who will receive the message; the receiver's job title*)

From: (*the name of the writer of the message*)

Subject/Re: (*the topic of the memo*)

Some companies purchase or print their own memorandum stationary with the five guide words mentioned above. This saves the writer some time when preparing memos.

Functions and types of memos

Memos usually serve the following purposes:

Give instructions or notify events which occurred;
Seek information;
Offer ideas & suggestions.

According to the above functions performed by memos, memos can be classified into:

Announcement memos
Instruction/directive memos
Request memos
Proposal memos
Report memos
Transmittal memos

Sample 1

MEMO

TO: All Employees
FROM: David Copper, Personnel Director
DATE: Nov. 22, 2010
SUB: Computer Purchase Program

In order to provide the necessary computer hardware and to encourage employees to learn how to use personal computers, we have designed the following computer purchase program.

► Employees must show that a computer will increase productivity in their jobs in order to participate.

► The computers will be mainly for work-related purposes.

► If the employee uses personal funds to purchase the computer, the company will lease the computer by paying a maximum of $500 over a 12-month period.

► The computer will become, in three years, the property of the employee who doesn't want to purchase one. Only after that, can these employees be allowed to use the computer for personal business and take it home if she/he wishes.

Proposals should be submitted to Cathy Carpenter, Personnel Director Assistant by sending an email to cathy123@163.com

Sample 2

MEMO

TO: All Employees
FROM: Alexandra Williams, Managing Director
DATE: Dec. 2, 2010
SUB: Unauthorized Use of Software—READ URGENTLY

In order to ensure that you do not intentionally or inadvertently violate the Copyright Law in this country, you should not copy any program installed on your computer for any purpose without permission from your immediate manager. Please carefully read and adhere to the following directions:

► To avoid placing yourself and the company at risk, please do not install software of any kind on your PC or the network.

► You are not allowed to upload or download unauthorized software from the Internet.

► Our IT personnel are the only people authorized to install software.

► If you want to use certain software programs at home, you must obtain written authorization from your immediate manager/IT Department to ensure our licenses permit this.

► Any employee found copying software illegally for their own or company use, or to give to any third party, including clients and customers, will be counseled and their position of employment reviewed/terminated.

Please uninstall all unlicensed copies immediately. If you require a particular software program, please consult your immediate manager or the IT Department to ensure the relevant software licenses are purchased for you. If you are in doubt, please also contact your immediate manager/IT Department.

Sample 3

MEMO

TO: Design Team #362
FROM: Sharon A. Doss
DATE: May 27, 2008
SUBJECT: Project Schedule

Purpose: This memo responds to your request that the weekly meeting be moved from 9. a. m. to 10. a. m. .

Summary: This request is satisfactory as long as it is approved by management.

Discussion: Management usually has no problem with the individual time changes in meetings, as long as meeting minutes are turned in by noon to Cathy.

Action: I have asked Cathy if she thinks this would be a problem and she said no, so all we need to do now is to get approval from Steve.

Sample 4

MEMO

TO: Dean of Journalism
FROM: Steve Nash
DATE: June 27, 2009
SUBJECT: Computer Lab

Purpose: This memo presents the findings of my visit to the computer lab at Clark C252.

Summary: In general, I felt that the lab needs much new equipment and renovation.

Problem: The inspection was designed to determine if the present equipment was adequate to provide graduate students with the technology needed to perform the tasks expected of them by their professors and thesis research.

Methods: I ran a series of tasks on SPSS and WordPerfect and recorded memory capacity and processing time for each task.

Results: The inspection found that the hardware used to run the computers is outdated and that the computers themselves are very slow.

Conclusions: This lab is inadequate for the everyday needs of graduate students in this department.

Recommendations: Four new computers running on Windows98 and a processing speed of at least 233mhz should be purchased immediately.

Sample 5

MEMO

Date: December 13, 2008
To: Annette T. Califero, General Office Director
From: Kyle B. Abrams, General Office Director Assistant
Subject: A Low-Cost Way to Reduce Energy Use

As you requested, I've investigated low-cost ways to reduce our energy use. Reducing the building temperature on weekends is a change that we could make immediately, that would cost nothing, and that would cut our energy use by about 6%.

<u>The Energy Savings from a Lower Weekend Temperature</u>

Lowering the temperature from 68 degrees to 60 degrees from 8 p.m. Friday evening to 4 a.m. Monday morning could cut our total consumption by 6%.

<u>How a Lower Temperature Would Affect Employees</u>

A survey of employees shows that only 7 people use the building every weekend or almost every weekend. 52% say they "occasionally" come in on weekends. People who come in for an hour or less on weekends could cope with the lower temperature just by wearing warm clothes.

<u>Action Needed to Implement the Change</u>

Provide a dozen portable space heaters to certain units. This would be a nice gesture towards employees who give up their weekends to work.

Begin saving energy immediately. Just authorize the lower temperature, and reset the controls for this weekend.

Sample 6

MEMORANDUM   August 16, 2009
TO: FLOYD JONES
FROM: DENNIS SMITH
SUBJECT: PURCHASING SHERATON MANUFACTURING

Purchasing Sheraton manufacturing

This memo is in response to your questions concerning the purchase of

Sheraton Manufacturing. (注释 memo) The memo will first explain goodwill and then discuss how to determine its value. By determining the value of Sheraton's goodwill you will have a dollar amount to help you determine how much you want to offer for the company as a whole.

What Is Goodwill?

Goodwill is an intangible asset made up of items which may contribute to the value and earning power of a company, but which are not listed on the company's balance sheet. Some possible items that may make up goodwill for Sheraton Manufacturing are:

(1) Highly capable engineering staff.
(2) Strong reputation for quality work.
(3) Good management.
(4) A large number of loyal customers.

These items are not listed on Sheraton's balance sheet. However, they obviously have value and therefore should be included in the purchase price of the business.

Determining the Value of Goodwill

The value of goodwill is established by comparing the present value of future cash earnings with the fair market value of a firm's other assets, less liabilities. The difference between the two is the value of goodwill.

The key to determining the value of goodwill is, of course, estimating the present value of future cash earnings. In the case of Sheraton Manufacturing, we can do this by accomplishing a cash flow analysis similar to the ones we perform in our capital budgeting process.

Let me know if you have any further questions about goodwill or the Sheraton Manufacturing acquisition.

Sample 7

Memo

To: John Smith, Production Manager
From: Susan Wang, Managing Director
Date: December 2, 2010
Subject: Making your suggestions on next year's production

The year of 2010 is one month away and it is time to plan for next year's production. Please have a think and make your suggestions on next year's production. Thanks.

Sample 8

Memo

To: Susan Wang, Managing Director
From: John Smith, Production, Manager
Date: December 21, 2010
Subject: Suggestions

Having checked our production capacity for the next year, I can suggest the following. Increase production by 10,000 bottles over a two-month period, while maintaining present production level of other lines.

Discontinue production of weaker line and use the shortfall capacity for mineral water.

I hope one of these suggestions is suitable.

Sample 9

Outgoing Memo

To: Jay Wang, Secretary
From: Rob Li, Marketing
Date: June 1
Re: My visit to Beijing to attend Agents Workshop

Can you look through the flight details from Travel World and book a flight which arrives early in the morning of the 12th?

Thanks.

Rob Li

Sample 10

Incoming Memo

To: Rob Li, Marketing
From: Jay Wang, Secretary

Date: June 6
Re: Your flight to Beijing
I've checked the flight details from Travel World and found Flight AF 202 which arrives at 6:45 is the most suitable. How do you like it?
Jay Wang

Sample 11

Memo

To: Health and Safety Committee
From: Joan Tam, Chairperson, Health and Safety Committee
Date: May 8, 2006
Subject: Time change for next meeting

Please note that the meeting on Monday May 15 has been changed to Wednesday, May 17.

Sample 12

Memorandum

To: Katherine Chu, Regional Manager
From: Stephen Yu, Sales
Date: June 19, 2006
Subject: Notification of My Resignation

I am writing to inform you of my intention to resign from G&S Holdings.

I have appreciated very much my four years working for the company. The training has been excellent and I have gained valuable experience working within an efficient and professional team environment. In particular, I have appreciated your personal guidance during these four years of my career. I feel now that it is time to future develop my knowledge and skill in a different environment.

I would like to leave, if possible, in a month's time on Saturday, July 22. This will allow me to complete my current workload. I hope that this suggestion arrangement is acceptable to the company.

Once again, thank you for your support.

Sample 13

Memorandum

To: All staff
From: Gloria dos Santons, Director
Date: December 2, 2005
Subject: Staff Christmas party

Please notice that year's Christmas party will be on December 18, from 11:00 to 15:00.

We will be having a picnic at the party across the road. You children and partners are welcome.

Please let Lily know by December 9 how many people from your family are coming. This will help with catering.

Sample 14

MEMORANDUM

To: S. M. Chan, General Manager
From: Samantha Ng, Ofiice Manager
Date: April 9, 2006
Subject: Purchase

(1) Introduction.

At the monthly staff meeting on Friday, April 7, 2006, you requested information about the possibility of purchasing a microwave oven. I would now like to present these details.

(2) Background.

Since the move to the new office in Kowloon Bay, our staff have diffculty in finding a nearby place to buy lunch.

(3) Advantages.

Providing a microwave oven in the pantry would enable our staff to bring in their own lunchboxes and reheat their food. Also, Staff members are less likely to return to work late after lunch.

(4) Staff Opinion.

A survey found that our staff would like to use the microwave oven.

(5) Cost.

Details of suitable models are given below:

Brand	Model	Price
Philips	M903	$280
Sharp	R-3R29	$260
Sony	6145 x	$240

(6) Request.

If this meets with your approval, we would appreciate it if you could authorize up to $300 for the purchase of the microwave oven.

Samantha Ng

Sample 15

MEMO

To: Golden Marxon
From: Jane Tam, Chairperson, Health Sciences Human Rources
Date: September 8, 2006
Subject: Formal Counseling Session Follow-up Memo

This is a follow-up to our formal counseling session held on August 22, 2006. Attached is the Action Plan, the outline of which we discussed in our meeting. You expressed some concerns about my expectation, but I am confident that if you apply yourself you will be able to meet them.

I will meet with you weekly for the next month to see how things are things are progressing. After that we will meet as needed but will have a regular meeting at least once a month. If you find that you need assistance in implementing the Action Plan, please let me know so that we can discuss any problems that you are having.

Thank you for your cooperation and I hope the Action Plan will be of assistance to you. Our first weekly meeting will be at 9:00 a. m. Next Monday.

Attachment
Cc: Health Sciences Human Recources

6.3.2 Useful Sentences

1. I am writing this memo to inform you that...

2. I am writing to inform you that...
3. I am writing to remind you that...
4. This is to remind you that...
5. Please note that...
6. Please notice that...
7. Until further notice...
8. Thank you in advance for your consideration/cooperation/help...
9. This will help with...
10. Please let...know...
11. We would appreciate if you could...
12. Thank you for support.
13. Your handling of this matter will be appreciated...
14. Please pass this information to...
15. In response to...
16. This memo is in response to...
17. This memo responses to your request that...
18. I appreciate that...
19. ...will be helpful/beneficial in...
20. Call sb. at...
21. Sponsored by...
22. Ring sb. on sth.
23. Be cordially invited...
24. Request the pleasure of the company of sb.
25. Appreciate its prompt delivery.
26. To acknowledge receipt of sth...
27. Prompt handling.

Task 6.3 Writing Practice

(1) Read and complete the following memo according to the Chinese given in the brackets.

Memorandum

DATE: 15 May 2012
TO: Training Personnel
FROM: George Zhang, Head, Training Dept.

Subject: Providing clear, complete Instructions

It has come to my attention that ＿＿＿＿＿＿＿＿（新雇员所做工作不是很令人满意）. This is the fault of the trainer, not the trainee. ＿＿＿＿＿＿＿＿（你们指导应更加明确完整）.

Please follow these guidelines:

Give an overview of the task. Make sure the task is understood.

Describe each step in order.

Describe each step thoroughly.

Ask questions at each step. Do not ask: Do you understand? Ask: How do we begin? What do we do next? etc.

＿＿＿＿＿＿＿＿（要受训人员复述指导）

(2) Write a Memo to Mr. Floyd Jones and give him a clear reply regarding the questions mentioned in the following situation.

Situation

Floyd Jones is the proprietor of the firm for which you work. Mr. Jones wants to acquire a manufacturing business. The business he wants to acquire, Sheraton Manufacturing, is insisting that Floyd pay not only for the identifiable net assets of the business, but also for "goodwill". Floyd asks you: "What is goodwill? Should I pay for it? If I should pay for it, how much should I pay?"

6.4　E-mails

Electronic mail, most commonly referred to as email or e-mail since approximately 1993, is a method of exchanging digital messages from an author to one or more recipients. Modern email operates across the Internet or other computer networks. Some early email systems required that the author and the recipient both be online at the same time, in common with instant messaging. Today's email systems are based on a store-and-forward model. Email servers accept, forward, deliver, and store messages. Neither the users nor their computers are required to be online simultaneously; they need connect only briefly, typically to an email server, for as long as it takes to send or receive messages.

An Internet email message consists of three components, the message envelope, the message header, and the message body. The message header contains control information, including, minimally, an originator's email address and one or more recipient addresses. Usually descriptive information is also added, such as a subject header field and a message submission date/time stamp.

In the business world, emails are widely used in both internal and external communications. In the former case, it may be interoffice memos or just simple messages between colleagues. In the latter, it may cover letters or complex reports between business firms and customers, or between firms and suppliers. Any business document, so long as it can be generated by, scanned into, or download onto a computer, can be sent as an email through cyberspace to anther computer. In this sense, an email is not only a type of writing, it may be considered a medium of business communication as well.

As an electronic message going online, an email may look different on different templates of email systems, a template being a pre-set form with empty fields to be filled in by the email writer. However, the basic components of an email are still the same, i. e. the heading and the body.

The heading of a business email is very similar to that of a business memo. It usually includes From, To, Cc, Subject, Date, and other information about the email. The header is separated from the body by a blank line. Each message has exactly one header, which is structured into fields. Each field has a name and a value. Informally, each line of text in the header that begins with a printable character begins a separate field. The field name starts in the first character of the line and ends before the separator character ":". The separator is then followed by the field value (the "body" of the field). The value is continued onto subsequent lines if those lines have a space or tab as their first character. Field names and values are restricted to 7-bit ASCII characters. Non-ASCII values may be represented using MIME encoded words. This section needs additional citations for verification. Please help improve this article by adding citations to reliable sources. Unsourced material may be challenged and removed.

To: The email address(es), and optionally name(s) of the message's recipient(s). Indicates primary recipients (multiple allowed), for secondary recipients see Cc: and Bcc: below.

From: The email address, and optionally the name of the author(s). In many email clients not changeable except through changing account settings.

Date: The local time and date when the message was written. Like the

From: field, many email clients fill this in automatically when sending. The recipient's client may then display the time in the format and time zone local to him/her.

The message header should include at least the following fields:

Message-ID: Also an automatically generated field; used to prevent multiple delivery and for reference in In-Reply-To: (see below).

In-Reply-To: Message-ID of the message that this is a reply to. Used to link related messages together. This field only applies for reply messages.

Common header fields for email include:

Subject: A brief summary of the topic of the message. Certain abbreviations are commonly used in the subject, including "RE:" and "FW:"

Bcc: Blind Carbon Copy; addresses added to the SMTP delivery list but not (usually) listed in the message data, remaining invisible to other recipients.

Cc: Carbon Copy; Many email clients will mark email in your inbox differently depending on whether you are in the To: or Cc: list.

The body of a business email is no different from that of a business letter or memo. Formal salutations such as "Dear Ms. Black" and "Sincerely yours" are suitable for letter-style business emails addressed to individuals with whom you are unfamiliar. When a business email functions as a memo, on the other hand, the salutation and complimentary close can be omitted altogether.

As an important medium of business communications, emails lie somewhere between telephones, face-to-face meetings, and written documents. They share advantages with each of these means of communication. Like telephone calls they are quick and easy. Like face-to-face meetings they allow a number of people to participate. Like written documents they can be downloaded and kept as a permanent record. But emails also share disadvantages with conversations and paper-based media. Like written documents, they reply on written language, which means the writer can only reply on the words to tell the recipient's reactions. Like conversations, it is possible for the writer to "say" in an email something that he or she will soon regret, just because it is so easy to send an email.

As such, emails tend to be sloppier, or less formal than communication on stationery. This is not always bad, of course, if you are writing the email simply to tell your co-worker to have lunch together. However, extra care is needed when you write to your superiors or in an external case, to a regular customer.

Business email typically follows a number of steps, including the following:

Subject of email

Opening and closing greetings

Beginning sentence

The main message

Ending

(1) Subject of email.

What's the problem with the following subjects?

Subject: [Blank]

Subject: "Important! Read Immediately!!"

Subject: "Simple question."

Subject: "Follow-up about last Friday"

Subject: "That file you requested."

Some often overlook is the proper use of a subject line. When filling in the subject line you have around 25 character spaces to get someone's attention. The best way to do this is to use capitals for the main point of the message, than followed by a short description of the nature of the main point.

For example: "meeting today", "DECISION NEEDED: We are choosing new product line today."

(2) Opening and closing greetings.

If you don't have a contact name:

Dear sir or Madam

Yours faithfully

If you know the name of the person:

Dear Mr/Mrs/Ms Jones

Yours sincerely

If you know the person as a friend or close business colleagues:

Dear James

Best wishes/regards

If you are contacting a company not an individual:

To Whom It May Concern

E-mail is meant to transfer information quickly, so it is purposely informal. Some people do not use capitalization. E-mail also makes use of a great deal of abbreviations to speed up typing.

u	you	hand	have a nice day
2	to	tyvm	thank you very much
bb	bye-bye	Ilu	I love you
f2f	face to face	ur	your
iow	in other words	fu	for you

Sample 1

Dear MS Johnston

Further to our telephone call this morning, I am writing to inform you of my availability for the above post. I am now free to take up the post from 1 April this year. I look forward to hearing from you.

Yours faithfully
Edward Bronson

Sample 2

Subject: Re: Ormet products agent in China

Mr. Yang,

Nice to hear from you. About Z interconnect technology, you may consult with Mr. Mason Law. He is our representative and familiar with it. His contact information is listed below. Thank you for your interest.

All the best

James Wang

Auster Circuits, Inc.

10080 Willow Creek Road

San Diego, Ca. 92131

845-803-0010 x311

James. Wang@ auster. net

(3) Ending.

Lastly, end your email with a professional signature line: who you are, your title and contact information.

Also remember to review your message thoroughly and be aware that if the email will be sent to many people? If my corporation or any other outside agency would see this email, could it be used against me in an investigation?

Sample 1

Subject: Ormet products agent in China
Dear Mr./Miss:
I am a member of R&D Department of Meadville group (Shanghai subsidiary company). Meadville Company is a special PCB manufacture supplier, we are very interested in Ormet conductive ink for Z-axis connection. We wonder if Ormet have the agents in China, and could you kindly provide with the Agents' E-mail or telephone number for us.

Thank you very much!
Best Regards
Tony Wang
Project & Development Department, Engineer
Shanghai Meadville Electronics Co., Ltd.
Tel:86-021-66610031 Fax.: +86-01066613035
Mobile Phone: 13088888899
Mail to: Tony.wang@126.com

Sample 2

Subject: Re: MEETING UPDATE.
Hello Mason:
We had a meeting last week, you remember? About the sample test we discuss last week, we have prepared well the test vehicle and material except for electronic conductive adhesion. Could you send us some sample for test as soon as possible? Anything need we do, please feel free to contact with us.

Thank you very much.
Best Regards.
Chris Li
Project & Development Department, Engineer

Shanghai Meadville Electronics Co. , Ltd.
Tel:86-021-66610031 Fax. : +86 - 021 - 66613035
Mobile Phone: 13988888899
Mail to: Gang. Li@ sme. meadvillegroup. com

Sample 3

Subject: O/E PCB Sample Order
Dear Chris,
Per your requirements, I have done some modification. The attachment is the O/E PCB survey. I will ask Mr. Liu to contact Huawei and collect the information of their design.
Best wishes
Xin Lei
R&D Department, Engineer
Shanghai Meadville Science and Technology Co. , Ltd.

Sample 4

Subject: O/E PCB Sample Order
Dear Dr. Tom,
I just got a phone call from Huawei (Mr. Wei Fang). He told me that they almost finished the design of their O/E PCB.

They will release their O/E PCB sample order in April. He said if Meadville could not provide the sample fabrication, he will release this order to some foreign suppliers first (say in Korea). The deadline of their O/E PCB project is this September 2009.

It seems that our schedule is a little behind their requirement. I'll be grateful if you could make the sample faster and have a new schedule to fulfill it. If you need any help, just let us know it.
Best wishes,
Samule Zhao
Marketing Department, Supervisor
Shanghai Meadville Electronics Co. , Ltd.
Tel:86-021-66610031 Fax. : +86 - 021 - 66613035

E-mail: Wei.Zhao@sme.meadvillegroup.com

Useful sentences

1. I am writing to confirm /enquire/inform you...

2. I am writing to follow up on our earlier decision on the marketing campaign in Q2.

3. With reference to our telephone conversation today...

4. In my previous e-mail on October 5...

5. As I mentioned earlier about...

6. as indicated in my previous e-mail...

7. As we discussed on the phone...

8. from our decision at the previous meeting...

9. as you requested/per your requirement...

10. In reply to your e-mail dated April 1, we decided...

11. This is in response to your e-mail today.

12. As mentioned before, we deem this product has strong unique selling points in china.

13. As a follow-up to our phone conversation yesterday, I wanted to get back to you about the pending issues of our agreement.

14. I received your voice message regarding the subject. I'm wondering if you can elaborate i.e. provide more details.

15. Please be advised/informed that...

16. Please note that...

17. We would like to inform you that...

18. I am convinced that...

19. We agree with you on...

20. With effect from 4 Oct., 2008...

21. We will have a meeting scheduled as noted below...

22. Be assured that individual statistics are not disclosed and this is for internal use only.

23. I am delighted to tell you that...

24. We are pleased to learn that...

25. We wish to notify you that...

26. Congratulation on your...

27. I am fine with the proposal.

28. I am pleased to inform you that you have been accepted to join the workshop scheduled for 22-24 Nov, 2012.

29. We are sorry to inform you that...

30. I'm afraid I have some bad news.

31. There are a number of issues with our new system.

32. Due to circumstances beyond our control...

33. I don't feel too optimistic about...

34. It would be difficult for us to accept...

35. Unfortunately I have to say that, since receiving your enquiries on the subject, our view has not changed.

36. We would be grateful if you could...

37. I could appreciate it if you could...

38. Would you please send us···

39. We need your help.

40. We seek your assistance to cascade/reply this message to your staff.

41. We look forward to your clarification.

42. Your prompt attention to this matter will be appreciated.

43. I would really appreciate meeting up if you can spare the time. Please let me know what suits you best.

44. Please give us your preliminary thoughts about this.

45. Would you please reply to this e-mail if you plan to attend?

46. Please advise if you agree with this approach.

47. Could you please let me know the status of this project?

48. If possible, I hope to receive a copy of your proposal when it is finished.

49. I would appreciate it very much if you would send me your reply by next Monday.

50. Hope this is OK with you. If not, let me know by e-mail ASAP.

51. Could you please send me your replies to the above questions by the end of June?

52. May I have your reply by April 1, if possible?

53. If you wish, we would be happy to...

54. Please let me know if there's anything I can do to help.

55. If there's anything else I can do for you on/regarding this matter,

please feel free to contact me at any time.

56. If you want additional recommendations on this, please let us know and we can try to see if this is possible.

57. I'm just writing to remind you of...

58. May we remind you that...?

59. I am enclosing...

60. Please find enclosed...

61. Attached hereto...

62. Attached please find the most up-to-date information on/regarding/concerning...

63. Attached please find the draft product plan for your review and comment.

64. If you have any further questions, please feel free to contact me.

65. I hope my clarification has been helpful.

66. Please feel free to call me at any time, I will continually provide full support.

67. Please let me know if this is suitable.

68. Looking forward to seeing you soon.

69. We look forward to hearing from you soon.

70. Hope this is clear and we are happy to discuss this further if necessary.

71. I look forward to receiving your reply soon.

72. Looking forward to receiving your comments in due course.

73. I'll keep you posted.

74. Please keep me informed on the matter.

75. For any comments/suggestions, please contact Nadia at 2552-7482.

76. I would like to apologize for...

77. I apologize for the delay in...

78. We are sorry for any inconvenience caused.

79. I am sorry for any inconvenience this has caused you.

80. I'm sorry about last time.

81. We apologize for not replying you earlier.

82. I'm really sorry about this.

83. Sorry, I'm late in replying to your e-mail dated Monday, April 1.

84. We apologize for the delay and hope that it doesn't inconvenience you too much.

85. Hoping that this will not cause you too much trouble.

86. Sorry if my voice message is not clear enough.

87. Thank you for your help.

88. I appreciate very much that you...

89. I truly appreciate it.

90. Thank you for your participation.

91. Thank you so much for inviting me.

92. Congratulations to all of you and thanks for your efforts.

93. Your understanding and cooperation is greatly/highly appreciated.

94. Your prompt response will be most appreciated.

95. Once again, thank you all for your commitment and support.

96. Thanks for your input/clarification/message.

97. Any comments will be much appreciated.

98. Thank you very much for everything you've done for me.

99. I would appreciate your kindest understanding with/regarding this matter.

100. Please convey my thanks to all the staff involved, they certainly did an excellent job.

101. If there's anything else I can do for you on/regarding this matter, please feel free to contact me at any time.

102. Attached please find my CV.

103. Please find attached my report.

Frequently Used Sentences for Professional Email Writing:

Tab 6.1

	Type	Frequently Used Sentences
1	Greeting message	Hope you have a good trip back.
		How are you?
		How is the project going on?

Continue Tab 6.1

	Type	Frequently Used Sentences
2	Initiate a meeting	I suggest we have a call tonight at 9:30 p.m. (China Time) with you and Brown. Please let me know if the time is okay for you and Ben.
		I would like to hold a meeting in the afternoon about our development planning for the project A.
		We'd like to have the meeting on Thu Oct 30, 03. Same time.
		Let's make a meeting next Monday at 5:30 p.m. SLC time.
		I want to talk to you over the phone regarding issues about report development and the XXX project.
3	Seeking for more information/feedbacks/suggestions	Shall you have any problem accessing the folders, please let me know.
		Thank you and look forward to having your opinion on the estimation and schedule.
		Look forward to your feedbacks and suggestions soon.
		What is your opinion on the schedule and next steps we proposed?
		What do you think about this?
		Feel free to give your comments.
		Any question, please don't hesitate to let me know.
		Any question, please let me know.
		Please contact me if you have any questions.
		Please let me know if you have any question on this.
		Your comments and suggestions are welcome!
		Please let me know what you think?
		Do you have any idea about this?
		It would be nice if you could provide a bit more information on the user's behavior.
		At your convenience, I would really appreciate you looking into this matter/issue.
4	Give feedback	Please see comments below.
		My answers are in blue below.
		I add some comments to the document for your reference.

Continue Tab 6.1

	Type	Frequently Used Sentences
5	Attachment	I enclose the evaluation report for your reference.
		Attached please find today's meeting notes.
		Attach is the design document, please review it.
		For other known issues related to individual features, please see attached release notes.
6	Point listing	Today we would like to finish following tasks by the end of today: 1....... 2.......
		Some known issues in this release: 1....... 2.......
		Our team here reviewed the newest SCM policy and has following concerns: 1....... 2.......
		Here are some more questions/issues for your team: 1....... 2.......
		The current status is as following: 1....... 2.......
		Some items need your attention: 1....... 2.......
7	Raise question	I have some questions about the report XX-XXX
		For the assignment ABC, I have the following questions.
8	Proposal	For the next step of platform implementation, I am proposing...
		I suggest we can have a weekly project meeting over the phone call in the near future.
		Achievo team suggests to adopt option A to solve outstanding issue......

Continue Tab 6.1

	Type	Frequently Used Sentences
9	Thanks note	Thank you so much for the cooperation.
		Thanks for the information.
		I really appreciate the effort you all made for this sudden and tight project.
		Thanks for your attention!
		Your kind assistance on this are very much appreciated.
		Really appreciate your help!
10	Apology	I sincerely apologize for this misunderstanding!
		I apologize for the late asking but we want to make sure the correctness of our implementation ASAP.

Tab 6.2

Purpose	Frequently Used Phase	Example
Indicating sequence	at first	At first I thought he was right; on second thoughts, I was sure.
	first of all	To do a good job, first of all you must keep your mind on your work.
	to begin with	To begin with, we ought to know what we are studying for.
	above all	You must, above all, set your heart on study.
	first, then, finally	First, we go over the story, then we make an outline of it, and finally we retell it.
	First, second, third	Why should we learn swimming? First, because it is a very good form of exercise. Second, it gives pleasure. Third, it may sometimes mean the difference between life and death.
	On the one hand, on the other hand	On the one hand he had to study, on the other hand he had a big family to support.
	in the first place, in the second place	In the first place, we should not delay our work. In the second place, we should divide our work to be done at regular times during the day.
Introducing topic	on the subject	On the subject of music, people nowadays love popular music rather than classical music.
	it is thought that	It is thought that some of the popular novels have bad effects on young people's mind.
	regarding	Regarding this matter, what's your opinion?
	concerning	Concerning their service, it needs improving.
	I'd like to point out	I'd like to point out that we are living in the 20th century.

Continue Tab 6.2

Purpose	Frequently Used Phase	Example
Indicating judgment	from my point of view	From my point of view, it is her mother's fault.
	in my opinion	In my opinion, the whole affair was a waste of time.
	in my view	In my view, she is a bit too slow to respond.
	as I see it	The difference, as I see it, is one of method.
	it seems to me that	It seems to me that this research plan will be very promising.
	I am certain that	I am certain that he will come out first in the contest.
	It is my belief that	It is my belief that there are living creatures on some other planets.
Indicating emphasis	actually	Actually, I find this subject rather interesting.
	practically	The two are Practically the same.
	as a matter of fact	As a matter of fact they kept in contact with each other for quite a long time.
	in reality	We once took him for an experienced worker. In reality, he was a student.
	in fact	It was, in fact, the most beautiful city I have ever seen.
	obviously	Obviously, there is much room for improvement in our work.
	equally	He was equally successful in gaining the prize.
	without doubt	Without doubt these theories were all wrong.
	anyway	That was not our fault, anyway.
	naturally	One will naturally ask why.
	simply	His arguments are simply water-tight.
	almost	The news is almost too good to be true.
	especially	Beijing is beautiful, especially in late autumn.
	Only	The failure only strengthened our determination.
	far from	Far from discouraged, we took added strength from our defeat. Indicating supplement and exclusion
	moreover	He refused to help me, moreover he laughed at me in public.
	furthermore	Furthermore, he never cared for other people's interests.
	what is more	What's more, I found, to my great surprise, a girl of six from Nanjing could speak good English.

Continue Tab 6.2

Purpose	Frequently Used Phase	Example
	and…as well	This old worker has experience and knowledge as well.
	apart from	Apart from oxygen, there are some other gases in the air.
	in addition to	In addition to "when", we can use "as soon as" to introduce this kind of sentences.
Indicating illustration	for instance/for example	Television, for instance, is a great invention in the 20th century.
	such as	There are many lovely parks in Beijing, such as the Summer Palace, Beihai and Zhongshan Park.
	take the case of	Take the case of cars, they use a lot of gas.
	in other words	In other words, the output has been increased fifty million tons.
	that is to say	That is to say we won't have enough time for a holiday.
	that is	He left last month—that is, in August this year.
	namely	Arabic is written in the opposite direction to English, namely from right to left.
	to be more exact	He came home very late last night, to be more exact, very early this morning.
Indicating purpose and result	as a result	The production, as a result, has begun to rise rapidly.
	at last	At last he obeyed the order silently.
	for the purpose of	For the purpose of learning, he visited many hospitals.
	therefore	The examination is still far away, therefore we plan to go for an outing.
	thus	He studied diligently, thus he got high marks.
	in this way	In this way you can get rid of bad habits.
Indicating Transition and concession	yet	Although this sounds strange, yet it is true.
	however	However, we will look into the matter later.
	nevertheless	Some of them hadn't for 36 hours. They went on working nevertheless.
	after all	What harm does it do after all?
	whereas	He thought I was lying, whereas I was telling the truth.
	even if	Even if we achieve great success in our work, there is no reason to feel conceited.

Continue Tab 6.2

Purpose	Frequently Used Phase	Example
Indicating Transition and concession	on the contrary	You think it simple, but on the contrary, it is complicated.
	no matter	No matter how difficult it may be, we are determined to carry the research to the end.
	in spite of	In spite of the cold weather, we went on digging the earth.
	all the same	He is not doing a very good job. All the same, you have to admit that he is doing his best.
Indicating conditions or cause	Once	Once you begin, you must continue.
	as long as	I will fight for the cause of Communism as long as I live.
	supposing	Supposing that yon were rich, what then?
	in case	In case I forget, please remind me about it.
	on condition that	We shall go to Guangzhou for our holiday, on condition that it isn't too expensive.
	on account of	On account of the bad weather, the harvest was poor.
	thanks to	Thanks to her ability, she has achieved great success.
	as far as	As far as I know, it is less valuable than diamond.
	owing to	Owing to his lack of experience, he didn't do the work well.
	but for	But for his help, we would have failed.
	according to	According to the weather report, it is going to snow tomorrow.
	considering	Considering that the time is short, you ought to go all out to fulfill the plan.
	it is understood that	It is understood that strict discipline is good for a student.
	it was noted above that	It was noted above that hard work and labor are often necessary to train a man's talent.
	it will be seen from this	It will be seen from this that the need for water is increasing day by day.

Task 6.4 Writing Practice

(1) Fill in the blanks with the appropriate sentences in the following

emails.

A

Request: technical parameters of your new products

Dear Tom, (*Purchasing manager*)

_____,
I'm pleased to discuss with you about the new type of HDI your company need. _____ offer me the technical parameters of your new products. And we are honored to invite you to attend the seminar about high-end HDI technologies held in our company on 12th, May next month.

Looking forward to hearing from you!

Yours faithfully

Brady

Sales representative

Shanghai Meadville Electronics Co., Ltd.

Tel: 021-52338899

B

Request again

Dear Mr. Tom,

_____,
especially this time of the year. However I would really appreciate it if you could send the technical parameters of your new products to me so that we can discuss about the cooperation between your company and our factory.

Thanks & Best regards

Brady

Sales representative

Shanghai Meadville Electronics Co., Ltd.

Tel: 021-52338899

C

Apologizing: late reply

Hi Brady,

_____.
Unfortunately, I cannot offer you the parameters of our new products, which are business secrets kept in our company.

If you have any other questions, contact me by phone below immediately.
Best wishes
Tom
Purchasing manager
Auster Circuits, Inc.
Tel: 0755-32456788

D

REMINDER: seminar about high-end HDI technologies on 12th, May
Dear Mr. Tom,

_____, we will hold a seminar about high-end HDI technologies on 12th, May next month. Would you please phone me before May 6 if we can count on you to participate?

I look forward to hearing from you!
Yours faithfully
Tom
Purchasing manager
Auster Circuits, Inc.
Tel: 0755-32456788

E

FW: REMINDER: seminar about high-end HDI technologies on 12th, May
Hi Brady,

Thanks for your reminding. _____ I'll take part in the seminar about high-end HDI technologies on 12th, May.

If there is some change, don't hesitate to inform me.
Best regards!
Tom
Purchasing manager
Auster Circuits, Inc.
Tel: 0755-32456788

(2) Write an email on behalf of President George Zhong of University of Zhongshan to congratulate Professor Denies Deng in the Natural Science Department on his recent reward of Fellows of the American Association for the Advancement of Science.

6.5 Reports

Reports play a crucial role in business practice as most major or decisive actions are based on business reports. On the other hand, reports are also quite often used as a device to exchange information in and among businesses, for instance, reporting to upper management, giving instruction to the divisions, making proposals, presenting a result of an investigation, etc. If reports are well written, that is, data collected thoroughly, analysis done perceptively and comment made correctly, solution can be expected to draw in a wise way.

Report is a common way of communication in many different professions. Businesspeople write a wide range of reports under various names, such as business plan, business proposal, project report, financial plan, and performance report, etc.

Business reports can be classified according to their different content. There are routine reports, investigation reports, progress reports, and feasibility reports. A routine report is a report presented to upper management on the day-to-day work; an investigation report is the description of the findings of an investigation; a progress report provides information of an ongoing program; a feasibility report is an assessment of the practicality of a proposed plan or method. Other kinds of reports include incident reports, supervision reports, sales reports, improvement reports, market studies and research reports.

Business reports can be formal or informal according to the degree of formality. They can be short or long. They may be delivered orally or through emails, memos or letters, though formal business reports are customarily submitted in print.

The most important elements of business report writing are accuracy and objectivity. Accuracy in business report writing means accuracy of information and that of writing. Since the information in a business report is used to make decisions, inaccurate information can lead to inaccurate decisions. Therefore, it is very important to make sure the facts are right. The accuracy of any report depends upon the correctness of the data gathered to prepare it. Sources used ought to be reliable and accurate in reporting all information.

The accuracy of writing depends on accuracy in writing mechanics (spelling, punctuation, and grammar) and accuracy in writing style. Formal style is usually adopted for writing business reports, so the passive voice, sentences beginning with "it", nominalizations and long learned words are commonly seen in business report writing.

In its most complete form, a formal business report includes three major parts with each containing sub-divisions.

(1) Front/Preliminary parts.

Title page: A title page is the front page of a report. On the title page should be included report title, name of the report writer, name of the report user, and date.

Letter of Authorization/Memo (a letter/memo by a person who authorizes the current report writer the task of writing the report)

Letter of Transmittal/Memo (a cover letter/memo responding to the call of a person who authorizes the report; briefly introducing key points of the report; expressing appreciation for anyone who helps in the completion of the report; expressing appreciation for the person who authorizes the report)

Table of Contents (a list of the sections in the report with the related page numbers)

List of Figures (a list/table of figures/diagrams/charts in the report)

List of Tables (a list of tables in the report)

List of Abbreviations (a list of abbreviations, e. g. scientific symbols, and their meanings)

Summary/Abstract/Synopsis/of Problem

Foreword/Introduction

(2) Middle/Body/Content parts.

Executive Summary (a quick overview of all the sections of the report)

Introduction

Text (the main body of the report identified throughout with headings and subheadings)

Conclusions/Summary

(3) Back/Extra parts.

References (a note for sources of information)

Bibliography (a list of citations)

Appendices (supplementary materials)

Glossary (an alphabetical list for technical terms)

Index (an alphabetical list of names and topics along with page numbers where they are discussed)

A short formal report is of special importance for beginners of report writing as it is more operable in format and content. It usually includes the following sections:

1) Terms of Reference/Introduction: This is an introductory part of the report answering questions like why the report is written, what the report is about, and when the report needs to be submitted.

2) Procedure/Method: This is where you explain how and where the information was gathered.

3) Findings: This section of the report should contain the information that you have found as a result of your procedure. You will need to include the facts and figures that you have been collected. You can use tables, graphs and charts.

4) Conclusions: This is where you show what you think of the information you have found. Make sure that you clearly show how you come to your conclusions, and that they are based on your findings. You should not introduce new points here.

5) Recommendations: This is where you must say how the problem can be solved. This must be based on the findings of the report.

6) Appendices: An appendix is the additional information you refer to in the report and wish to conclude as evidence or demonstration of the full findings.

7) Bibliography: The bibliography is a list of references.

An informal report is usually written in the format of a memo for internal communication, particularly within departments and for dealing with routine issues. Therefore, there is also a heading consisting of "TO", "FROM", "SUBJECT" and "DATE". The body of an informal report usually includes: Title; Background/Introduction/Situation; Findings/Analysis of Situation; Action/Solution/Conclusion.

The purpose of a formal report is to present a problem or condition, give supporting facts, provide analysis of the circumstances, and summarize the information. The result of the report is to draw a conclusion based on everything presented, and make proper recommendations.

Keep the content of the report free of opinions and biases. Back up the conclusion or recommendations with facts. If there appears to be more information needed, do more research to see if any more facts do exist. Make sure the facts are accurate and your thinking is logical. Make effective use of graphs, illustrations and charts to make important points. This is especially useful when facts are abundant and not easy to follow.

Business report writing often uses statistical data and their interpretation. Statistics are key building blocks of many reports. They must be rock solid to guarantee the integrity of your report. Treat these hard-earned data with the respect they deserve.

After you have finished the first draft, make sure you do the following editing:

Clearly state the scope of the report in the introduction;

In the body of the report, fully develop all the points in the introduction;

Develop the points logically and completely;

Present a clear discussion of the stated problem or condition, and the solution;

Write a report in plain language so that your audience will understand;

Properly title all tablets and figures, and place them correctly within the report;

Remove all grammar and spelling errors;

Have the report reviewed by your colleagues;

Edit it again.

Sample 1

To: Mile Johnson, Sales Manager
From: Sarah Liu
Date: July 2, 2010
Subject: Sales Performance of the Shanghai Branch
Introduction
Following your instruction, we examined the cause of the decline in sales of Shanghai Banch. We visited the office and most of their major customers there. These are my findings.
Findings
Some of the major customers in Shanghai have closed down, and some

have moved to other areas.

Other customers are planning to move to new Hangzhou or Ningbo as business there is booming and they can enjoy favorable policy from the local government there.

The Shanghai Office has not kept an up-to-date mailing list for sending circulars to existing customers who have moved out of Shanghai, or to potential customers moving in.

Conclusions

A more favorable after-sale mix is needed to keep our customers there.

An up-to-date mailing list for sending circulars should be made.

Recommendations

Upon the basis of the above findings and the conclusions, I recommend:

A traveling sales representative be positioned in Shanghai as this person will keep contact with customers who have moved out of Shanghai but may still purchase our goods.

Technical support be given in Shanghai Branch to deal with information or data sorting.

Sample 2

Report on Recommendation for a One-day Training Session

Introduction

The aim of this report is to recommend a one-day training session called "Familiarity with Your Post" for the sales representatives of the Sales Department.

Reasons

We have recruited several sales representatives recently. In spite of former sales experience, they are not familiar with their new working environment and may need quite a period to adapt to everything. Such a one-day training session seems to be necessary and urgent.

Contents and Benefits

There are many items relevant to the one-day training session for the sales representatives, which is designed to highlight work efficiency in the company.

Some brief information of the company should be given, such as the company's history, its organization structure and financial structure. The current situation of the company should be emphasized too. These would probably develop their loyalty and affection to the company.

They must be informed of the company's main products, its annual sales volume, and the sales target of this year. Clear recognition of this can help them adjust their personal goals and it will be served as great motivation.

Then, the course can focus on our customers. High value should be put on the types and characteristics of the target customers. Their needs are also expected to be transmitted to the sales representatives, which will help them to be more responsive and adaptive when selling products.

They should be given a brief introduction to the people whom they are working together with since coordination and teamwork can greatly contribute to the company.

Recommendations

We strongly recommend that training be arranged as soon as possible. And it could not be held on weekends, or it may occupy their spare time.

Task 6.5 Writing Practice

(1) Write a report on the topic of "Satisfaction with Employee Benefits" to Mr. Andy Chen, Director of Personnel.

You will first gather some information from employees at different levels in the company. Obtaining such information may involve looking through the past files regarding this problem. It may involve interviewing employees from different levels. Next you will analyze the situation in light of all you have learned about it. Then you will develop some recommendations to the situation. You may want to investigate the following aspects:

Overall satisfaction

Problem when dealing with the personal department

Suggestions for improvement

Problems when dealing with Health Maintenance Organization

(2) Rewrite the following sentences to make them more formal in style.

1) I am glad to enclose a check for you.

2) I am glad to tell you that your application for a post as a secretary was successful.

3) I am sorry to tell you that we cannot deliver the goods on time.

4) Could you tell me your prices?

5) Here is our invoice.

(3) Complete the following sentences by choosing the expressions given in the box.

| conclusion | conclusions | sum up | It is clear that |

1) To _____, my investigation indicates that investment in the ABC Company is not as reliable or beneficial as investment in the field we have been engaged in.

2) In _____, the purchase of new laptops is necessary at present.

3) _____ the English proficiency of our marketing staff is far from satisfactory.

4) No _____ were reached regarding the solution to the problem.

6.6 Minutes

Minutes of meetings are not just written for absent-minded participants to do their homework afterwards. They also keep permanent and formal records of discussions and decisions at meetings. Finished soon after the meetings, they are approved by the participants, signed by the chairperson and may be sent to archives for others to read long after the meetings. In business communication, minutes can keep people updated, track ongoing issues, and record business activities.

There are some common misunderstandings about minutes of meetings. First, minutes are less effective than a tape recorder. It is true that a tape recorder can take down every word said at the meetings. But it is not true that every word at the meeting makes sense. A lot of utterances, such as "er" and "ah" made by speakers at the meeting only indicate hesitations or uncertainty instead of making any points. No participants would like to read a tape transcription of their ramblings at the meeting. Second, minutes should not be in a verbatim manner, i.e. word by word. Even experienced minutes-takers with good shorthand skills can sometimes fail to keep up with some fast speakers, especially those with bad logic in their speeches. Minutes note down only the points and events instead of the necessary repetitions and nonsense words. Third, minutes may be taken by participants. Minutes should be impartial and objective records of what happens at the meeting. If taken by participants, it is not impossible that minutes will be influenced consciously or unconsciously by comments and opinions, as it is a duty of participants to give their opinions at the meeting. Minutes are usually taken by secretaries who will not speak at the meeting.

Finally, minutes may be corrected by people other than participants. People who were not present at a meeting didn't hear what said what. How could they decide whether to accept the minutes or not?

When our meetings aren't effective, we waste valuable time figuring out what we are trying to accomplish in them.

When our meeting minutes aren't effective, we waste the time we spent in meetings. Without good meeting notes or minutes, we may not remember or recognize:

- What we decided in the meeting
- What we accomplished in the meeting
- What we agreed to in terms of next steps (action items)

And when we can't remember the items above, we end up going in different directions and then meeting again for the same original purpose!

To avoid wasting your time spent in meetings, be sure your notes and minutes answer these 10 questions:

1. When was the meeting?
2. Who attended?
3. Who did not attend? (Include this information if it matters.)
4. What topics were discussed?
5. What was decided?
6. What actions were agreed upon?
7. Who is to complete the actions, by when?
8. Were materials distributed at the meeting? If so, are copies or a link available?
9. Is there anything special the reader of the minutes should know or do?
10. Is a follow-up meeting scheduled? If so, when? where? why?

Minutes need headings so that readers can skim for the information they need. Your template may include these:

Topics

Decisions

Actions Agreed Upon

Person responsible

Deadline

Next Meeting

Date and Time

Location

Agenda items

6.6.1 Do's and Don'ts

Do write minutes soon after the meeting—preferably within 48 hours. That way, those who attended can be reminded of action items, and those who did not attend will promptly know what happened.

Don't skip writing minutes just because everyone attended the meeting and know what happened. Meeting notes serve as a record of the meeting long after people forget what happened.

Don't describe all the "he said, she said" details unless those details are very important. Record topics discussed, decisions made, and action items.

Don't include any information that will embarrass anyone (for example, "Then Terry left the room in tears").

Do use positive language. Rather than describing the discussion as *heated* or *angry*, use *passionate*, *lively*, or *energetic*—all of which are just as true as the negative words.

Do have a new year filled with productive meetings captured efficiently in crisp, clear meeting notes.

6.6.2 How to Write Minutes

(1) Completeness.

Your minutes must cover every pertinent discussion during the meeting. Although you need not record every word spoken, you need to capture all the relevant topics discussed, issues and questions raised, as well as resolutions or plans of actions which have been agreed upon and laid down.

(2) Conciseness.

While it is vital that you record everything that has been discussed during the meeting, it is also equally important to make your minutes as brief as possible. You must be able to capture all the important issues discussed in a brief, organized and comprehensive manner. This skill can be acquired after writing several minutes.

(3) Accuracy.

It is very important that your minutes reflect accurate information. Always make sure that what you put into your report is correct and valid. If you're not sure as to the accuracy or validity of a certain issue, do not hesitate to ask those who. During my first few weeks with the company, there were terms and issues I simply had no idea about. So I sought clarification before writing the minutes. Remember that the minutes serve as a record of the meeting so that everyone involved—whether present or absent during the meeting—will have a good grasp of all the important issues that have been discussed.

(4) The Structure of the Minutes.

The form and structure of your minutes should also be considered carefully. I was fortunate enough to be provided with a template to work on when writing the minutes of our teleconferences. If you are allowed to make your own template, then you can be a little creative in formatting the structure of your minutes. In doing so, you need to bear in mind that minutes must be brief yet organized, comprehensive and accurate.

It would be best to use a columnar structure wherein you have separate columns for topics, issues raised, resolutions and plans of action, as well as for names of the person/s responsible for such actions.

Naturally, a good minute report must also reflect all the key elements such as the date and time, venue, attendees and facilitator, as well as the duration of the meeting. The schedule of the next meeting must also be recorded.

Sample 1

Meeting minutes document about the leaders of forage grass station of
Tianjin Animal husbandry office visit and inspect

(August 25, 2012)

August 25 of 2012, the head of forage grass station of Tianjin Animal husbandry office which is Xun Guirong Lady and the deputy director of Wuqing

Animal husbandry and aquatic office which is Mr. Fu Weitian, a group of people visited the location of Zhuoda Agricultural project where is nearby Tianjin Zhuoda endowment community, inspected the project of the New Zealand grass.

At the meeting, city, district leadership and the major managers of Zhuoda agricultural group Mr. Di Chengming, Mr. Liang Yanqiu, Mr. Jiang Wanying and Mr. Li Jianping of my Zhuoda company Conducted an in-depth exchange of views about the grass project development prospects, government to my company agriculture policy support and financial support. Finally, the city, district leadership gives a positive affirmation in both sides of the development of grass project and core competence of enterprise.

Finally, we preliminary reached a common opinion which are application about 1,333 hectares (9,000 CNY/ha) grass planting subsidies for my enterprise; apply for 15 million CNY city low-interest agricultural assistance loan for my enterprises, etc.

(1) In the meeting, the head of forage grass station of Tianjin Xun Guirong lady said:

First of all, to the development planning operation mode of Zhuoda agricultural group gave high evaluation and affirmation. In the United States, grassland agricultural economy is the fourth big pillar industry. Because of the past grass market of China does not distinguish between quality and price, lead to grow only in order to volume of production and output many low quality products.

Alfalfa is the king of the grass, the purpose of the alfalfa is very great, it contains an unknown factor, it has very big effect for female animals. National issued a document about development project of high quality dairy, we must develop high quality forage grass. Chairman of grass industry and dairy industry the experts urged, don't solve the problem about grass quality and industry, dairy industry can't one foot to walk, to ecological development is the most important factor to ensure the food safety.

In the 90 centuries, Tianjin Dagang development district has planted 2,667 hectares of grass as a project, but in final project was failure, the main reason is that the grass and livestock quantity does not match. From 2004 to 2006, countries do not grant subsidies to the planting of grass, only grant subsidies to the planting of grain, so it cracked down on the grass industry. At present the national annual production of grass is about 400 thousand tons, imports about 300 thousand tons. Based on past experience, to promote the development of grass industry will need to common fit of grass industry and animal husbandry department which can promote the whole industrial chain, otherwise, it will damage two industry.

In the policy, at present the country has took out $520 million use for development of 34,667 acres grassland. Countries give 133.3 acres shares of Tianjin, the mainly reason is that countries to Tianjin mature animal husbandry hope is very high, in addition comparing with other city, the development of dairy industry of Tianjin in the national is more leading, it can be digested in the locality.

Otherwise, large grass project has played an important role on local government GDP growth. It also made a positive contribution for farmers to increase production and income. For example: in Inner Mongolia Eduoke county circulates the land to the enterprise, and let the farmers found the cooperatives of cooperatives and the cooperatives of agricultural machinery, the company set standards to let farmers to operation and implementation, thereby solve the contradiction between the land and farmers, finally the province was attaches great importance to, the government is also strong support.

At present animal husbandry industry of Guandong has the great quality, because the high quality of alfalfa planting played a key role. As the project of enterprise, if you can do a long time, this is the most concern of government's. If you want to do a good job in this industry, you must have confidence and determination, specific still need to see the situation of the ultimate technology to carry out, these is expectations of Tianjin Animal husbandry office to enterprise.

The early stages investment of the project is very little for Real estate firm, but for farmers is too big. Planting need choose high yield varieties, because the land is more expensive and the management cost is higher than farmer, so we need to use the high cost to create a high income. As long as the capital already have enough, market have a plenty of, when the time comes we apply for more than 10 million CNY city low-interest agricultural assistance loan to make project high starting point start, let the future owner of Surrounding buildings experience true harmony between man and nature which will achieve by the development of Wuqing project.

(2) The deputy director of Wuqing Animal husbandry and aquatic office Mr. Fu Weitian said:

According to the current situation of the Tianjin breeding, each cow per year needs 1 ton alfalfa forage, now Tianjin has 150,000 head, Wuqing has 52,000 head, it is not even including the other aquaculture varieties of animal husbandry industry. Last year, the demand of grass of Tianjin is more than 30 thousand tons, according to the calculation of the Wuqing grass yield can local digestion, nearby digestion.

The good development of animal husbandry is an innovative mode of promotes agricultural development. Wuqing is a big district, however, the ecological environment is very poor, the modernization development of agriculture is too slow. If there is no large enterprise promoting, the mode of farmers' family planting cannot go to modern industry scale. Land circulation potential is very great, we need to put grass industry as industrialization industry rather than agriculture, and play a leading role from two element structure to three element structure transformation, and is a great help to increase the farmers' income. At the same time promotes the large model of green food safety, and pays special attention to the green food quality, implements the three industry linkage as final development mode of future.

(3) As interactive exchange the president of our company Mr. Di Chengming from the group's overall level said:

Zhuoda is three industry linkage, that is agriculture, new building materials, endowment demonstration project, meanwhile, Zhuoda also want to do the first-class city operators. The first thing of our development is to think of the life security for urban residents, life convenient supporting for farmers, the transformation of employment and five insurance, the greening and beautification of urban. Containing negative oxygen ion of our new material products is common building materials 10 times to 12 times. This can solve the worries and concerns of personal healthy security in home.

Cooperation with group headquarters' idea of 'three industry linkage', in all parts of the country such as Shijiazhuang, Tianjin, Shandong, Wuhan, Hainan, Shanxi, Nanjing and other places will do the strategic layout. In the recent, our agriculture group will try my best to do two things: one is to be a benchmarking of ecological animal husbandry demonstration of China, the other one is to be a high scientific and technological content in modern safety agriculture which is also large scale and industrialization. We are cooperating with large fertilizer, forage breeding company ROVENSDOWN which owned by New Zealand state, together found the project of 'China Zhuoda New Zealand ecological pasture'. This is a large industrialization cluster projects, and mainly is combination the high technology organic fertilizer and grass varieties combination. With the project attached, it also has professional technical of agriculture cooperation with New Zealand university of Lincoln, in the other hand, the cold fresh meat and dairy cooperation with South Island Pasture Alliance and the Western dairy industry will also expand. I have a final dream; it is to let the kids of Chinese who can drink the infant milk powder of New Zealand, and Let Chinese athletes to eat on our ecological beef and to drink on our healthy milk.

Our firm and the largest modern agriculture company of the United States, which is ST Company, is underway negotiations to cooperate, in the beginning, it is mainly embryo cattle and capital cooperation. Just now our chat is also talking that, Chinese dairy cow's production of milk is only in 4.5 tons to 5 tons per year, however; the whole American embryo cattle's production of high quality milk is reaching up to 10 tons per year. This value has more than doubled, because of the high quality will make the benefit more apparent. Because of the time limit, I won't discuss more about large-scale security agriculture. On the pasture project, our team has a word that is 'planting high quality grass, breeding the high quality cow, producing the high quality milk, feeding and making people health'.

Get to the point, for the project of forage grass be born Tianjin, we are still very carefully. In the beginning of project, we did market research for more than three months. We separately visited the farm and ranch of place such as Xinjiang, Inner Mongolia, Heilongjiang, Shandong, Hebei. And on July 5th in Beijing we invited 10 domestic chief scientists and experts about animal husbandry, industry and market to discuss and argue the feasibility of project, Internal also discussed for more than a month, comprehensive all research and argumentation results, preliminary conclusion is that the project is feasible and can implement. As for the back project implementation process, New Zealand aspects will rely on the advantage of international high-end brand and patent, along with the project process, according to the need for project reconstructs the available facilities and resources of the whole industry chain of project peripheral.

Our appeal of agriculture group is to let all of the surrounding buildings' owners who can eat the safe and high cost performance agricultural products, in addition, gradually and obviously raises the level farmers' income, perfecting the community and form a complete set for environment, meanwhile. The key is to realize the upgraded of the industrialization of farmers in the true sense, and to be a new type of industrial workers. We cooperates with New Zealand. Our goal is to reach 134 thousand hectares, at that time, no matter in scale, technology, brand or in the industry has the absolute right.

According to conservative estimates, the profit of planting grass is 3 times to 4 times than planting corn and other crops, our goal is listed. Of course it also depends on the local government whether can provide some land, capital and policy support.

(4) The vice President of our company Liang Yanqiu from real estate development supporting level said:

In 2006 Zhuoda began to participate in project of Tianjin, in 2007 we came to Wuqing District; we have been established two big projects until now. For positive response national development policies, we are occupying an area of 200 square kilometers land to build Beijing-Tianjin new city where is close to the Beijing, there are 100 square kilometers for agricultural to create natural new town, planning agricultural land is 453 hectares in the first period.

The Beijing-Tianjin new city covers a total of 5 area, the center of new city is in Hexiwu town and Gaocun village, that is creative Taiwan area, Zhuoda involved in two of the five.

(5) The vice president of our company Mr. Jiang Wanying mainly from present situation and market feedback of grass industry level said:

At present Zhuoda mainly rely on agriculture, the agricultural industry, capital operation and market sales as some big plate of operation mode. In the enterprise, these three elements are often difficult to gather together, however Zhuoda has all of these.

Planting alfalfa is fully staffed, which not only can improve the environment that plays the role of vegetation protection, but also it is economic product which is rich nutrition and rich in protein, so the grass industry attracted a large number of enterprise to investment it. In the past two years it has appeared many in the scale of the high starting point planting, all of these are the entire automated machinery plant operation. (in addition the localization of agricultural machinery equipment also have corresponding subsidies of agriculture)

In the market, if you want to purchase cooperation with a big company such as Mengniu, you need to have a major grass base and grass green reserves can enough at least 3 months or above usage, that can achieve supply requirements of cooperation with Mengniu. By this, large scale of planting can be digested in local and nearby. In 2007 the price of alfalfa imported from the United States is 2,100 to 2,200 CNY/ton, currently alfalfa imported from the United States is more than $400 a ton, combine with transportation and other costs to China port price is 3,200 CNY/ton. According to the supply and demand of domestic and foreign market, the planting prospects of high quality alfalfa planting prospects are very broad.

(6) The common opinion with government

1) We preliminary reached that are application about 1,333 hectares (9,000 CNY/ha) grass planting subsidies for my company; apply for 15 million CNY city low-interest agricultural assistance loan for my enterprises, etc. oral intention.

2) With Tianjin Animal husbandry office, Wuqing Animal husbandry and aquatic office and Wuqing dairy cow association set up the mechanism of regular consultation and discussion.

3) Tianjin Animal husbandry office will assist our agriculture group that applies demonstration projects of large agricultural machinery to the national ministry of agriculture.

4) Forage grass station of Tianjin Animal husbandry office will unit Tianjin dairy cow association to buy our production of Zhuoda New Zealand ecological pasture.

Sample 2

COMPANY

Meeting of the Board of Directors to be held on Wednesday, April 3, 2009 at 10:15 A. M. in the The Company Boardroom

AGENDA

1. Apologies for absence
2. Minutes of the meetings held on March 2, 2009

3. Points arising from minutes as read

4. Report by the Chairman (a copy of the report is attached to this agenda)

5. Resolution or Motion

6. Date of next meeting

7. To transact any other business that may come before the meeting

Minutes of the monthly meeting of a board of directors

Minutes of the Board of Directors of the XYZ Company held on Wednesday, April 3, 2009, at 10:15 A. M. in the company boardroom. Chairman John Brown presided.

PRESENT: Brad Schaffner (Harvard), Cathy Zeljak (George Washington), Brian Baird (H. F. Group), Diana Brooking (Washington), Adam Burling (ACRL), Jackie Byrd (Indiana), Jared Ingersoll (Columbia), Sandra Levy (Chicago), Dan Pennell (Pittsburgh), Janice Pilch (Illinois), Emily Ray (Yale), Kay Sinnema (Library of Congress), Andy Spencer (Wisconsin), David Woodruff (Getty Research Institute).

APOLOGIES: Apologies for absence were received from Rina Dollinger and Alfred Kessel.

MINUTES: The minutes of the March 2, 2009, meeting were read by the secretary and approved.

REPORT BY CHAIRMAN: The Chairman reported that he had met Mr. Nathan Rosenberg concerning XYZ's interests in computer software development and the services Mr. Rosenberg is prepared to extend to aid XYZ in developing these interests. For the information of the Chairman, Mr. Rosenberg outlined the growth of the software industry from the time he launched ABC Software Company in 1987 until today.

REPORT BY GENERAL MANAGER:

Thomas Kilroy summarized his detailed discussions with Jay Jefferson, Chief Executive Officer of Hudson Audiovisual Productions ("Hudson") and BZN's interests in audiovisual instructional materials. The classroom use of audiovisual instructional materials in the United States, Canada, the United Kingdom, and other countries of the European Union has been a major educational trend and has had phenomenal growth. A trend that educators in North America and Western Europe predicting is likely to continue.

Since there are many ways that Hudson can help BZN develop an international audiovisual program for use in English-speaking countries and with translation for other parts of the world, Mr. Kilroy made the following proposal, seconded by Nichols Raines, to authorize a feasibility study to cover the following:

1) The present educational audiovisual marketplace in the United States, Canada, and the United Kingdom, and its potential for expansion.

2) Present companies operating in this marketplace and their share.

3) Growth patterns of different types of audiovisual materials and their potential for continued growth and change.

REPORT BY MARKETING MANAGER:

Thomas Kilroy gave a summary of a study on the feasibility of acquiring an audiovisual instructional materials company in North America and the United Kingdom. Results indicate more investigation is needed.

1) To select the companies that seem to offer the best opportunities to BZN and to investigate the possibility of acquiring them.

2) To inquire about the terms of sales from the owners of the companies selected by BZN and report these terms to BZN.

MOTION: Chairman Brown proposed a motion, seconded by Sharon Moretti, that an ad hoc committee of directors should be instituted to study Mr. Rosenberg's involvement in greater detail. The board agreed to vote on this motion at the next meeting.

RESOLUTION: A resolution authorizing the company's transfer agent to issue new shares was unanimously adopted by all members.

NEXT MEETING: It was agreed that the next meeting will be held on May 2, 2009, at 10:30 A.M., in the company boardroom.

There being no further business, the meeting closed at 11:45 A.M..

6.6.3 Useful Sentences

    The vote encompassed approval...
    The chairman highlighted the background of...
    The chairman kicked off the discussion by...
    The president called meeting to order.
    The members inclined to provide more information about...
    The information reviewed at the June meeting suggested that...
    The manager reported on recent developments of...

Participants expressed concern about...
Participants observed that...
Others noted that...
Participants also discussed the role of...
Participants interpreted the incoming...
Several participants pointed out that...
In their discussion of..., participants observed that...
In their discussion of..., meeting participants saw...as...
In light of the possibility that...
In their discussion of...
The staff forecast prepared for...
The Committee unanimously approved the minutes of...
With regard to the Committee's announcement to be released after the meeting, members expressed some difference in views about...

Task 6.6 Writing Practice

(1) Translate the following sentences.

1) Mr. Mark maintained that the Financial Department was not responsible for the fall in sales.

2) The president announced two upcoming international conferences.

3) Annie explained that, as prospects for the future appeared sound, she should strongly recommend an increase in staff salaries.

4) The meeting was called to order by Zhao Ying at 9:00 a.m..

5) The next meeting was provisionally arranged for Tuesday, October 5.

6) Several appointments and dismissals were announced at the meeting.

(2) Take a minutes for a meeting held recently in your class. Pay attention to the format and all necessary elements of the minutes.

Answers

Part 1

Chapter 1
Task 1.1

The daring <u>life</u> and unexplained <u>death</u> of an American pilot, Amelia Earhart, have intrigued people for decades. Her love <u>affair</u> with airplanes bloomed when <u>Amelia</u> attended an air show in California with her father. <u>Amelia</u> received a parade and a medal from President Herbert Hoover in 1932 after <u>she</u> became the first woman to fly alone across the Atlantic Ocean. Her most treasured <u>goal</u>, however, was to be the first pilot ever to circle the earth at the equator. Amelia, along with her copilot, Fred Noon, took off from Miami in June 1937. <u>Articles</u> and <u>photographs</u> for American newspapers, together with letters to her husband, were sent by Amelia throughout her journey. The <u>public</u> followed Amelia and Fred's progress eagerly. <u>Everyone</u> was stunned when their <u>airplane</u> suddenly vanished one month after their <u>quest</u> began. The two <u>flyers</u> had completed 22,000 miles of the mission. A final <u>message</u> from Amelia to a Coast Guard ship indicated that her <u>plane</u> was near New Guinea, in the South Pacific. Neither the <u>plane</u> nor its <u>pilots</u> were ever found, though <u>squads</u> of Army planes and Navy ships searched thoroughly. Numerous <u>adventurers</u>, <u>scholars</u>, and Earhart <u>fans</u> have launched their own unsuccessful searches. <u>Rumors</u> about the pilots' disappearance continue to circulate today. <u>Some</u> say that Earhart dove into the ocean deliberately, while <u>others</u> claim <u>she</u> was on a spy mission and was captured by the Japanese. Nevertheless, many modern female <u>pilots</u> cite Earhart's courage and achievements among their reasons for learning to fly.

Task 1.2

Cheese rolling |has been known| as one of Britain's most unusual customs for centuries. Each year, Gloucestershire, England, |is invaded| by thousands of fans who |can't wait| for the contest. They |are thrilled| to watch perfectly sane men and women chase seven-pound wheels of Gloucestershire cheese that |are rolled| down Cooper's Hill. Once the spectators |see| the athletes line up along the crest of the hill, they |begin| chanting " |Roll| that cheese!" When the master of ceremonies |has blown| the whistle, the athletes |give| their cheeses a push and |scramble| after them. The hill |is| steep and lumpy, so contestants |know| that they |might get injured|; broken bones and sprains |are reported| each year. Some competitors |win| only by accidentally tumbling down the hill, past their more careful peers. At times, the cheese |rolls| into the crowd and |strikes| someone, but no one |is hurt| and the cheese |is kicked| back onto the course. The winner |gets| a fine prize: the cheese that he or she |has chased|. Cheese rolling |may have evolved| from early harvest or fertility rituals, and it |may date| back to the ancient Britons or Romans who |lived| in the area.

Task 1.3

Many <u>animals</u> |are| friendly, helpful, or amusing, but <u>others</u> |possess| venom <u>that</u> |can cause| their victims pain or even death. Rattlesnake <u>bites</u>, for example, |can cause| severe pain, swelling, and temporary paralysis. Several old horror <u>movies</u> |feature| Gila monsters, a type of venomous lizard <u>that</u> |frequents| the southwestern United States and Mexico. <u>Bites</u> from Gila monsters |can bring| horrible pain and dangerously low blood pressure. Many <u>people</u> |are| allergic to bites from bees, wasps, hornets, and even ants. Allergic reactions can include swelling and rashes. Some victims are so allergic that they may die of shock within minutes of being bitten. Though most spiders' bites cause only itching and swelling, others are much more harmful. Black widow spider bites cause severe pain, weakness, and convulsions, though survival from their bites is likely. The brown recluse spider is often called a "fiddleback" because of its oblong body.

Task 1.4

1. Tom's car alarm (are, is) a source of irritation for her neighbors.
2. For years, a problem facing the city (was, were) killer bees.
3. On the curb (was, were) sitting my brothers.
4. The topic of my essay (was, were) the various kinds of tropical fish, as well as how to care for them.
5. Goalies, rather than defensive players, often (receive, receives) the most media coverage.
6. Cable news channels sometimes (announce, announces) the winner of an election before all citizens have gone to the polls to vote.
7. In his movies, Johnny Depp always (know, knows) when the outlaws are about to attack.
8. On his Web site, Carlos (offer, offers) cell phone accessories at discounted prices.
9. Why (is, are) there so much traffic on Interstate 405?
10. Many tourists are surprised to learn that there once (was, were) a lot of steelhead trout in the canyons of Malibu, California.
11. People now (begin, begins) smoking at a younger age than ever before.
12. Senator Diaz (has, have) promised not to raise taxes.
13. Did you know that cross-country skis (is, are) much cheaper than downhill skis?

14. The Ice Hotel, built each winter in Arctic Sweden, (melt, [melts]) in May or June.
15. To win horseracing's treasured Triple Crown, a horse (have, [has]) to win the Kentucky Derby, Preakness, and Belmont races.
16. At nearly one hundred years old, Lloyd Moore ([is], are) Nascar's oldest former driver.
17. The founder of Craigslist.com, one of America's twenty most popular Web sites, (are, [is]) actually a man named Craig Newmark.
18. Laker player Kobe Bryant won the league's Most Valuable Player award in 2008, and many fans thought it ([was], were) long overdue.
19. Just how many chiles (was, [were]) in those enchiladas we ate?
20. We all know not to disturb Caitlyn when her favorite show, *Desperate Housewives*, ([is], are) on.
21. To ascend the St. Louis Arch, you must ride in a cramped capsule that (resemble, [resembles]) an egg.
22. After watching a season of *Boston Legal*, Linda ([has], have) decided to become an attorney.
23. The television special *Lewis and Clark* ([has], have) lured many people into learning about early American explorers.
24. Tim said that there (is, [are]) two assignments due next Monday.
25. ([Has], Have) anyone met the new dormitory advisor?

Task 1.5

1. She dusted the shelf before putting the antique ceramic plate on it. (She dusted the antique ceramic plate before putting it on the shelf.)
2. I did not go to the depressing solo concert. (It is depressing that I did not go to the depressing solo concert.)
3. I checked the weather forecast yesterday, but it didn't predict the sleet we are having today.
4. When my dog kept barking at the parrot, I put the dog in the other room.

(When my dog kept barking at the parrot, I put the parrot in the other room.)
5. Anyone who is interested in volunteering at village-schools should write his or her name on the list.
6. I had a good time collecting shells on the beach. When I looked carefully at low tide, I could see many different kinds of shells.
7. Because she had decorated her living room with posters from chamber music festivals, her date thought that she was interested in classical music. Actually she preferred rock.
8. In my high school, students didn't need to get all A's to be considered a success; they just needed to work to their ability.
9. Zoe told Amy, "I am worried about your mother's illness." ("... about my mother's illness")
10. Though the little boy cried for several minutes after colliding with a chair, eventually his crying subsided.

Task 1.6

1. When the rhythmic gymnast asked for a volunteer partner, everyone in the men's gym class raised his hand.
2. The faculty of the foreign languages school was praised by the president for its dedication to the college.
3. Each of the children was responsible for arrange their own stationery.
4. For a child, stories are magical, and they improves the child's imagination.
5. A parent reading aloud to his or her children fosters lifelong love of reading in them.
6. When studying a foreign language, one should avoid translating each word separately into his or her own language.
7. C
8. All of the airline passengers must pass through the security check before they may board the airplane.
9. Those kinds of puzzles make me confused.
10. Many a student earn his or her tuition by working part time.

Task 1.7

1. Believe it or not, there is a set of rules about how to display the American flag, which the War Department wrote in 1923.
2. Citizens may display their flags any time they want to although it is traditional to fly them only from sunrise to sunset.
3. The White House is unusual because its flag flies both day and night.
4. C
5. No other flag may be flown above or to the right of the U. S. flag except at the United Nations headquarters in New York City.
6. A rule that most Americans are familiar with is that the flag should never touch the ground or floor.
7. A flag may cover the casket of military personnel or other public officials if it is not permitted to touch the ground or be lowered into the grave.
8. Disposal of a worn or damaged flag in a dignified way is preferably by burning.
9. C
10. Politicians still debate whether American schoolchildren should be required to pledge their allegiance to the flag although reciting that oath is not mandatory now.

Task 1.8

1. Wind power for the home is a supplementary source of energy. It can be combined with electricity, gas, or solar energy.
2. C
3. In the Middle Ages, the streets of London were dangerous places. It was safer to travel by boat along the Thames.
4. "He's not drunk," I said. "He's in a state of diabetic shock."
5. If you are able to endure extreme angle turns, high speeds, frequent jumps, and occasional crashes, then supermoto racing may be a sport for you.

Task 1.9

1. Rodney's goal is to take piano lessons and play in the school orchestra, and then he'll try to make some spending money by playing in local jazz clubs.
2. Smiling and clapping her hands, he is clearly a healthy and happy baby.
3. The Lagat family of Kenya have produced several of the world's top distance runners.
4. C
5. As we arrived too late to the movie theatre, Rico and Zack had arrived on time and gone inside without us.
6. Yankees player Robinson Cano telephones his father in the Dominican Republic. After every game they dissect Robinson's batting performance swing by swing.
7. C
8. The humidity was high, so the children did not feel like playing outside.
9. Cesar bought Lisa a sweater that matches her new skirt perfectly.
10. You won't believe what Jack just told me. Go ahead try to guess!

Task 1.10

1. When we watch an exciting movie on television, commercials are especially irritating.
2. Raised in Colorado, Mike naturally misses the snow-covered mountains.
3. Although only a sophomore, Kathy was selected by the field hockey team as its captain.
4. C
5. When he was a child, his father bought him a violin in the hope that he would become a violinist.
6. While I was walking on the beach, the sand warmed my bare feet.
7. While I was walking across the manicured golf course yesterday, the sprinklers suddenly came on.
8. After I offered a toast to the guest of honor, dinner was served.
9. C
10. Driving across the country last summer, I could detect the differences in re-

gional accents.

Task 1.11

1. Many students graduate from college with debt totaling more than fifty thousand dollars.
2. It is a myth that humans use only 10 percent of their brain.
3. A cool-hunter is a person who can find the next wave of fashion in the unnoticed corners of modern society.
4. The bank robber was described as a short man weighing 175 pounds and wearing a baseball cap.
5. Kevin found some mold growing at the bottom of the swimming pool.
6. On the wall above his desk is a photograph in a gold frame of his daughter.
7. The patient with symptoms of heart disease was referred to a cardiac specialist.
8. At Fairview College, Professor Jenkins is teaching a course on criminal behavior.

Task 1.12

1. In computer class, Phuong learned to build web pages and use the Internet.
2. Trisha complained that her counselor did not have an understanding of students' problems and did not like people.
3. Owning a home requires not only a lot of maintenance and time but also a great deal of expense.
4. Wally's ideas are clever, original, and practical.
5. The ambassador from Iran would neither apologize nor promise to accept the demands of the United Nations.
6. C
7. C
8. The governor said that his hobbies were fly-fishing and playing video games with his grandchildren.
9. Many people join health clubs for exercise, relaxation, and romance.
10. Nicholas Cage is admired as an actor because he is good not only in dramatic roles but also in comedies.

11. My Aunt Clara swears she has seen Elvis snacking at the deli, browsing at the supermarket, munching at the pizza parlor, and selecting the cookbook at a local bookstore.
12. According to my husband, summer air in Louisiana is 2 percent oxygen, 8 percent water, and about 90 percent mosquitoes.
13. Smart people learn from their own mistakes; smarter people learn from others' mistakes.
14. Theater class helped me overcome my shyness, make new friends, and improve my confidence to do other activities.
15. The writer Oscar Wilde, the dancer Isadora Duncan, the painter Max Ernst, and the rock star Jim Morrison, are all buried in the same Paris cemetery.

Task 1.13

1. I enjoy pizza much more than Garth does.
2. The Tim McGraw CD is more expensive than the Faith Hill CD.
3. C
4. Clothes are more fashionable at Tommy Hilfiger than at other stores.
5. We'd rather listen to blues than to other kinds of music
6. The neighbors near our new house in Brownsville are friendlier than the neighbors near our old house in Boston.
7. Sipping coffee with my English instructor is more enjoyable than with a super model.
8. C
9. The defense attorney's case is stronger and more interesting than the prosecutor's.
10. Judy's flu has grown worse since yesterday OR worse than it was yesterday.

Task 1.14

1. Using radiation – proof clothes was a precaution taken by the rescuers in Japan to prevent nuclear radiation.
2. A career in medicine, which many young people are pursuing, requires at least ten years of challenging work.

3. I did it is because they asked me to do it.
4. Raised in Inner Mongolia, Ling loves the prairie.
5. This box contains the favorite toys of my son's.
6. By early diagnosis, gastric cancer is often curable.
7. We determine our distance of travel depending on the weather condition.
8. Wearing thongs in PE class, Jenny sprained her ankle.
9. On seeing the birthday gift on her desk, my little daughter was pleasantly surprised.
10. Being confident in her language gift, Kate decided to major in English-teaching.

Task 1.15

1. simple sentence
2. simple sentence
3. compound sentence
4. complex sentence
5. complex sentence
6. compound-complex sentence
7. simple sentence
8. compound sentence
9. complex sentence
10. simple sentence
11. complex sentence
12. simple sentence
13. complex sentence
14. compound-complex sentence
15. complex sentence
16. compound sentence
17. simple sentence
18. simple sentence
19. complex sentence
20. compound-complex sentence

Task 1.16

1. Willie had a long, bushy beard and a droopy moustache.
2. The man handed me a torn and faded photograph of a young woman.
3. The photograph instantly brought back fine old memories.
4. The torn and faded photograph of a beautiful young woman instantly brought back fine old memories.

Task 1.17

1. Monroe and I strolled through the graveyard, the most peaceful spot in town.
2. We were waiting outside the prison cells, a row of sheds fronted with double bars, like small animal cages.
   (George Orwell, "A Hanging")
3. Outside beneath my window, my father whistled for Reggie, our English setter.
4. We arrived at a small group of peasant houses, low yellow constructions with dried-mud walls and straw roofs.
   (Alberto Moravia, *Lobster Land: A Traveler in China*)
5. A great many old people came and knelt around us and prayed, old women with jet-black faces and old men with work-gnarled hands.
   (Langston Hughes, "Salvation")
6. I led a raid on the small, shabby grocery of Barba Nikos, a short sinewy Greek who walked with a slight limp and sported a flaring, handlebar moustache.
   (Harry Mark Petrakis, *Stelmark: A Family Recollection*)

Task 1.18

(Keep in mind that in most cases more than one effective combination is possible.)
1. The first alarm clock, which woke the sleeper by gently rubbing his feet, was invented by Leonardo da Vinci.
2. Children who have not received flu shots must visit the school doctor.

3. Success, which encourages the repetition of old behavior, is not nearly as good a teacher as failure.
4. I showed the arrowhead to Rachel, whose mother is an archaeologist.
5. Merdine, who was born in a boxcar somewhere in Arkansas, gets homesick every time she hears the cry of a train whistle.
6. The space shuttle is a manned rocket that can be flown back to earth and re-used.
7. Henry Aaron, who played baseball with the Braves for 20 years, was voted into the Hall of Fame in 1982.
8. Oxygen—which is colorless, tasteless, and odorless—is the chief life-supporting element of all plant and animal life.
9. Bushido, which is the traditional code of honor of the samurai, is based on the principles of simplicity, honesty, courage, and justice.
10. Mary danced on the roof of her trailer during the thunderstorm that flooded the county last night.

Task 1.19

1. Because the species is unknown in Egypt, it is unlikely that Cleopatra actually committed suicide with an asp.
2. The boy hid the gerbil where no one would ever find it.
3. Since our neighbors installed a swimming pool in their backyard, they have gained many new friends.
4. On a hot August evening, my parents and I watched in awe as erratic bolts of lightning from a distant storm illuminated the sky.
5. Whenever Benny played the violin, the dog hid in the bedroom and whimpered.
6. Natural rubber is used chiefly to make tires and inner tubes because it is cheaper than synthetic rubber and has greater resistance to tearing when wet.
7. By ancient custom, when a Peruvian woman finds an unusually ugly potato, she runs up to the nearest man and smashes it in his face.
8. Credit cards are dangerous because they encourage people to buy things that they are unable to afford and do not really need.
9. Some day, when the clouds are heavy, and the rain is coming down and the pressure of realities is too great, I shall deliberately take my glasses off and

go wandering out into the streets, never to be heard from again.
(James Thurber, "The Admiral on the Wheel")

Task 1.20

1. A common myth about the nature of mathematical ability holds that one either has or does not have a mathematical mind.
(Sheila Tobias, "Who's Afraid of Math, and Why?")
2. Where cross-country skiing differs most fundamentally from downhill skiing is in the way you get yourself uphill.
(Thomas J. Jackson, "Happy Trails")
3. Geologists believe that radar scanning will be valuable for detecting modern waterways lying near the surface in arid areas.
4. What an American values is not the possession of money as such, but his power to make it as a proof of his manhood.
(W. H. Auden, "The Almighty Dollar")
5. Politicians should be encouraged to stand for what they believe in, not formulate their principles on the basis of opinion polls.
6. One of the saddest things is that the only thing a man can do for eight hours a day, day after day, is work.
(William Faulkner)
7. Happiness is not having what you want, but wanting what you have.
(Hyman Judah Schachtel, *The Real Enjoyment of Living*)
8. The truth is that when we are in trouble we discover swiftly and painfully what kind of inner resources, what imperishable treasures of mind and heart we have deposited in the bank of the spirit against this rainy day.
(A. Whitman, "Resources to Last a Lifetime")
9. In practice nobody cares whether work is useful or useless, productive or parasitic; the sole thing demanded is that it shall be profitable.
(George Orwell, *Down and Out in Paris and London*)
10. Nonverbal communications signal to members of your own group what kind of person you are, how you feel about others, how you'll fit into and work in a group, whether you're assured or anxious, the degree to which you feel comfortable with the standards of your own culture, as well as deeply significant feelings about the self, including the state of your own psyche.

(Edward T. Hall, "The Sounds of Silence")

Task 1.21

1. Sitting on the ground in a shady corner with my back against the wall, I took small sips from a can of Coke.
2. Sitting on the widow ledge overlooking the narrow street, I watched the children frolicking in the first snow of the season.
3. Published by the U.S. Government in 1914, the first edition of *Infant Care* recommended the use of peat moss for disposable diapers.
4. The gray, weather-worn house sat stately upon a hill surrounded by barren tobacco fields.
5. Fearing that some member of the gang might see me, I washed the windows in a fever of fear, whipping the squeegee swiftly up and down the glass.
6. "Goldsmith smiled, bunching his fat cheeks like twin rolls of smooth pink toilet paper."

(Nathanael West, *Miss Lonelyhearts*)

7. The medieval peasant—distracted by war, weakened by malnutrition, exhausted by his struggle to earn a living—was an easy prey for the dreaded Black Death.

Task 1.22

1. It being freezing cold,...
2. ... her little son following her.
3. There being something wrong with his computer,...
4. She having finished her composition, we went home.
5. ..., with his clothes covered with snow.

Task 1.23

1. Ed and the little man climbed the stairs together, each lost in his own strange world.
2. I sat on the highest limb of a sturdy oak tree, its branches reaching to the clouds as if to claim a piece of the sky.

3. The dog trots away, his head and tail erect, his hips slightly to one side and out of line with his shoulders.
4. Her slender front paws reaching ahead of her like the hands of an experienced swimmer, the raccoon goes down on all fours and strides slowly off.
5. Their faces old and beautifully lined, their gray heads almost touching, my grandparents were holding hands in a New York City subway train.
6. Half listening to what the grownups were saying and half lost in a daydream, I sat huddled on the steps, my cheeks resting sullenly in my palms.
7. One sunny morning I whipped down the Roxbury Road on my bicycle, the front spokes melting into a saw blade, the wind shrilling tunes through the vent holes in my helmet.
8. An elderly woman, her ash-blond hair slightly askew and showing tuffs of thin gray hair, shuffles slowly to a park bench and sits down heavily.
9. A pencil poking out from behind his ear, Arthur fidgets on his high-legged chair in his box-like office in the old Loft's candy factory on Broome Street.
10. Between 90 million and 100 million years ago, several species of turtle took to the sea, their stubby legs adapting into streamlined flippers.

Chapter 2

Task 2.1

I am not against all schools. I am very much in favor of schools that consist of groups of porpoises or similar aquatic animals that swim together. I only wish that I had been to one. No, I'm thinking more of school in the dictionary sense as an institution or building at which children and young people receive education. That dictionary definition tells the story. What a school of porpoises do is play. Skool is for work. It is an institution. Why put children in an institution? The real reason is that it gets the brats out from under parents' feet. The purported reason is that this is the best way to get useful information into the skulls of the little darlings. How absurd! Children are more intelligent than adults and wiser. Instead of instilling into them the accepted knowledge and wisdom of the past, what we ought to be doing is learning from them. That would be my idea of a good school: one run by children—or porpoises.

(Adapted from "Down With Skool!" by Richard Boston. *Guardian Weekly*, April 22, 1990)

Task 2.2

1. The cold, impersonal atmosphere of the university was unbearable.
2. An ambulance threaded its way through police cars, fire trucks, and irate citizens.
3. C
4. After two broken arms, three cracked ribs, and one concussion, Ken quit the varsity football team.
5. C
6. NASA's rovers on Mars are equipped with special cameras that can take close-up, high-resolution pictures of the terrain.
7. C
8. C
9. Love, vengeance, greed, and betrayal are common themes in Western literature.
10. Many experts believe that shark attacks on surfers are a result of the sharks' mistaking surfboards for small injured seals.

Task 2.3

1. When Mt. St. Helens erupted in the 1980s, many people in Seattle worried about the status of Mount Rainier.
2. My sister, who plays center on the Sparks, now lives at The Sands, a beach house near Los Angeles.
3. Being written in haste, the composition is full of mistakes.
4. I had the pleasure of talking to a woman who had just returned from India, where she had lived for ten years.
5. C
6. A member of an organization that provides job training for teens was also appointed to the education commission.
7. Crocodiles, in fact, do not particularly like human flesh.
8. All our savings gone, we started looking for jobs.

9. Brian Eno, who began his career as a rock musician, turned to meditative compositions in the late 1970s.
10. Their room was on the third floor, its window overlooking the sportsground.

Task 2.4

1. Cricket, which originated in England, is also popular in Australia, South Africa, and India.
2. At the sound of the starting pistol, the horses surged forward toward the first obstacle, a sharp incline three feet high.
3. After seeing an exhibition of Western art, Gerhard Richter escaped from East Berlin and smuggled out many of his notebooks.
4. Corrie's new wet suit has an intricate blue pattern.
5. The cookies will keep for two weeks in sturdy, airtight containers.
6. On June 15, 2013, our office moved to 30 Peace Road, Mudanjiang 157099.
7. C
8. Ms. Carlson, you are a valued customer whose satisfaction is very important to us.
9. Mr. Mundy was born on July 22, 1939, in Arkansas, where his family had lived for four generations.
10. C

Task 2.5

1. Cows will not eat hay that has a musty odor; therefore, farmers must make sure that it is dry before they bale it.
2. Professor Kgosi showed us slides of his trip to Zanzibar, Tabora, and Linga in Tanzanina; Nairob, Nakum, and Mombasa in Kenya; and Jube, Waw, and Kartoum in Sudan.
3. I will have to find a job this semester, or I will have to get a loan to pay for my tuition.
4. C
5. Jessica quit her job at the bakery last week; she plans to move to Cedar Rap-

ids to take over her father's farm.
6. The music that the disc jockey played was from the 1950s, so I decided to listen instead of dance.
7. Tran speaks English at school; at home, however, he speaks Vietnamese.
8. Monaco has no famous colleges or universities; however, it has a ninety-nine percent literacy rate.
9. One moment he was friendly, even warm; the next he was coldly indifferent.
10. If an animal does something, we call it instinct; if we do the same thing, we call it intelligence.

Task 2.6

1. Although Barbara and I were in Boston for just one day, we were able to achieve our goal: a tour of the city's historical sites.
2. C
3. The North End and Beacon Hill possess quaint features of a bygone era: cobbled streets, gaslights, and treacherous brick sidewalks.
4. C
5. C
6. I was amazed by the New England Aquarium's four-story circular glass tank, which houses the aquarium's main attractions: sharks, turtles, eels, and hundreds of tropical Fish.
7. We next visited the Old North Church, whose steeple contained the two lanterns that sparked the famous midnight ride of Paul Revere.
8. Next we toured the 1713 Old State House to see tea from the Boston Tea Party, one of John Hancock's coats, and the east front where the Boston Massacre occurred.
9. Handwritten documents, tape recordings, and the actual Oval Office desk: these mementos at the John F. Kennedy Library touched us deeply.
10. As dusk descended on Boston, Barbara and I strolled to the Public Garden for our final treat: a ride in one of the famous swan-shaped boats.

Task 2.7

1. Our favorite barbecue restaurant is Poor Richard's Ribs.

2. C
3. The innovative shoe fastener was inspired by the designer's young son.
4. Each day's menu features a different European country's dish.
5. Sue worked overtime to increase her family's earnings.
6. Ms. Jacobs is unwilling to listen to students' complaints about computer failures.

Task 2.8

1. Gandhi once said, "An eye for an eye only ends up making the whole world blind."
2. As for the advertisement "Sailors have more fun," if you consider chipping paint and swabbing decks fun, then you will have plenty of it.
3. C
4. After winning the lottery, Juanita said that she would give half the money to charity.
5. After the movie, Vicki said, "The reviewer called this flick 'trash of the first order.' I guess you can't believe everything you read."
6. C

Task 2.9

1. For several weeks in 2009, the Black Eyed Peas held the top two spots on the music charts with their songs "I Gotta Feeling" and "Boom Boom Pow".
2. Last week we read "A Modest Proposal", an essay by Jonathan Swift.
3. Last week we read "A Modest Proposal"; this week we're reading Shirley Jackson's short story "The Lottery".
4. In a famous *New Yorker* essay in October 1998, Toni Morrison referred to Bill Clinton as "our first black president".
5. Bonnie asked, "Are you going to the concert without me?"
6. Bonnie asked if we were going to the concert without her. (no quotation marks)
7. In the words of comedian Steve Martin, "Talking about music is like dancing about architecture."
8. The indie folk band Deer Tick sang "What Kind of Fool Am I?"

9. Was it Dylan Thomas who wrote the poem "Fern Hill"?
10. Uncle Gus said, "I heard your mother singing 'Tutti Frutti' out behind the barn at three O'clock in the morning."
11. "I've memorized several poems," Merdine said, "including 'The Road Not Taken' by Robert Frost."
12. "All our failures," wrote Iris Murdoch, "are ultimately failures in love."

Task 2.10

1. DollarXmy pet dogX is not allowed to enter the house.
2. Law, navigation, politics, medicine, war—Shakespeare wrote about all of these topics.
3. If we win the championship gameXand the critics say we won'tXit will be a tremendous victory for our athletic program.
4. My oldest brotherXthe computer programmer who lives in Rockville CentreXis unable to attend our cousin's wedding.
5. Earl claims that it was her intelligenceXnot her wealthXthat attracted him.
6. The most common American slang termsXaccording to an authority on language deal with money, sex, and drinking.
7. Only one obstacle kept Con from a career in music—talent.
8. I read an article in the *Times*Xor maybe it was *Newsweek*Xdescribing the tornado in Kansas last week.
9. Kent's fatherXan acupuncturistXlives in San Antonio.
10. Our dinner last nightXsalad, steak, a vegetable, and dessertXcost only five dollars with a special coupon.

Task 2.11

1. Social insects, bees—for example—are able to communicate complicated messages to one another.
2. A client left his or her (*or* a) cell phone in our conference room after the meeting.
3. The films we made of Kilauea on our trip to Hawaii Volcanoes National Park illustrate a typical spatter cone eruption.
4. C

5. C
6. Of three engineering fields—chemical, mechanical, and materials—Keegan chose materials engineering for its application to toy manufacturing.

Task 2.12

1. Zola's first readers were scandalized by his slice-of-life novels.
2. C
3. The swiftly moving tugboat pulled alongside the barge and directed it away from the oil spill in the harbor.
4. C
5. Your dog is well known in our neighborhood.
6. Roadblocks were set up along all the major highways leading out of the city.

Task 2.13

1. C
2. The story of the sinking of the *Titanic* is the subject of the movie *The Titanic*.
3. I learned the Latin term *ad infinitum* from an old nursery rhyme about fleas: "Great fleas have little fleas upon their back to bite 'em, / Little fleas have lesser fleas and so on *ad infinitum*."
4. In the film *The Postman* the leading character wins a woman's heart by quoting from the poems "Walking Around" and "Leaning into the Afternoons" by the poet Pablo Neruda.
5. C
6. *Song of Myself*, Walt Whitman's famous long poem, was published in 1855.

Task 2.14

1. Marion Cotillard, the French film actress, won an academy award for best actress in the movie *La Vie en Rose* in 2008.
2. The 1964 civil rights act established as law equal rights for all citizens in voting, education, public accommodations, and federally assisted programs.
3. Applicants for the sales position were required to pass written examinations in

English, Spanish, and Japanese.

4. C

5. The oldest university in the united states is harvard, which was founded in 1636.

6. Happy birthday, aunt mary.

7. The commencement speaker was chief justice souter of the supreme court.

8. Colin Powell, a retired general in the united states army, was born in New York.

9. For many years the irish, italians, and jews were the dominant ethnic groups in new york city.

10. My uncle Dan told me many stories about fishing along the banks of the mississippi river.

11. Many african americans celebrate the festival called Kwanzaa, which means "first fruits of the harvest" in the african language Swahili.

12. Munich is the capital of bavaria in southern Germany and is located on the isar river.

Chapter 3
Task 3.1

1. c
2. a
3. b
4. c

Task 3.2

1. (b) *The Hunger Games* is a morality tale about the dangers of a political system that is dominated by the wealthy.

2. (b) While cell phones provide freedom and mobility, they can also become a leash, compelling users to answer them anywhere and at any time.
3. (b) College students looking for part-time work should begin their search by taking advantage of job-finding resources on campus.
4. (a) For the past three decades, coconut oil has been unjustly criticized as an artery-clogging saturated fat.
5. (b) Despite its title, *Bram Stoker's Dracula*, a film directed by Francis Ford Coppola, takes considerable liberties with Stoker's novel.
6. (a) There are several steps that teachers can take to encourage academic integrity and curtail cheating in their classes.
7. (a) J. Robert Oppenheimer, the American physicist who directed the building of the first atomic bombs during World War II, had technical, moral, and political reasons for opposing the development of the hydrogen bomb.
8. (b) The iPad, with its relatively large high-definition screen, has helped to revitalize the comic book industry.
9. (a) Like other addictive behaviors, Internet addiction may have serious negative consequences, including academic failure, job loss, and a breakdown in personal relationships.
10. (b) Every Sunday we visited my grandmother, who lived in a tiny house that was undeniably haunted.

Task 3.3

1. Before humans learned to farm, they were nomads, moving from place to place in search of game and vegetation. Each group consisted of about thirty to fifty people. <u>Once farming was developed, the beginnings of cities appeared.</u> Farming provided steady sustenance, which allowed people to live in larger groups and in permanent settlements. Each group had to make rules for civil coexistence, for divisions of labor, and for trade. People began to base their identities less on family ties than on geographical or cultural ties, and they placed growing value on the interests of the larger community.

2. <u>My mother is neither tall nor heavy, but she's the biggest person in my life.</u> There has been no other person with a greater influence on me. Most mothers feed, wash, and clothe their children, and my mother is no exception. But more than this, she made sure that I received the finest education possible. This

education was not at expensive schools or famous universities, but at home, by her knee, patiently. My mother explained to me the difference between right and wrong; the virtues of generosity, honesty, and hard work; and the importance of family and social ties. From her I understood who I was, where I belonged, and how I should spend my energies. No matter how big I might grow to be, I hope to be as great as my mother.

3. <u>Reasons for the popularity of fast-food chains appear obvious enough.</u> For one thing, the food is generally cheap as restaurant food goes. A hamburger, French fries, and a shake at McDonald's, for example, cost about one-half as much as a similar meal at a regular "sit-down" restaurant. Another advantage of the chains is their convenience. For busy working couples who don't want to spend the time or effort cooking, the fast food restaurants offer an attractive alternative. And, judging by the fact that customers return in increasing numbers, many Americans like the taste of the food.

Task 3.4

Original Topic Sentences:
My life may be a box full of frustrations, but learning how to overcome them has given me the gift of patience.

Task 3.5

1. <u>Almost every wedding tradition has a symbolic meaning that originated centuries ago.</u> For example, couples have been exchanging rings to symbolize unending love for over a thousand years. <u>Most often, the rings are worn on the third finger of the left hand, which was thought to contain a vein that ran directly to the heart. The rings in ancient times were sometimes made of braided grass, rope, or leather, giving rise to the expression "tying the knot".</u> Another tradition, the bridal veil, began when marriages were arranged by the families and the groom was not allowed to see his bride until the wedding. The tossing of rice at newlyweds has long signified fertility blessings, and the sweet smell of the bride's bouquet was intended to drive away evil spirits, who were also diverted by the surrounding bridal attendants. Weddings may vary enormously today, but many couples still include ancient traditions to signify their new life

together.

2. <u>Adlai Stevenson, American statesman and twice an unsuccessful presidential candidate against Eisenhower, was well known for his intelligence and wit.</u> Once on the campaign trail, after he had spoken eloquently and at length about several complex ideas, a woman in the audience was moved to stand and cheer, "That's great! Every thinking person in America will vote for you!" Stevenson immediately retorted, "That's not enough. I need a majority!" Frequently a reluctant candidate but never at a loss for words, Stevenson once defined a politician as a person who "approaches every question with an open mouth". <u>Stevenson was also admired for his work as the Governor of Illinois and, later, as Ambassador to the United Nations.</u>

Task 3.6

Suggested Answers:
The following sentences support the topic sentence with precise descriptive details:
1. It is a Madeira folk guitar, all scuffed and scratched and finger-printed.
4. At the top is a bramble of copper-wound strings, each one hooked through the eye of a silver tuning key.
6. The strings are stretched down a long slim neck.
7. The frets on the neck are tarnished, and the wood has been worn down by years of fingers pressing chords.
11. The body of the Madeira is shaped like an enormous yellow pear, one that has been slightly damaged in shipping.
14. The blond wood has been chipped and gouged to gray, particularly where the pick guard fell off years ago.

Task 3.7

The originals:
1. Retirement should be the reward for a lifetime of work. *Instead*, it is widely viewed as a sort of punishment for growing old.
   (Carll Tucker)
2. In recent years viruses have been shown to cause cancer not only in chickens

but also in mice, cats, and even in some primates. *Therefore*, it is a reasonable hypothesis that viruses might cause cancer in humans.

3. We do not seek solitude. *In fact*, if we find ourselves alone for once, we flick a switch and invite the whole world in through the television screen.
(Eugene Raskin, "Walls and Barriers")

4. We were not irresponsible. *On the contrary*, we were trained to think that each of us should do something that would be of genuine usefulness to the world.
(Lillian Smith, *Killers of the Dream*)

5. Little girls, of course, don't take toy guns out of their hip pockets and say "Pow, pow" to all their neighbors and friends like average well-adjusted little boys. *However*, if we gave little girls the six-shooters, we would soon have double the pretend body count.
(Anne Roiphe, "Confessions of a Female Chauvinist Sow")

6. We drove the wagon close to a corner post, twisted the end of the wire around it one foot above the ground, and stapled it fast. *Next*, we drove along the line of posts for about 200 yards, unreeling the wire on the ground behind us.
(John Fischer, "Barbed Wire")

7. We know very little about pain and what we don't know makes it hurt all the more. *Indeed*, no form of illiteracy in the United States is so widespread or costly as ignorance about pain.
(Norman Cousins, "Pain Is Not the Ultimate Enemy")

8. Many of our street girls can be as vicious and money mad as any corporation president. *Moreover*, they can be less emotional than men in conducting acts of personal violence.
(Gail Sheehy, "$70,000 a Year, Tax Free")

9. The historical sciences have made us very conscious of our past, and of the world as a machine generating successive events out of foregoing ones. *For this reason*, some scholars tend to look totally backward in their interpretation of the human future.
(Loren Eiseley, *The Unexpected Universe*)

10. Rewriting is something that most writers find they have to do to discover what they have to say and how to say it. There are, *however*, a few writers who do little formal rewriting because they have the capacity and experience

to create and review a large number of invisible drafts in their minds before they approach the page.

(Donald M. Murray, "The Maker's Eye: Revising Your Own Manuscipts")

Task 3.8

1. A society that has no heroes will soon grow enfeebled. *Its* purposes will be less elevated; *its* aspirations less challenging; *its* endeavors less strenuous. *Its* individual members will "hang loose" and "lay back" and, so mellowed out, the last thing of which *they* wish to hear is heroism. *They* do not want to be told of men and women whose example might disturb *them*, calling *them* to effort and duty and sacrifice or even the chance of glory.

(Henry Fairlie, "Too Rich for Heroes." *Harper's*, November, 1978)

2. **The Fortune Teller**

The fortune teller moved *her* dry, shriveled hands over the glass ball that *she* had bought at a dollar store a long time ago. *She* could hear the laughter and the occasional shouts of the children as *they* ran outside from ride to ride and from tent to tent. *They* never came in to see *her*. Instead it was always the face of a laid-off dock worker or a romantic teenager that peered through the entrance way of *her* tent. The unemployed dock workers wanted to hear about winning lottery tickets and new job opportunities. The teenagers were eager to hear stories about far away places and dark, mysterious strangers. And so the fortune teller always told *them* what *they* wanted to hear. *She* liked giving *them* something to dream about. *She* tried to fill *their* minds with great expectations. Just then, a young man appeared in the entrance way. *He* was nervous, and *his* smile was timid. *He* shuffled into the dark tent, *his* head full of dreams and yet, at the same time, innocently empty. The fortune teller took *his* trembling hands into *her* own hands and peered at the revealing lines etched on *his* palms. Then, slowly, in *her* cracked, ancient voice, *she* began to speak of new job opportunities, far away places, and dark, mysterious strangers.

Task 3.9

1. recommendation

2. prediction
3. final thought

References

［1］蔡慧萍.语类—过程英语写作教程［M］.杭州：浙江大学出版社，2012.
［2］陈立平.新编英语写作教程［M］.西安：西安交通大学出版社，2002.
［3］丁往道，吴冰.英语写作基础教程［M］.第2版.北京：高等教育出版社，2005.
［4］顾曰国.高级英语写作［M］.北京：外语教学与研究出版社，2000.
［5］姜亚军，马素萍.英语写作教程［M］.北京：高等教育出版社，2008.
［6］李太志.商务英语写作教程［M］.苏州：苏州大学出版社，2009.
［7］刘隆宇.新编英语写作速通［M］.武汉：武汉大学出版社，2009.
［8］徐小贞.商务英语写作［M］.北京：外语教学与研究出版社，2007.